Race, Class & Struggle

Race, Class & Struggle

Essays on Racism and Inequality in Britain, the US and Western Europe

Louis Kushnick

Rivers Oram Press
London and New York

First published in 1998 by
Rivers Oram Press
144 Hemingford Road, London N1 1DE

Distributed in the USA by
New York University Press
Elmer Holmes Bobst Library
70 Washington Square South
New York, NY10012-1091

Set in Sabon by
NJ Design Associates, Romsey, Hants
and printed in Great Britain by
T.J. Press (Padstow) Ltd

British Library Cataloguing in Publication Data
A catalogue record for this book is available from the British Library

ISBN 1 85489 096 4 (cloth)
ISBN 1 85489 097 2 (paperback)

This book is dedicated to the memories of Bessie and Meyer Levin and Evelyn and Al Kushnick who taught me by example that it wasn't necessary to be a racist in a racist society, and to Patricia Kushnick for her commitment and partnership in the fight against racism.

Contents

Acknowledgments   ix

Introduction   1

1 Race, Class and Power: The New York   26
  Decentralisation Controversy

2 Race, Class and Civil Rights   46

3 British Anti-discrimination Legislation   79

4 Parameters of British and North American Racism   114

5 The United States: The Revocation of Civil Rights   136

6 Racism, the National Health Service and the   147
  Health of Black People

7 The Political Economy of White Racism in   165
  Great Britain

8 Racism and Anti-Racism in Western Europe   183

9 The Political Economy of White Racism in the   203
  United States

Notes   224

Index   243

Acknowledgments

The essays in this collection have been written over a twenty-seven-year period. These years have been marked by struggle and progress and by reactionary and racist politics and resistance. I hope that this book captures these developments and struggles. If they do, it is because I have been informed and influenced by those struggles and by the work and lives of many individuals.

The education, comradeship and support I have received over the past three decades from my colleagues at the Institute of Race Relations has been the most important influence upon my work. Their willingness to work with me and bring me along, and to turn my convoluted prose into readable English, has been exemplary. The political and intellectual leadership provided by A. Sivanandan has not only informed my work but been a model of committed scholarship, linking research and writing with struggle, based on the understanding that the function of knowledge is to change reality.

The political commitment of my partner, Patricia, has informed her work as an educator and neighbourhood worker in inner-city Manchester. Her involvement with, and commitment to, inner-city, multi-racial working-class communities has helped to anchor me in the realities of the British class and race-stratified society — and to the need to change it.

I would like to thank the large number of activist scholars whose work has informed mine and whose commitment has been a model to me, and whose criticisms and suggestions have helped me develop my analysis. Among them are: Abdul Alkalimat; Huw

Beynon; Benjamin P. Bowser; Lee Bridges; Mary Ellison; Evelyn Hu-DeHart; James Jennings; Simon Katznellenbogen; Manning Marable; Jacqueline Ould and Melanie Tebbutt.

I would like to acknowledge the financial assistance provided by the Nuffield Foundation Small Grants Scheme in the Social Sciences and by the University of Manchester Fund for Research in the Humanities and Social Sciences.

I would like to thank Kristin Armstrong, Dave O'Carroll and Laura Turney for their sterling work trying to organise me and ensuring a high standard of finished work and my publishers, Elizabeth Fidlon and Katherine Bright-Holmes, for their enthusiasm, support and hard work to make this book possible, and for their confidence in me.

I want to thank Alex and Simon and John and Delia for their love, support and encouragement.

Introduction

The plight of the white working class throughout the world today is directly traceable to Negro slavery in America, on which modern commerce and industry was founded, and which persisted to threaten free labor until it was partially over thrown in 1863. The resulting color caste founded and retained by capitalism was adopted, forwarded and approved by white labor, and resulted in subordination of colored labor to white profits the world over. Thus the majority of the world's laborers, by the insistence of white labor, became the basis of a system of industry which ruined democracy and showed its perfect fruit in World War and Depression.[1]

The unifying theme of the essays in this volume is the centrality of racism in the creation and reproduction of hierarchical and unequal class-based societies. The research has focused primarily on Britain and the United States, but also includes a study of racism and anti-racism in contemporary Western European countries. These studies are based on the understanding that *race* is a social and political construct rather than a scientific category.[2] Racism does not require different physical characteristics, such as skin colour, to justify the distribution of resources in favour of particular groups at the expense of others. At different points in European history, for example, groups have been defined in racial terms without having different skin colour. It was developed as part of the triumph of England over the Celtic periphery, which Michael Hechter calls 'Internal Colonialism', over the Irish, the Scots and the Welsh.[3] The ideology which accompanied and justified this new world system was in part based on the construction of racialised categories and explanatory systems of thought established on these categories — as well as upon the validation of expropriation, enslavement and exploitation.

In the case of the conquest and expropriation of the land of the Catholic Irish Celts, Rolston argues that

> By the time the Elizabethan planters (settler-colonists) were moving into Ulster, they were carrying the legacy of almost half a millennium of racist beliefs with them as cultural baggage. In addition, they had their own contemporary reasons to denigrate the native Irish and thus reduce the likelihood of guilt in dispossessing them of their land and rights. Given the intensity of the Elizabethan thrust to plant Ireland, the old stereotype was given a new and more sinister lease of life.

He adds that

> the view of the Irish as ignoble savages took on an intensity under the Elizabethan conquest that it had never had before. Previously, it was reason for segregation; now it became the justification for genocide.[4]

> Elizabethan adventurers wrote of the Irish as a 'wicked race' which could only 'be subdued by force'. As 'pagans', they were a legitimate 'sacrifice to God'. They were a lower order of humanity who 'live like beasts, void of law and all good order ... brutish in their customs'.[5]

Such beliefs not only justified displacement and slaughter, it absolved those who carried out such actions of 'all normal ethical considerations' — and became part of a strategy of slaughter which was being carried out against Native Americans at the same time. There was a high degree of ideological and structural intertwining of actors and ideas in creating this new world system. Nicholas Canny is quoted by Rolston on this interconnection:

> The same indictments being brought against the Indians, and later the blacks, in the New World ... had been brought against the Irish .... Both Indians and blacks, like the Irish, were accused of being idle, dirty and licentious.[6]

The development of this system of 'Internal Colonialism' provided the structural basis of the ideological racism which continued as the unequal relationship between England and the Irish Catholic Celts proceeded, and as that relationship came to include the migration of the Irish to Britain as cheap labour. One crucial point is that seemingly obvious differences in secondary racial characteristics, in physiognomy and skin colour were not, and are not, necessary for the construction and reproduction of racism. The construction of the 'Irish' as a distinct racial group with specified racial characteristics did not require the Irish to be of a different colour. It is interesting to note that many of the stereotypes applied to Africans, and used to justify their enslavement, had first been used against another European group of people. Thus, the common-sense arguments about 'natural' responses, fears, antagonisms and the like of members of one *racial* group to members of another *racial* group do not accurately explain the processes through which racism is constructed. Race is a social construct — not a biological one — and how people are defined is the result of the interplay of structures, interests and ideology.

In the twentieth century, however, skin colour and its presumed associated traits have been, because of the history of colonialism and imperialism, in the words of Susan J. Smith, 'particularly salient'.[7] Plantation economies based on slavery in the New World provided for the development of manufacturing in the centre of the world system, particularly in Britain. The triangular trade was a stimulus for British manufacturers and for economic development in the British settler colonies in North America. Africans were bought with British manufactured goods. Those who survived the middle passage in British ships had to be clothed and fed by British firms and the crops they produced on the plantations provided both the raw materials for industry and capital for investment in new plant and equipment in the South and New England.[8] Winston Churchill identified the trade's importance in the following terms:

> The West Indies, two hundred years ago, bulked very largely in the minds of all people who were making Britain and making the British Empire. Our possession of the West Indies, like that of India — colonial plantation and development, as they were then called — gave us the strength, the support, but specially capital, the wealth, at a time when no other European nation possessed such a reserve, which enabled us to come through the great struggle of the Napoleonic Wars, the keen competition of the commerce of the eighteenth and nineteenth centuries, and enabled us not only to acquire this worldwide appendage of possessions we have, but also to lay the foundations of that commercial and financial leadership which, when the world was young, when everything outside Europe was undeveloped, enabled us to make our great position in the world.[9]

The importance of the slave trade can be gauged by the following quotation from a Liverpudlian authority writing in 1797:

> This great annual return of wealth may be said to pervade the whole town, increasing the fortunes of the principal adventurers, and contributing to the support of the majority of the inhabitants; almost every man in Liverpool is a merchant, and he who cannot send a bale will send a bandbox. It will therefore create little astonishment that the attractive African meteor has from time to time so dazzled their ideas that almost every order of people is interested in a Guinea cargo.... People used to say that 'several of the principal streets of Liverpool had been marked out by chains, and the walls of the houses cemented by the blood of the African slaves'. The Customs House sported carvings of Negroes heads. 'It was the capital made in the African slave trade that built some of our docks', wrote a late Victorian Liverpool essayist. 'It was the price of human flesh and blood that gave us a start'.[10]

Professor H. Merrivale, who delivered a series of lectures at Oxford in 1840 on the theme 'Colonisation and Colonies', asked two important questions and gave an equally important answer:

> What raised Liverpool and Manchester from provincial towns to gigantic cities? What maintains now their ever active industry and their rapid accumulation of wealth? ... Their present opulence is as really owing to the toil and suffering of the Negro as if his hands had excavated their docks and fabricated their steam engines.[11]

Bailey quotes the view of a mid-eighteenth century British merchant Malachi Postlethwayt, which provides support for Merrivale's conclusion:

> Is it not notorious to the whole World, that the Business of Planting in our British colonies, as well as in the French, is carried on by the Labour of Negroes, imported thither from Africa? Are we not indebted to those valuable People, the Africans for our Sugars, Tobaccoes, Rice, Rum, and all other Plantation Produce?[12]

The only 'black' spot on the horizon of this profitable economic system was that it was based on slavery. This was potentially particularly dangerous at that point because capitalism in its struggle against feudalism was evolving an ideology, alongside the political dimension, of liberation based on individuals. In this new system, individual transactions in the market place formed the basis of economic activity and societal progress — with each individual 'free' to sell his or her labour to any would-be purchaser. People were to be freed from their previous feudal ties to the land and, in their drive to maximise profitable use of the land as a commodity, landowners would be free to displace labour no longer required. How, then, is it possible to create a new economic and political and philosophical system dedicated to individualism, freedom and profit on the backs of slaves? James Walvin addresses this question in the following way:

> It was one thing to concede the economic importance of the African, it was quite another to justify the treatment to which he was subjected and yet the relevant literature tried constantly to fulfill both tasks .... Whenever varied interest groups sought to advance their own claims to a share in the African trade they generally presented their case not as a simple economic proposition, but as a moral enterprise, justifiable on the grounds of an alleged inferiority of the Negro. The distinctive qualities of the African, noted in the sixteenth century, became the hallmarks of inferiority by the eighteenth century. Even by the late sixteenth century British commercial practice, and the legislation defending that commerce, was actually treating the African as a form of subhuman; a species of property, or a simple commodity. Alongside this commercial fait accompli, through a multitude of tracts, pamphlets, handbills and books whose purpose was to defend and justify that commerce.[13]

These 'tracts, pamphlets, handbills and books' provided a 'solution' to the moral questions posed by Equiano and Montesquieu, among others. Equiano, an ex-slave and one of the leaders of the anti-slavery movement in eighteenth-century Britain, posed the problem: 'Can any man be a Christian who asserts that one part of the human race were ordained to be in perpetual bondage to another?'[14] Interestingly enough, on the other side of the Channel, the French philosopher Montesquieu articulated the problem in similar terms when he wrote: 'It is impossible for us to suppose these creatures to be men, because, allowing them to be men, a suspicion would follow that we ourselves are not Christians'.[15]

The resolution of these problems lay in the ending of slavery and of the slave trade only when economic change and the resistance of the slaves made the ex-slaves' free labour a satisfactory alternative. In a development similar to that adopted earlier *vis-à-vis* the Irish

Catholics, whose land and freedom had been taken by England, all of the victims of these processes, whether Irish or African, were defined as ape-like, less than human, savage. This 'solution' — slavery — has had fundamental and continuing consequences. It facilitated these barbaric practices by justifying their use in terms of the superior civilisation of the British and other Europeans. The rationalisation was subsequently used to justify imperial conquest of Africa at the end of the nineteenth century and has been a constant theme of British education and in popular culture since. Significantly, in 1983, when Prime Minister Margaret Thatcher, in full glory of her victory over the 'Argies' and of her putting the 'great' back into Britain again, was revelling in 'Victorian values' during one 'Question Time' in the House of Commons, a Labour MP challenged her by asking which Victorian values was she referring to: poor houses and gin-soaked mothers? Thatcher responded immediately and with vigour that it meant bringing civilisation to countries of the world which would not have it without Britain. It is equally significant that she included this assertion in her famous Bruges speech, where she asserted Britain's sovereign right to limit further integration.

Racism has functioned to legitimise inequality and hierarchy in class-based systems by rationing scarce resources in a racialised fashion. In this way it legitimates both rationing itself and the way available resources are defined, gaining the acceptance and loyalty of the majority of the dominant group on the basis of their receiving, 'deservedly', more than members of the dominated group. The key issue, then, becomes not the high degree of inequality among the members of the dominant group but the distinctions between lower-level members of the dominant group and members of the dominated group. Black sociologist Charles S. Johnson has argued that institutional racism is a response to the contradictions inherent in a society based upon 'capitalistic liberty', that it is 'a commitment to exclude the Negro from power in order to protect the limited expansion of equal rights to others'.[16] The following quotations will help facilitate an understanding of this dynamic in operation.

> I wonder the working people are so quiet under the taunts and insults offered to them. Have they no Spartacus among them to head a revolt of the slave class against their political tormentors? *Cobden*[17]
> ... it was 'our ignorance of society and of government — our prejudices, our disunion and distrust' which was one of the biggest

obstacles to the dissolution of the 'unholy compact of despotism'.
London Working Man's Association[18]

Ignorance, disunion and distrust are central components of and also
the consequences of the dominant racist ideology into which successive generations of British and American people — and people in
other race-centred societies — are socialised and which serves to
maintain the capitalist world system.[19] As John Stanfield has written: 'Race-centred societal members are socialized in mundane ways
to presume certain populations are naturally inferior or superior due
to social and cultural attributes attached to physical features.' He
identifies the two dimensions of racism 'as a central aspect of human
development in America and in other race-centred societies ...
racialism and racial discrimination'. Racialism is a product of
developmental and everyday socialization; and racial discrimination 'occurs when a dominant population creates, legitimates, and
reconfirms its superiority through labelling outsiders as inferior
races and through dehumanizing them through withholding crucial
resources such as property ownership, gainful employment, investment capital, and human dignity'.[20] Thus, this is not an argument
about dumb workers, dumb whites being manipulated in a way that
they are too stupid to understand but which is clear to white intel-
lectuals. Neither is it an argument which asserts the primacy of
ideology over material forces, nor, we hope, an argument which is
so deterministic and instrumentalist that it constructs inevitable
outcomes and ignores struggle. The dominant ideology and the
extent of effective democracy that exist in any society at any point
are the results of previous conflicts between classes and other
forces, conflicts which have produced reforms, changes, concessions. Therefore, ideological and psychological processes, on the
one hand, and material forces on the other are engaged in the
dynamics of class relations. Concessions won by working-class militancy in one historical period may not be secure in another period
characterized by a lower level of consciousness and militancy.

The organisation of power and distribution of resources along
racial lines determine the conditions and chances of people in these
societies. Therefore, the shape of class relations in these societies are
the consequences of state power and action. State racism (that is,
racism which is sustained in a variety of ways by state action)
underpins and legitimates popular racism, itself transmitted by

institutions under the control of the state and of capital. The dominant ideology — regularly reinforced by the political institutions and the media — can 'explain' events and provide an agenda for action, no matter how wrong-headed and contradictory to the material reality and interests of white workers. Thus, for the white working class in the metropole, racism, in both its material and ideological aspects, provides privileges at the cost of the continuation of a system which exploits its members, limits human development, maintains insecurity, and largely leaves the working class powerless to contest for power or even to maintain the material privileges won in previous periods. For the metropolitan ruling classes, however, racism has provided greater, and more sustainable, material benefits. Through their ability to set agendas, determine what is natural or normal and to define common sense, they have been able to establish a degree of control over the minds and consciousness of the metropolitan working class. This advances the bourgeoisie's political control of the state and society. Racism has enabled the bourgeoisie to establish the race-stratified labour forces in the metropole, which facilitates the super-exploitation of racially oppressed workers as well as the continuing exploitation of white workers.

One of the clearest examples of the operation of state racism, its role in constructing race-stratified societies and legitimating the common-sense racist ideology, together with creating 'the facts on the ground' which then structure future relations between people, is the forging of what D.S. Massey and N.A. Denton in the 1990s called 'American Apartheid'. Detailed studies of the construction of the first and second ghettos found the local state and the national state integrally involved, along with banks, savings and loan institutions, insurance companies and real estate and property development interests, in constructing those ghettos.[21] Hadjor identifies the role played by the 'property buyers' bibles' — *Babcock's Valuation of Real Estate* (1932) and *McMichael's Appraising Manual* (1931) — which indicated that the presence of 'undesirable elements' was 'sufficient grounds to refuse a loan'. He argues that this policy 'was not only an effective sanction against prospective black buyers, but was also a good way to put pressure on white homeowners to help keep blacks out and so protect the value of their property'.[22]

Hadjor also identifies the role played by the Home Owners Loan

Corporation (HOLC), created by the Roosevelt Administration, which institutionalised 'red-lining'. It instituted a system of grading for neighbourhood factors, which determined mortgage-granting decisions. The grades ranged from 'A' — 'areas in demand in good times and bad and were homogenous, i.e., American business or professional men' — 'B' — 'still desirable' — 'C' — 'declining' — to 'D' — 'declined'. Black areas were invariably put in 'D' while those areas 'within such a low price or rent range as to attract undesirable elements' were put in 'C'.[23] The Federal Housing Administration (FHA) and the Veterans Administration (VA) fuelled the post-World War II suburbanisation programme which led to the construction of over $120 billion worth of private, owner-occupied housing by 1965, 98 per cent of which was owned by whites. The FHA's *Underwriting Manual* (1939) emphasised the importance of keeping out 'inharmonious racially or nationality groups' and recommended the use of 'subdivisions, regulations, and suitably restrictive covenants' to achieve their exclusion.[24]

The result, along with racially segregated high-density public housing in the inner-cities, was, for Massey and Denton, 'Black reservations, highly segregated from the rest of society and characterized by extreme social isolation'.[25] Hirsch identifies the role of racism in allowing competing class interests among whites to be resolved at the expense of blacks and identifies public housing to become an officially sanctioned 'second ghetto ... solidly institutionalized and frozen in concrete' where 'government took an active hand not merely in reinforcing prevailing patterns of but in lending them a permanence never seen before'.[26]

Hadjor concludes that

> suburbanization has taken place within a social environment and political climate that have ensured that this moment took on racial overtones. With economic and political discrimination ensuring that blacks were concentrated in ghettos, it was not difficult to attack racial implications to the mass movement of white people away from those areas. Black neighborhoods were associated with deprivation and crime in the public imagination. For most whites, self-improvement became closely linked with putting distance between their family and the places where black people lived.[27]

With jobs and public services following the whites to the suburbs, it is not surprising that politicians cultivated the suburban white voters and that these voters used their suffrage to ensure the continuing flow of public resources. The inner-cities, meanwhile, continued to be starved of public resources and to be defined in racially derogatory terms. Crime, welfare and social dislocation were racialised and became the basis of a politics of scapegoating and of destroying the legitimacy of 'big government', while Military Keynesianism — the system of pump priming the economy via massive military spending rather than spending on civilian physical and human infrastructure — continued unopposed. Public policies continued throughout the Cold War to privilege the giant corporations, the 'industrial' component of what President Eisenhower called the 'military-industrial complex' and the largely white strata of well-paid professional, scientific and management elites employed by these corporation. The political Right in the US in both its 'Old' and 'New' forms, attacked income transfer programmes benefiting the poor as examples of wasteful governmental expenditures which coddled the shiftless and lazy poor and increased the taxes on the hard-working, decent people.

As African-American families were increasingly faced to rely on programmes such as Aid for the Families with Dependent Children (AFDC) because of the operations of structural racism in the labour market, in housing and in education, these attacks increased in ferocity. As economic restructuring began to erode the benefits which had accrued to white politics appealing to white working-class and lower middle-class people, particularly men, from the operation of this racialised system, the racialised attacks became even more central to white politics, appealing to white suburban voters and to divert the attention of those large groups of white working people from the real causes of their declining standard of living on to appropriate scapegoats.[28] These racialised attacks on 'dependency, welfare queens', and the underclass thus fed into the right-wing and corporate strategy of dismantling large parts of public provision and the Social Wage by scapegoating the black and Latino poor. It would thus allow Reagan and Thatcher to focus the attention of white working people on 'legitimate' enemies and gain their votes while carrying out an agenda constructed by, and for the benefit of, corporate capital.[29]

In Britain, the continuing definition of Afro-Caribbeans and Asians as 'the Other', as 'outsiders', as 'them' rather than 'us' served to enable Thatcher, Major, et al. to play the 'race card' in successive elections and facilitate the same restructuring. One of the most obvious examples came in the run-up to the 1979 General Election, when, in 1978, Thatcher declared her belief that 'the British people had a legitimate fear of being swamped by an alien culture'. She obviously had a limited definition of who constituted the 'British People' and of an 'alien culture'. Clearly, the latter was made up of Coke, Pepsi, McDonalds or Kentucky Fried Chicken and the former equally clearly constituted whites. The language of 'swamping', 'floods of immigrants', etc. were emotive and threatening. On election night, 1987, former Conservative Prime Minister Edward Heath said that immigration was one of three key reasons for the third consecutive Tory victory. How accurate was this assessment and, more to the point, what exactly did Heath mean when he spoke of immigration? Immigration had come to mean black immigration in the most specific sense in the British political system, certainly since the late 1950s. But there had been virtually no black primary immigration into Britain since 1973, when the 1971 Immigration Act — passed by Heath's own government — came into force. Further, between 1965 and 1972 there had been only an average of 6500 black primary immigrants entering Britain a year as a result of the Labour Government's 1965 Immigration White Paper. Thus, if the former Prime Minister were correct, and I believe he was, both he and a significant proportion of the white British public and political elites must have meant something beyond black immigration when they spoke and wrote about immigration. That term had come to mean the very presence of black people in Britain. Thus, a more accurate statement would be that racism was one of the key factors ensuring a third successive Conservative victory, much as it was in the victories of Ronald Reagan and of George Bush.

The fourth consecutive Conservative victory, on 9 April 1992, provides additional support for an argument that racism played a central role in late twentieth-century British politics. In the year before the General Election, the Conservative Government and its allies in the press again raised the issue of immigration — or in their terms the spectre of Britain being flooded by bogus asylum-seekers. The Prime Minister, John Major, the Foreign Secretary, Douglas Hurd, the Home Secretary, Kenneth Baker and myriad of lesser Tories all warned of the threat of millions of economic migrants flooding into Britain and Europe and calling for more and more restrictive immigration controls both on the European level and on the national level. Britain began more openly co-operating with the Schengen Agreement nations within the European Community — France, Germany, Belgium, Luxembourg, the Netherlands, Portugal, Spain and Italy — which have agreed on the abolition of border controls, a common visa policy, common rules on which country should decide on asylum applications and the creation of the Schengen Information System, a powerful database which will hold details on several categories of individuals of interest to the police and other agencies, including foreign nationals deemed 'undesirable'.[30] On the British front, the government introduced the Asylum Bill on 31 October 1991. The Bill, designed according to the government, to deal with an increase in applications for asylum from 5,000 in 1989 to over 20,000 in 1990 — although there is no evidence to support the Home Office claim that the increase is owing to 'bogus' refugees — provided for compulsory fingerprinting of all refugees, fast-track removal of 'bogus' applicants, stiffer credibility tests on refugees claiming asylum — failure to apply immediately on arrival, failure to make prompt and full disclosure of the facts, and lack of a proper passport or travel document — refusal on the basis of the applicant's getting involved in political activity in Britain which might upset the authorities in their own country, removal of rights to legal aid and lawyers of applicants' choice, and removal of family right to council housing until case decided. Frank Krenz, the London representative of the United Nations High Commissioner on Refugees, said the new rules were 'tendentious and biased against the applicant' and could damage the chances of *bona fide* refugees who needed protection under the 1951 UN convention. The Commission for Racial Equality informed the Home Secretary that the plans to remove eligibility to legal aid was illegal under the Race Relations Act. Human rights and welfare organisations, such as Amnesty International, the British Refugee Council and the Medical Foundation for the Care of Victims of Torture, as well as the Archbishop of Canterbury, George Carey, and the Roman Catholic Archbishop, Basil Hume have condemned the measures proposed in the Bill. The government withdrew the bill just before the 1992 General Election because there was no time to complete its legislative processes — but used it, as did the Tory papers such as the *Daily Mail*, the *Daily Express*, the *Sun*, the *Daily Star*, as a weapon against Labour in the election. Labour was accused of planning to allow into the country thousands of bogus refugees. Only a Conservative victory would save Britain from being swamped with undesirables, that is non-white people. Both Foreign Secretary Hurd and Home Secretary Baker played this card during the campaign.

An interesting parallel to the Tory Press playing the race card in this way can be found in the Southern United States near the end of the nineteenth century when there was the 'danger' of poor white and poor black farmers and labourers coming together. To stir up racial discontent, the *Advertiser* on election day fell back on its tried and tested formula — race-baiting. The front page of the *Advertiser* was filled with reports of assaults by blacks on white women. 'The Negroes', reported the *Advertiser*, were 'getting very troublesome' in Mississippi. 'Several Negro women of Tuscumbia' were reported to 'have addressed a very insulting letter to several respectable white ladies.'... The 'white men of Lawrence County' were urged ... to 'do' their 'duty' to 'protect the white race from this animalism'.[31]

The same processes were apparent in the run-up to the 1997 General election with similar Conservative expectations of success. The Home Secretary, Michael Howard, introduced yet another Immigration and Asylum Bill in 1996, designed to tighten still further regulations denying entry to asylum-seekers. The Government and its friends in the media continued the process of labelling asylum-seekers as bogus and denying their legitimacy. Howard was joined by the Social Security Minister, Peter Lilley, in this attack and Lilley introduced measures to deny all benefits to asylum-seekers who failed to apply for asylum at the port of entry. In September 1995, Andrew Lansley, a Conservative Party official, wrote in the *Observer*, that the Conservatives had successfully played the race card in the 1992 General Election and in the 1994 European Parliamentary elections, and would do so again in the next General Election.[32]

The continuing centrality of racism in Britain, the United States and in Western European countries is striking. This racism in found in the disproportionate number of African-Caribbean youngsters being expelled from British schools; the disproportionate number of African-American men and women imprisoned in the United States; the disproportionate number of African-Caribbean men and women imprisoned in Britain; in differential access to bail hostels in Britain; in the refusal of Congress to accept the recommendations of the Sentencing Commission to end the massive disparities between crack and powder cocaine possession levels before mandatory sentencing commences — a difference of 100; in differential levels of deaths in custody and at the hands of the police; in differential funding of public services; differential location of investment and in location of toxic waste dumps and incinerators; in continuing racial discrimination in employment; in continuing and increasing differential levels of illness, disease and mortality; in differential levels of unemployment, underemployment and poverty. In the United States in 1996, tapes of a meeting of senior executives of Texaco Inc., exposed racist contempt for the firm's black employees and a willingness to destroy documents demanded in a Federal lawsuit. Executives were heard referring to black employees as 'black jelly beans' and 'niggers':

> This diversity thing, you know how all the black jelly beans agree .... That's funny .... All the black jelly beans seem to be glued to the bottom of the bag.[33]

From the late 1980s, the Reagan/Bush Supreme Court, under Chief Justice William Rehnquist, has undermined the effectiveness of measures taken by the Second Reconstruction designed to provide racial justice to the victims of institutionalised racism. David Kairys concludes after analysing the Court's decisions in this area that:

> The Court has reversed the social roles that shaped the history of American racism: whites have become the presumed victims and African-Americans the presumed racists. To rationalize this reversal of social roles, the Court has employed the history, language, and moral force of the progressive struggle against racism. Thus, while challenges to discrimination against minorities or women are greeted with scepticism, deference to government officials, restraint and an obliviousness to reality, affirmative action is an occasion to 'smoke out racism' and remedial redistricting draws a charge of 'segregation'.[34]

> .... Perhaps the hallmark of our time is the use of the ideal of color-blindness as a non-racist symbol and rationalization for halting and reversing the process of integration of African-Americans into the economy and society. In the cruelest of ironies, color-blindness has become a code-word not for inclusion or integration — words and ideas not heard much lately — but for the separation and segregation that increasingly characterize American society as we move toward

what looks like a developing American apartheid. This is not a reaction or response to equality that has gone too far, but to the first substantial entry in our history of African-Americans into the economy and social life of the nation.[35]

Throughout the European Union there has been both increasing state racism and an escalation of racist violence and support for far-right parties. The connection between these two phenomena in Western European countries is similar to that identified in the United States and in Britain. The combination of economic and social dislocation following attempts at restructuring and in the face of cheaper imports from other areas of the integrated and transnational, corporate-controlled world economy, plus the failure of the left organisations in the workplace or in the polity to challenge the increasingly dominant free-market ideology, has led to an escalation in the scapegoating of immigrants and settlers from the periphery. They are blamed for the loss of jobs; for the loss of secure jobs; for cuts in the social wage and consequent insecurity; for the growing fears for the future; in short, they are blamed for the consequences of globalisation and the collusion of national elites in the process and for the resulting increase in income and wealth inequalities caused by these economic and political forces. The national elites using their dominance of the state and the media have been constructing new definitions of national and European identity, identities which are racially constructed and oppositional to the constructed Other. Europe is, therefore, Christian rather than Muslim, white rather than black, civilised rather than backward and primitive. Europe must defend itself against Islamic Fundamentalism and from Economic Refugees posing as political refugees or asylum-seekers. Within this framework, the European Union has been constructing Fortress Europe to keep the hordes of 'racially inferior' on the outside. Among the measures taken, which in practice mean a betrayal of international agreements and United Nations charters on rights of refugees, are: the Schengen Agreement, the 'Safe Third Country' rule and fines imposed on airlines bringing refugees or asylum-seekers into EU countries without proper papers and visas — even if it is impossible for such people, fleeing from repressive regimes, to obtain visas or to leave their countries using proper papers.

This racism is becoming one with a common, European culture, 'which defines all Third World people as immigrants and refugees, and all immigrants and refugees as terrorists and drug-runners, [which] will not be able to tell a citizen from an immigrant or an immigrant from a refugee, let alone one black from another. They all carry their passports on their faces.'[36] As Sheila Allen and Marie Macey have written of British blacks in the New Europe:

> Formally, these people will enjoy all the rights of free movement as befits their British citizenship. But in a climate which equates race and ethnicity particularly with being black, and being black with being an immigrant (and a potentially illegal one), it is difficult not to foresee an increase in racial harassment and control not only at Europe's external borders, but internally as well.[37]

The experience of those at the cutting edge, the migrants and refugees, provides further validation of this crucial analysis. The Refugee Forum and Migrants Rights Action network found that it is no coincidence that countries such as Italy which did not experience racial attacks on its North African workers, began to see vicious attacks at the time when its government began imposing immigration restrictions. '*Unlike wealth, racism does 'trickle down' from the top, and when governments define peoples as unwelcome and undesirable, their populations follow.*' [Italics added][38]

Given such leadership towards racism from elites and the state, it is not surprising that support for the far right is growing. The *Front National* in France, for example, has won a growing number of town halls and is increasing its membership in areas of previously strong Communist Party membership. They are increasing their membership among police, prison officers and among college students and are seeking seats on housing association councils. The *FN* has recently launched a 'campaign against globalisation' and have supported demonstrations against cuts in defence industries.[39] They are attempting to fill the void left by the Left after the Mitterrand years. In Germany, the Social Democrats have not only supported the restrictive legislation proposed by the Christian Democratic Government of Chancellor Kohl restricting rights of entry and asylum but have tried to play the anti-immigrant card themselves. Throughout the Union, and in non-EU countries such as Switzerland, such political measures have been followed by increasing police violence against migrants and settler communities; increasing levels of imprisonment of young people from these communities; increasing levels of racial violence against these communities; and increasing activities by far-right organisations and parties.

The fundamental argument, therefore, is not only that racism has blighted the lives of tens and hundreds of millions of people of colour all over the world, but that is has also functioned worldwide to maintain class-stratified societies.[40] This racist system has, however, been contested terrain for its entire history. Individual whites, as well as people of colour, and organised groups of whites and groups of people of colour, and integrated groups have resisted the imposition of the racist ideology and the racialised organisation of society.[41] It is important to study that resistance and to understand the conditions within which whites opted for a more inclusive, not racially limited identity — as opposed to the racially exclusive basis of identification which has been the dominant mode for most of the period under review.

Summary of Themes

The chapters in this collection have addressed issues of racism since 1969. 'Race, Class and Power: The New York Decentralisation Controversy' was a study of the interconnections of race and class in the nature and outcomes of the New York City school system. It focused on the struggles around desegregation, decentralisation and community control which pitted parents of colour against the bureaucracy of the school system and the bureaucracy of the teacher's union. It analysed the centrality of racism in terms of the rationing of educational resources; in terms of an ideological justification for the racialised outcomes of the educational system; and in terms of the vested interests of a section of white society, particularly educational professionals and administrators in the maintenance of that racialised system. It also analysed the struggles of the African-American and Latino communities and of whites who had political identities and practices separate from racial privilege. This analysis was based upon an understanding that poor people, and people of colour and anti-racists are protagonists in their own history and make their own history, but not under terms and conditions of their own choosing. This chapter was recently recommended by James Jennings as one of three articles providing an understanding of this episode in the history of Puerto Rican activism.[42] I chose it for this collection because, unfortunately, the central issues I discussed in 1969 are still shaping the educational experiences of a large proportion children of colour throughout the United States. The patterns of racial segregation, constructed and maintained by state action short of a legally required system of segregation, not only continue but are being reinforced. Recent research carried out by the Harvard Graduate School of Education found that schools in the US are more segregated in 1997 than at any time since the 1950s, with children of colour increasingly confined to low-achieving classrooms in poor areas. State action is as integrally involved in the production of these outcomes as it was under the pre-*Brown* v. *Board of Education of Topeka* decision of 1954 which declared the 'separate but equal' system of *de jure* segregation unconstitutional. The researchers found that federal court rulings in the early 1990s which allowed schools to abandon busing — taking children by bus to schools in other racial/ethnic areas — have limited black and Hispanic pupils to these segregated, low-achieving schools. They found that after busing was introduced in 1971, 63.6 per cent of black students were in schools where less than half the pupils were white — the latest figure is 67.1 per cent. For Hispanics, the current position is that three out of four Hispanic pupils are in schools whose pupils come mainly from an ethnic minority background. The report concludes that:

> For both black and Latino students, the contact with whites is going down .... We are at a historic turning point in terms of the access to opportunity in American schools.[43]

The issue now, as it was in New York City in the 1960s, is not primarily whether children of colour sit at the next desk to white children. The issue is the nature and quality of education these children receive. The differential funding regimes continue to favour grossly suburban, white middle-class children [of course, the privileges of the children of the elite are taken as given] and to equip them to succeed in the 'meritocratic' race and to have greater and greater amounts of resources spent on their education and to ensure their success in the competitive labour markets. We either recognise this reality and the need to challenge it — as has social commentator and researcher Jonathan Kozol who has documented the extent of these differentials and their educational and personal, attitudinal consequences for both the privileged and the deprived youngsters in his book *Savage Inequalities*[44] — or we blame the victim using a variety of forms of scientific racism. The mainstream media's uncritical acceptance of the deeply flawed and victim-blaming, *Bell Curve*.[45] One of the major academic critiques of *The Bell Curve* analysed Herrnstein and Murray's basic premises and concludes that none of them 'can be established utilizing any approximation of the scientific method, their program reduces itself to only right-wing ideology, a right-wing ideology whose prescriptions need to be taken very seriously'.[46] Therefore, the choices facing the society about equality and education I discussed in 1969 in the first essay in this book are even more starkly facing the society in the post-Civil Rights era.

The next article, 'Race, Class and Civil Rights', also deals with issues of race and class in the United States. The development of the Civil Rights Movement CRM is examined and the analysis relates that development to struggles of African-Americans — and their allies among other groups in society — for racial justice and to ideological and structural and economic forces in American society at the time. The ending of the re-established plantation system and its dependence upon labour-intensive production was a major factor in the successful struggle to overcome the Jim Crow system of *de jure* segregation; the increasing diversification of the Southern economy and entry of new economic forces from the rest of the country brought new players into the game who understood that institutional racism could successfully replace Jim Crow in maintaining racial hierarchy and a weakened working class; the 'good war' against fascism had removed the moral justification for Jim Crow; the determination of the United States government to create and dominate a new world system created foreign policy imperatives to remove legal segregation from the statute books so as to deny the Soviets an ideological weapon to use against the United States in the two-thirds of the world which wasn't white; the anti-Communist politics of the post-war period silenced voices, black and white, which wanted to address issues of race and class, and legitimated those which focused on the removal of *de jure* segregation and which demanded incorporation into the existing liberal democratic institutions. This analysis identified the limitations inherent in such a set of demands and such a strategy in terms of the maintenance of structural racism and the consequences both for the majority of African-Americans, particularly for working class and poor African-Americans, and in terms of the reproduction of ideological and structural racism and for white working-class people.

I chose this essay for the collection because the continuing centrality of racism is apparent in everyday life: in the nature of the political process; in the imprisonment statistics — with an African-American male being five times more likely to be imprisoned in the US than an African male in South Africa; in continuing and escalating levels of class inequality and the increasing scapegoating of affirmative action and 'special interests' by both Democrat and Republican politicians; by the ignoring of the needs of the people living in the inner-cities; by the racialising and feminising of poverty so that the safety net becomes shredded and we end 'welfare as we knew it'.[47] These characteristics of contemporary US society illustrate the need to go beyond formal legal and constitutional rights to a more encompassing definition of rights and freedom and the inescapable need to link economic and political democracy.

'British Anti-Discrimination Legislation', was published in 1971, as an analysis of the passage of the 1965 and 1968 Race Relations Acts in Britain. It formed part of a collection of essays entitled, *The Prevention of Racial Discrimination in Britain*, which was sponsored by the United Nations Institute for Training and Research and the Institute of Race Relations. It was an attempt to study the response of the British state to the contradictions inherent in the recruitment of people of colour from the former colonies of the Caribbean and the Indian subcontinent to fill vacancies as cheap labour in the post-war period. It analysed the social and political costs of the popular racism which had rendered such labour cheap in the first place and the state racism which had historically created that popular racism and reinforced it through failing to challenge stereotypes. The situation was worsened by resource-allocation decisions that created and escalated infrastructure shortages which then became racialised. The chapter analysed the limits of the state response and the dominant ideology shaped in part by lessons drawn from state action in the United States.

I chose this essay because it illustrates my misguided optimism at the time about the *bona fides* of the British state. Since it was written it has become more and more apparent that structural racism has been shaping the experiences and opportunities of black British people, including the children and grandchildren of the post-war migrants, and that the British state was unwilling to forego the advantages of racial stereotyping and scapegoating. The politicians continued to define black people as outsiders, as 'the problem' and to play the 'race card' in election after election and to refuse to provide the agencies established to implement anti-discrimination legislation with the necessary powers to make a fundamental change in the operation of racialised labour markets. These factors were addressed in essays written after this one and which are included in this volume. [See Chapters 4, 6 and 7.]

'Parameters of British and North American Racism' was published in a special issue of *Race and Class* on the 1981 uprisings in British inner-cities. It analysed the causes of the uprisings and related them to the uprisings in the United States in the 1960s. The article studied the official responses in the United States, in particular the administration's establishment of the Kerner Commission and its responses to the Commission's recommendations. It identified the priority given to the implementation of those recommendations to do with policing and intelligence-gathering and the failure to address seriously those dealing with structural racism. It was in this context that the Scarman recommendations were reviewed and likely British governmental responses were identified.[48] Lord Scarman made a number of recommendations about recruiting more members of the ethnic minorities into the police; the establishment of consultative machinery between the police and the community; more community policing; more effective complaints procedures to deal with complaints against the police; and urgent actions was required if the social conditions which underlay the disorders in Brixton and elsewhere were to be corrected. He did not, however, accept that institutional racism was present in Britain.

I chose this essay because of its continued relevance in the face of repeated urban uprisings in both Britain and the United States and the political struggle over the meaning of these uprisings. The most dramatic of these uprisings was, of course, that of Los Angeles in 1992 following the acquittal by the suburban jury, made up of 11 whites and one Asian-American, of the four police officers who had been videoed severely beating Rodney King, an African-American. There were recent examples of urban unrest in

Britain in December 1995, following the death of the second black man at the hands of the police in Brixton within three months, and in a predominantly black area of St Petersburg, Florida in October 1996, just days before the presidential election, after police shot and killed a second black young man in a week. In these instances, in both countries, as in the US following the 1992 LA uprising, the dominant discussion ignored the fundamental issues of structural racism, police violence and injustice and focused on the supposed shortcomings of the rioters, their violence, their unwillingness to work, and on looting. One commentator on these developments concluded:

> The main point to come out of all the arguments and opinion exchanges that unrest such as the Los Angeles riots of 1992 is now considered to have far more to do with morality than with poverty. The real evil is, therefore, the act of riot, not the degradation of human life in the ghetto. While playing brief lip-service to the structural problems of the inner-city, the post-liberal consensus plays down those social factors that create poverty and emphasises instead that the cause of the problem is the breakdown in the moral code among individuals.
>
> The reorientation of the post-riot discussion in this fashion helps to divert attention away from a critique of the way in which American society is organised and run, and pile it on to a moral condemnation of the urban poor. The fact that the conservative opinion-makers have been able to achieve this so successfully despite the glaring weakness and vulgar prejudices underlying many of their own arguments, demonstrates the extent to which traditional liberal ideas have not been marginalised.[49]

In 'Revocation of Civil Rights' there was an analysis of the repeal of large sections of the Second Reconstruction through actions of the Reagan and Bush administrations and through a series of Supreme Court decisions by the Reagan/Bush Court. The limitations in the gains of the CRM, which I identified in Chapter 2, were examined and found crucially to have allowed this process of revocation, seen by many analysts as similar to the repeal of much of the First Reconstruction. The failure of both Reconstructions to challenge the economic organisation of society, a system of racialised capitalism, meant that the political gains could not be protected when the coalitions which had come together, under pressure from African-Americans, to institute the reforms broke apart. When the goals were achieved of those for whom the changes were tactical, designed to maintain the unequal hierarchical system they dominated, the change-oriented movement divided and a significant portion of its leadership was coopted.

I chose this article because I feel that it correctly identified these processes and raised questions about the implications for race and class inequality. The triumph of the 'post-liberal consensus' has meant that the election of a Democratic President in 1992 and his re-election in 1996, the first time a Democratic President has been re-elected since 1944, has not meant a fundamental challenge to the deteriorating position of large parts of African America.[50]

'Racism, the National Health Service and the Health of Black People', which was given 'top priority' for publication by the referee, was published in 1987 in the *International Journal of Health Services*. It analysed the nature and consequences of racism for black people as patients and as employees in the National Health Service and identified the interconnections between structural and ideological racism shaping their experiences in both categories. Racism in education, employment, housing and the criminal justice system all have health consequences and consequences for employment within the NHS and racism in the popular culture and state racism all affect the treatment of black people as patients and consumers.[51] I included this article because the issues I raised have continued to shape the experiences of black people. It is interesting and disturbing to note that a recent investigation by the Commission for Racial Equality has found patterns of racial discrimination in the appointment of consultants and senior registrars similar to those discussed in this article.

> Although almost every respondent had an equal opportunities policy covering the recruitment and selection process, in almost every case there was a big gap between policy and actual practice .... Taken together with the consistently low success rates for ethnic minority applicants for senior medical posts, the selection practices found among health authorities and trusts can give little confidence to ethnic minority applicants that their applications will be treated fairly.[52]

There is concern about racial harassment of black health workers and a lack of consideration and support by managers and supervisors; about the large gap, as described above in the case of consultants and senior registrars, between equal opportunities statements and implementation; and widespread discrimination in the allocation of training and promotion of nurses.[53] Recent research by the MSF union has found that there has been a short drop in the number of black nursing, midwifery and health visiting staff. This is particularly apparent in the numbers employed in the under-25-year-old category, 0.8 per cent, compared with those between 55 and 64, where the figure is 8.7 per cent,[54] the authors of this report conclude:

> Racial discrimination operates at all levels in the NHS, right from the processing of application forms through to top jobs. It presents a concrete ceiling which keeps many talented and qualified ethnic minority staff from the positions they could be filling. Racism operates also on other levels, be it racial harassment and abuse from patients or unequal disciplinary measures applied to ethnic minority staff. No statistic can ever measure the resulting waste of talent and opportunity, nor the indignities balk and ethnic minority people are experiencing daily.[55]

The need to place equality at the heart of the new, decentralised NHS has thus become ever more apparent. The problem of forcing institutions to prioritise equal opportunities and to move beyond mere symbolism is a major one and the experience in the area of the health-care delivery system is not an encouraging one. Similar issue need to be addressed in other areas of public life, such as education, policing, housing and employment. In each of these areas, black people are being denied equality in terms of employment, treatment and service delivery. As the power of democratically elected Local Education Authorities is eroded in favour of local management of schools, the problem of how equal opportunities policies are to be administered and monitored in such a multiplicity of locations is one that has not yet been seriously addressed — but clearly needs to be.

The last three articles in this collection, published in 1995 and 1996, take the analyses developed in the previous articles and apply them to explain contemporary race and class relations. They are based upon an understanding that in the years since the Civil Rights Movement in the United States and since the passage of the 1965, 1968 and 1976 Race Relations Acts in Britain — and more crucially, since the passage of the Immigration Acts of 1962 and

1971 and the Immigration White Paper of 1965 and the Kenyan Asian Act of 1968 — there has been a massive increase in racial polarisation in the United States, Britain and the rest of Europe, both East and West. There has been an increase in racial violence in these areas and increasing scholarly recognition of the centrality of racism in the organisation of modern Western societies.[56] The successful playing of the race card in election after election has been accompanied by a rightward shift of mainstream political parties and a narrowing of the parameters of legitimate political discourse in the United States and Western Europe.[57] This rightward shift in political and governmental action has led to an increase in popular racism. Politicians then used this increase as a justification for further racist state actions, which in turn exacerbated popular racism .... This growth of racism has accompanied, and made politically possible, greater class inequality and a restructuring of the political economies of the advanced capitalist countries at the expense of the working classes. All these events were anticipated in the earlier articles and are central to the analysis in 'Racism and Anti-Racism in Western Europe', published in 1995; 'The Political Economy of White Racism in the United States', published in 1996 in the Second Edition of *Impacts of Racism on White Americans*; and 'The Political Economy of White Racism in Britain' — published as an Occasional Paper in 1996 by the Trotter Institute.

The challenge facing our societies is the construction of social and economic justice. without racial justice, it will not be possible to create just societies. Without justice there will be no peace, Nor will there be effective democracy. Without effective democracy, there will be no control over the activities of the transnational Corporations and their Political Allies in power in the national state and in the international agencies such as the IMF, the World Bank, the World Trade Organisation, and in the impending European Monetary Union. The choice facing us is a stark one, I hope that the issue raised in this collection will have moved the debate forward and help in the chose of justice over barbarism.

1 Race, Class and Power
The New York Decentralisation Controversy

Racial and religious tension and conflict in New York City dramatically increased in the latter half of the 1960s. Charges of 'black anti-Semitism' and 'white racism' abound, while meaningful communication between the races is less than it has ever been. The general context within which the situation has developed has been that of the growth of the Black Power concept and the resulting black challenge to the white economic, political and educational power structures. This challenge, so different from the glorious days of the civil rights decade of the 1950s when blacks and whites marched together in the South, represents a realisation among black leaders that the basic problems of jobs, housing and education in the urban ghettos of America have to be solved before there can be any real progress of black Americans as a group. This, however, brings them into conflict with whites with vested interests to protect, and the resulting controversy has been bitter. An example of the break-up of the old civil rights coalition following the presentation of a challenge to white self-interest can be seen in the mobilisation of the majority of Reform Democrats of the FDR-Woodrow Wilson Club to defeat plans to pair PS84, a predominantly white elementary school, and a nearby black and Puerto Rican school. David Rogers, in *110 Livingston Street*, quotes one disappointed club member saying: 'All their old liberalism went by the boards. They are liberal in the abstract, and when the problem is far away, say in Selma, Jackson or Birmingham, but not for their children or their schools and neighbourhoods.'[1] The same, as we shall see, could be said of the 'liberal' United Federation of Teachers.

The latest round in this battle, and perhaps the most significant, has been the fight over the attempt to decentralise the New York City school system into between thirty and sixty school districts, each with a locally elected system. The conflict which resulted from this plan has received very wide press coverage not only in the United States but in Britain and the rest of Europe as well. Much of the coverage has concerned itself with the dramatic events of the confrontation blacks who are reported to be anti-Semitic; Mayor Lindsay being hustled out of a side door after intense barracking at a Jewish Community Centre by Jews irate at what they considered his surrender to black militants; and a series of teachers' strikes which virtually closed the city's school system for three months from September 1968. The interesting questions raised by this conflict are not merely over the types of, or control of, New York's educational system. The importance of this particular issue lies in its relationship with the broader fight for power of a previously powerless group in society. Rhody McCoy, the unit administrator or supervisor of one of the experimental school districts, that of Ocean Hill-Brownsville in Brooklyn, cogently declared that 'if anyone walking the streets of New York is under the impression that the teachers are on strike over an educational issue, he is grossly misinformed. The issues are politics and labour.'[2]

This attempt by the powerless to obtain power is part of a wider problem facing not only the United States but Western Europe as well. It is the growing sense of individuals that the bureaucrats who run the large units of government are too distant from them and that they are not really accountable to those they are supposed to serve. There is a pressure throughout the developed world for some form of devolution of power to bring control close to the individual and the region or community. This involves a revaluation of the expertise of the professionals and a decline in the previously almost automatic deference to that expertise. There is a class element in this attitude — a feeling that the middle-class professionals do not understand or value the way of life and aspirations of working-class people. But it is not restricted to any one class. For example, the President of the American National School Board Association said recently: 'The average citizen feels he's getting further away from influencing anything ... the schools have not found many effective ways to relate to the community.' *Education News* went even further when it declared that 'the invisible people also inhabit the wealthy suburb and the dusty farm town. And whether and when and how they will influence their schools is a national issue.'[3]

But imagine how much more invisible and powerless most urban black ghetto residents are. They are faced with an educational system which is segregated, inferior and, most of all, unresponsive to their legitimate demands. They live in segregated, overcrowded, substandard and expensive neighbourhoods, pay more for inferior merchandise and have twice the national unemployment rate. Their votes are solicited and then taken for granted and their wishes constantly ignored in favour of those of more powerful groups or in favour of administrative convenience and economy. They have been able to bring their grievances about the failures of the educational system to the fore, and to be in a position to have a say in the operation of the system in at least three areas, because their alienation from the present system coincided with the rejection of that system by outside white and powerful groups. It was this combination of previously powerless blacks, fed up with the system's failure to respond to their needs, and of foundational political figures, concerned about the failure of the education system, which led to the decentralisation controversy of the past two years in New York City.

II

It is important to sketch in the background to this controversy if we are to understand the form it took and its implications. Probably the single most important factor underlying the black demand for decentralisation and community control was the almost complete failure of the New York City school system to educate the majority of its black or Puerto Rican pupils. David Rogers, in his penetrating study of the system, concluded that the New York City schools have failed in ghetto areas, in most desegregated communities as well. 'One out of three pupils in the system is a year or more retarded in reading and arithmetic .... Public education was for previous ethnic groups a prime means for social mobility, but for the Negro it tends to block mobility and to increase socio-economic and racial segregation.'[4]

The schools that black children attend are overwhelmingly segregated. In 1969, fifteen years after the United States Supreme

Court declared that school segregation based on law was unconstitutional, *de facto* segregation in the North generally and in New
York City in particular is the norm. Sixty-five per cent of New
York City's black children attend schools which are over 90 per
cent black, while 80 per cent of the city's white school children
attend almost all-white schools.

Despite almost ten years of effort, civil rights groups were
unable to move the city's educational institution to integrate the
schools. There were, to be sure, a multitude of agreements in principle, policy statements and declarations of intent, but there was
little actual mixing of bodies in the schools. Most white groups
and school officials did not want the various desegregation plans
to succeed and these programmes were subverted by acts of omission as well as of commission. Not only were children not, in any
significant way, moved from black to white schools, but new
schools were consciously built in the heart of white and black
neighbourhoods so as to perpetuate segregated schooling.[5]

The importance of this failure to take positive zoning decisions
cannot be overestimated, for, as Rogers argues:

> A conventional interpretation of school and city officials, and of
> social scientists and urban planners, is that housing segregation is the
> primary cause of school segregation. It is assumed that school
> segregation was not deliberately planned, but just came about as a
> result of residential patterns. My evidence suggests that this is not
> totally the case in New York City and that the Board of Education's
> own actions contributed to the tipping of some residential areas that
> had previously been integrated. I am suggesting that school
> construction and zoning practices of the board were a cause not only
> of increased school segregation but of housing segregation as well.'[6]

> The educational system came up with a number of desegregation
> plans, such as Open Enrolment, which were sabotaged. The following
> comments are illustrative of the techniques which were used to
> sabotage these programmes. A Brooklyn civil rights leader said, 'In
> almost every school I have anything to do with, Open Enrolment was
> not only not pushed but talked against. Parents got lectures about
> how hard it is to travel and go to school far away.' A human relations
> staff person in the Bronx reported 'Open Enrolment proposals were
> always announced at the last minute, with a notice sent home the last
> two weeks of school with an invitation to visit new schools. They
> know that the parents don't have time on two weeks' notice to get
> involved. So in a way, it was doomed to failure before they started.'[7]

Not only were black parents thus discouraged from enroling their children in the programme but if they did attempt to transfer their children further difficulties were put in their way. Forthcoming pupils would often be placed in slow and/or segregated classes or streams, more disciplinary measures would be used, and often little attempt was made by principals and supervisors to obtain extra services for the incoming students. Probably the most damning comment about the treatment received by the incoming pupils is the following account by a Bronx civic leader: 'A few years ago, about 30 to 35 kids were bussed into an elementary school here. They went on one bus and were deposited at a particular door, never in the school yard where the rest of the kids were. They went directly to their room and from 8.30 until 3.30 they stayed there. They ate their lunch in the room and did exercises there rather than recess. They left the room only to go to the bathroom and were taken directly to the bus and home at the end of the day.'[8]

The failure of these desegregation plans meant that the black children remained in segregated schools. But not only were they segregated in inferior schools with the highest percentages of substitute and temporary teachers and with the highest rate of daily teacher absenteeism. In the Ocean Hill-Brownsville schools, the daily absentee rate in the year before decentralisation was 25 per cent. Teachers who were found unacceptable to principals and supervisors in other, mainly white, areas were regularly transferred from school to school until they wound up in ghetto schools. This is not to say that all the teachers in these schools were like this, but enough of them were to do damage and to set the tone of the schools. The results were as could have been expected. Not only are black children behind whites in reading and arithmetic, but the longer they stay in the school system, the farther behind they fall. So children who were half a year behind at first grade level are two years behind by the sixth grade, and almost three years behind by the twelfth grade. Three times as many black teenagers as white are high-school drop-outs and even among those blacks who stay on to graduation, a majority do not receive either academic or commercial diplomas, but receive instead a general diploma which is largely useless in the job market.[9] The children in such a situation are largely alienated from the school system and one of the main tasks facing Rhody McCoy and the others running the decentralised districts is, in McCoy's words, to get 'these youngsters to understand that these are schools'.

This massive school system, involving over 1.1 million pupils, over 900 separate schools and over 56,000 teachers, is run by an enormous and largely unaccountable and inflexible bureaucracy. The educational bureaucracy has been unresponsive to the changing nature of the population of New York with 59 per cent of the schoolchildren now either black or Puerto Rican. The bureaucracy is still overwhelmingly white and Jewish — over 60 per cent of the teachers, and an even greater percentage of supervisors and headquarters bureaucrats, are Jewish. At the same time, only 9 per cent of the teachers are either black or Puerto Rican. This disparity is even more dramatic at the supervisory levels, where until 1967 there were only four black principals out of 865 — a little less than 0.5 per cent — and only 12 black assistant principals in the 1500 positions at that rank. This educational bureaucracy, which includes the faculty in the city colleges, as well as the bureaucrats and teachers, is phenomenally inbred. A recent study found only one top level headquarters bureaucrat who had been in the school system for less than ten years, and most had been in the system for twenty or thirty years. Certain ethnic groups are, as we have seen, over-represented. Both of these factors help to explain the crux of the problem of the school system, which is the system's unwillingness or inability to respond to the new demands being made on it. A United States Office of Education study of the school system concluded that it appeared 'paralysed' by its problems and that it had failed to stem a precipitous downhill trend. They also found that the system has not made any meaningful changes in curriculum, administrative structure, general organisation and teacher recruitment, appointment and training for at least three decades. This large, cumbersome school system has been hindered by a congested bureaucracy and has suffered from inertia and has responded dilatorily to new major demands being made on it.[10]

The bureaucracy, having used the claim of professionalism to defeat political interference by the big-city political machines many years ago, still clings to it as a shield against criticism. In this, they have been joined by the teachers, who use it as a defence against what they call interference from parents, especially lower class parents. This determination to cling to the facade of professionalism is probably more obstinate because there is really so little substance behind the façade. One astute observer of the school system has declared: 'While teachers and principals may know more about education than most laymen, ... they don't know very much. There is no codified body of knowledge that educators can learn and apply, as there is in medicine and law. There is little expertise to apply despite any myths to the contrary.'[11] Faced with the failure of the school system either to integrate the schools or to educate their children properly in ghetto schools, black parents have become increasingly more resistant to the bureaucracy's claims of professionalism and expertise. Indeed, they are basing their opposition to professional control not merely on the grounds of the failure of the professional but on broader theoretical considerations as well. Reverend C. Herbert Oliver, President of the Ocean Hill-Brownsville governing board, has said that the responsibility to educate the nation's young is the parents'. 'We have lost sight of this principle. It is not the duty and responsibility of the professional to educate children. Parents may employ professionals but it is their own function to see that their children are educated. The professionals have taken on the job and said to parents, particularly poor black parents, you get out. This must never be. Parents must educate children.'[12] In addition, their demands are based on the view that segregated schools are the given — that the real choice facing black parents is whether their children will go to good segregated schools or bad segregated schools — at least for the near future. Preston Wilcox, a Professor of Social Work at Columbia University, has said that 'most schools teach white nationalism; black children should be exposed to black nationalism. We have a dual system of education now but both are controlled by whites.'[13]

III

Given this situation the blacks turned from desegregation to questions of quality of education and of local control, which was seen as a necessary condition for quality education. They saw the necessity of limiting the powers of the school professionals if they were to accomplish their goals. This shift in emphasis in the black community coincided with Mayor Lindsay's attempt in 1967 to obtain more money from New York State for the city's school system by proposing the decentralisation of the system into five, borough-wide districts. The state legislature agreed to increase the State's contribution on the condition that a fully fledged decentralisation plan be worked out. Mayor Lindsay appointed a Panel on Decentralization under the Chairmanship of McGeorge Bundy, President of the Ford Foundation. In November 1967 the Panel reported in favour of decentralisation not into five very large units, but into between thirty and sixty smaller units of between 12,000 and 40,000 pupils. They recommended that local governing boards be established, chosen in part by parents in the district and in part by the Mayor. These local boards were to have control over expenditure, curriculum development, book and supply purchasing, and appointments. The main limitations on the latter power were that teachers already having tenure would be assured of its continuance and that all new teachers would have a New York State teaching certificate.[14] The Ford Foundation at the same time agreed to finance three experimental demonstration districts: one in East Harlem called the Intermediate School 201 Complex, Two Bridges in the Lower East Side of Manhattan, and one in Brooklyn, destined to become the centre of the fight over decentralisation, Ocean Hill-Brownsville. Each district was built around one or two intermediate schools with their feeder elementary schools.

These proposals were not universally welcomed and the fight over decentralisation began almost immediately. The central Board of Education, the United Federation of Teachers, and the Council of Supervisory Associations — the supervisors' trade union — all part of New York City's educational bureaucracy, responded to the attempt to decentralise the city's school system with determined and unscrupulous opposition. The stakes of this battle with the black community were very high-control of a billion dollar educational budget, control over many thousands of non-teaching jobs, the dominance of the teachers' union, lucrative construction contracts, and in the long run the continued dominance of the white power structure. These were all at risk if the decentralisation experiment was successful and if the entire system was decentralised. The tactics of these groups were based on the attempt to discredit decentralisation by proving that it led automatically to chaos, union-busting and racism, especially anti-Semitism. Each of these tactics was designed to mobilise particular groups: liberals and educationists by showing the chaos that would result; the city's powerful union movement by showing the union-busting; and the liberals and, most importantly, the city's large and influential Jewish community by showing widespread anti-Semitism inherent in decentralisation. This last has been the single most publicised aspect of the conflict, not only in New York and the United States but in Britain as well.

The central Board of Education and its mammoth bureaucracy, with all it had to lose from decentralisation and community control, played a crucial role in the battle. Their role as the all-powerful centre of the educational system would be destroyed if decentralisation succeeded, for they would be left as a rump organisation with limited powers and limited resources. Their role was crucial because the three demonstration districts, IS 201 in East Harlem, Two Bridges in the Lower East Side, and Ocean Hill-Brownsville in Brooklyn, had to establish the limits of their powers and their detailed terms of reference with the central Board. The Board, however, in the words of the New York Civil Liberties Union ' ... attempted to scuttle the experiment in Ocean Hill-Brownsville [the first of the districts to begin operations] by consistently refusing to define the authority of the local Governing Board'.[15] They refused to co-operate with the local board, utilising their bureaucratic expertise in delay and obfuscation. For example, when the steering committee in Ocean Hill-Brownsville, in accordance with a time-table laid down by the Ford Foundation, attempted to obtain the names and addresses of parents in their area so as to register them for an election for the Local Governing Board, the central Board refused. After further pressure and delay they agreed to allow two secretaries at the central headquarters to obtain this information. The local people were required to pay the secretaries for this operation. But, after agreeing, they were informed that the two secretaries were on holiday, and would not be back until after the election was due to be held. The local people did the best they could without this list: they sent notes home with the schoolchildren, and volunteer teachers canvassed the neighbourhood. After the election, in which 25 per cent of those eligible voted — a figure, incidentally, which was almost double the normal turnout in local elections in that district — the central Board refused to recognise the elected body, on the ground that they were not representative. By failing to define clearly the authority of the Local Governing Board and by refusing to co-operate with them, the central Board was ensuring that at some point the local people would overstep their authority and thus come into conflict with the central Board. This ploy worked, as we shall see, and it played a major part in the conflict over decentralisation.

The local Boards' main public protagonist has been the United Federation of Teachers under its President, Albert Shanker. While publicly declaring their support for the principle of decentralisation on a limited basis, they have consistently worked against any meaningful decentralisation programme. They lobbied extensively, expensively and effectively in the New York State Legislature in the Spring of 1968 against all strong decentralisation bills — bills that would have created between 30 and 60 local districts run by locally elected boards, with effective powers. Instead, they supported the bill, which finally passed, which postponed the decision for a year, and which kept the three demonstration districts under the jurisdiction of the central Board and of the State Commissioner of Education. They then proceeded to use that year to prove not only that decentralisation meant chaos, in which their prime ally was the central Board, but that it meant union-busting and anti-Semitism as well. Before discussing their tactics, let us look, for a moment, at their motivation.

The first, and most obvious, reason for their opposition to a far-reaching decentralisation scheme is a straightforward trade union one. They have established a productive relationship with the central Board of Education — productive in terms of improvements in pay and conditions — and do not want to lose the relationship. The alternative — having to negotiate with between 30 and 60 separate districts — is one which they obviously do not desire. This reason, however, is not sufficient to explain the virulence of their opposition, for if the will were there it should be possible to work out a mutually satisfactory structure — for example, something like the Burnham Committee — under which the union would negotiate a central contract for the entire system. One could also have an appeal procedure, chaired by an independent party to evaluate transfer policies and the like. But there was no such desire on the union's part. Shanker, believing in the domino theory, was determined to crush decentralisation in the bud rather than let it succeed in one place and spread to the rest of the system. It seems clear that his and the union's motivation was based on something much broader than that which we traditionally consider trade union self-interest. They have been determined to maintain the shield of professionalism against potential interference. At the heart of the black demands for decentralisation and community control, and indeed of the Bundy Committee's recommendations, was the idea that the parents had to be brought into the educational system in a significant way. This the UFT rejected, perhaps out of fear or perhaps because they saw how threadbare the cloak of professionalism really was and feared exposure. In their response to the Bundy recommendations the UFT declared that it was 'anti-professional' to allow a situation in which 'charges could be brought against a tenured faculty member by a community board of laymen with no professional expertise'. They also declared that 'the Bundy report ignores the new power and integrity of the professional teacher who will not continue to teach in any school or district where professional decisions are made by laymen'.[16] Why this fear of laymen and parents? Could it be that the teachers, having failed to reach these people's children, feared that they would then hold the teacher responsible? Could it be that deep down the teachers themselves felt a sense of failure that was not totally assuaged by their defence mechanisms and rationalisations? The evidence seems to indicate that this is the case and that this is a crucial part of the motivation for their fanatical opposition to decentralisation. Edmund Gordon placed the teachers' concern with what they call 'professionalism' into its proper context when he wrote:

> Professionalism is based on specialised competence, on independence of judgement concerning professional matters, on quality of services rendered, and on responsibility for that competence, that independence of judgement and that service. The concern with professionalism among educators has tended to favour the former two to the neglect of the latter two.[17]

Instead of consciously accepting responsibility for the failure of the system to educate black children, the teachers have erected, on very shaky foundations, a structure of rationalisations accounting for this failure. This shifts the full burden of blame on to the children, the parents and the neighbourhood. It is argued that these children are 'culturally deprived', that their parents are not only uninterested in education and therefore not supporters of the school but that they are often antagonistic, so that the teachers, doing the best they can, are faced with an all but impossible situation.

Despite the surface plausibility of these assertions there are major internal weaknesses in their case which threaten this entire defensive edifice and which, if linked to successful decentralisation, can only topple it. The assertions about parental indifference are supported neither by survey data (which show the very high expectations black parents have of education), nor by experience of parents in the decentralised districts. Outside observers as well as those running these districts have been struck by the response of these supposedly uninterested parents to real opportunities for participation. Even in districts which have not yet decentralised but which hope to be included in the wider plans for decentralisation there has been a tremendous response of parents. The United Bronx Parents Association has been holding a series of meetings in the Bronx and on a bitterly cold December evening over 800 parents attended one of their meetings in a low-income black and Puerto Rican area. They listened to detailed lectures on various aspects of decentralisation and broke up into work groups to discuss particular problems of curriculum development, teacher and pupil rights, and book and supply purchasing. This meeting lasted for well over three hours, and these supposedly are the parents who do not support the schools. Until now, no one has tried in any constructive way to enlist their support.

Another crack in the edifice has been occasioned by the growing evidence showing the importance of teacher expectations for pupil performance. One recent and major study found that the performance of a randomly selected group of children was significantly improved merely by changing teacher expectation of these children. The authors of this study have argued that

> the disadvantaged child is a Negro American, a Mexican American, a Puerto Rican or any other child who lives in conditions of poverty. He is a lower-class child who performs poorly in an educational system that is staffed almost entirely by middle-class teachers. The reason usually given for the poor performances of the disadvantaged child is simply that the child is a member of a disadvantaged group. There may well be another reason. It is that the child does poorly in school because that is what is expected of him. In other words, his shortcomings may originate not in his different ethnic, cultural and economic background, but in his teachers' response to that background.[18]

They found that the results obtained by changing teacher expectations were greater than were obtained by programmes using Title
I money under the Elementary and Secondary Education Act of
1965 which was designed to provide special programmes directed
toward disadvantaged children. The importance of teacher-expec-
tation and self-fulfilling prophesies cannot be overstressed.
Howard Kalodner, a New York University Law Professor and legal
counsel to the Bundy Committee, has said that the first pre-
requisite for a chance at success for the decentralised districts is
'some way to destroy the professional educational bureaucracy.
Seventy-five to eighty per cent of the educators do not believe that
black and Puerto Rican children can learn. You can't have a professional educational system like that.'[19]

This, of course, is precisely what those in favour of community
control wish to do. They want to bring into their schools teachers,
regardless of race or religion, who will be sympathetic and understanding and not begin with low expectations of their children.
And if they find teachers with these negative attitudes they want to
be able to transfer them out of their district. The sum total of these
threats to the teachers' defensive rationalisations is magnified by
the fear that, if the schools in the decentralised districts succeed
when they have failed, these rationalisations will be exposed. This
has led to their unprincipled opposition to the experiment. As one
UFT teacher with painful honesty put it: 'Either I buy a great big
bag of guilt or I become a self-protective bigot ... and I am not prepared to buy the bag of guilt.'[20] This attitude and these fears can
explain, but can never exonerate, the union's tactics, which, however successful they may have been in the short run, can only do
major damage to race relations. In order to mobilise opposition
from other unions against decentralisation, the union consistently,
and very largely successfully, misrepresented the attempt by the
Ocean Hill-Brownsville board to transfer 19 teachers out of the
district. This is a common practice in the New York City school
system, yet the central Board denied Rhody McCoy as demonstration district supervisor the powers normally given to district
supervisors. The union claimed that these teachers had been
unfairly dismissed in violation of their tenure rights and due
process. They claimed this so often that soon the Mayor, the central Board and the press were all talking about the teachers who
had been fired — despite the fact that none of the teachers had lost

a single day's pay, that the letter informing the teachers of their transfer both offered an opportunity to appeal and instructed them to report to the central Board for reassignment. The New York Civil Liberties Union declared that 'there is no question that under present standards the United Federation of Teachers created the due process issue out of thin air'.[21] Another study of this controversy, under the chairmanship of the President of the Bank Street College of Education, found that under normal circumstances the Demonstration project might have been able to accomplish the transfer of 'unsatisfactory' personnel informally, but a larger struggle was being waged in the New York State Legislature over a general proposal to decentralise the entire school system.[22]

Thus it is clear that the UFT and the central Board were using this issue as a way of discrediting decentralisation in the eyes of the rest of the city and in the New York State Legislature. The UFT then tried to get an added bonus by escalating their demand for settlement of the ensuing series of teachers' strikes to include provisions which if the local board accepted would discredit the local board in the black community and if they did not accept them would provide justification for the continuation of the strikes and the suspension of the local board and of Rhody McCoy. All of the latter happened when the Ocean Hill-Brownsville people refused to abide by the terms of settlement of one of a series of city-wide teachers' strikes that closed the schools for 36 days from September 1968. They had had no part in drawing up this settlement, which would have had the local board welcome back, rather than merely allow the return of, the striking teachers. Another requirement was that the local board agree in advance to accept all orders and recommendations of the central Board. All of these were impossible if the local board was to retain any standing in the local community. Consequently the Ocean Hill-Brownsville Board is under suspension, although it is in fact still running the schools in the district.

The union strategy during the series of strikes was geared to the attempt to discredit and destroy the decentralisation experiment because Shanker saw it as part of a domino theory. If it succeeded in Ocean Hill Brownsville it would spread to the rest of the city. Proof that this was his goal, rather than a settlement of the outstanding issues, can be seen in his firing of one of his vice-presidents, John T. O'Neill, who had attempted, and almost succeeded, in working out a settlement with McCoy.[23] The union's other main tactic was to convince the political leaders and the city's whites, and especially its Jewish population, that decentralisation was racist and anti-Semitic in origin and nature. The New York Civil Liberties Union has condemned this tactic in the following words:

> the UFT leadership, and in particular Albert Shanker, systematically accused the Ocean Hill-Brownsville Board and Rhody McCoy of anti-Semitism and extremism, and then 'proved' those accusations only with half truths, innuendoes and outright lies.[24]

An analysis of the material distributed by the hundred thousand by the union shows a large part of it to be fraudulent — either in terms of its having been concocted or in terms of two unrelated pieces of literature being put together on the same sheet in such a way as to imply that they belonged together. This approach has succeeded in mobilising the city's Jewish community against decentralisation and against Mayor Lindsay; he was prevented from completing a speech at a Jewish Community Centre by intense barracking by Jews convinced that he had sold out to the black anti-Semites. This inevitably exacerbated an already tense racial situation. It also succeeded in convincing the mass media that black anti-Semitism was a major problem worthy of magazine cover stories and leader-page articles deploring it. It even succeeded in becoming such a firm part of what is conceived to be common knowledge that the British Prime Minister, the Rt Hon Harold Wilson, in a speech on 10 March 1968 celebrating the twentieth anniversary of the *Jewish Vanguard*, declared, almost in passing:

> God help this country if anti-racialism were to breed a racialist backlash which could lead one section of the persecuted to strike out blindly, such as the manifestation, deplored and resisted, for example, by all decent Americans, under which black power becomes anti-Semitic.[25]

In fact, the truth about the Ocean Hill-Brownsville Board, and indeed about black anti-Semitism in general, is somewhat different from the UFT line which has been so widely accepted. Rhody McCoy and the local board issued a statement in which they declared that they have never tolerated nor will they ever tolerate anti-Semitism in any form. They further declared: 'Anti-Semitism has no place in our hearts or minds and indeed never in our schools'. Their actions as well have hardly been consistent with anti-Semitism and racism. Of the 350 new teachers they hired in the summer of 1968, 70 per cent were white and 50 per cent were Jewish. Over three-quarters of the district's teachers took a full-page advertisement in the *New York Times* supporting the local board and attacking the UFT and Mr Shanker for the unfounded charges of anti-Semitism and for the attempt to destroy decentralisation. The UFT succeeded in mobilising Jews as Jews to oppose decentralisation by playing on the growing Jewish fears of anti-Semitism in the black community. This blurred the essential fact that when Jewish teachers and Jewish administration opposed decentralisation they did so as teachers and administrators rather than as Jews. This mobilisation of Jews *qua* Jews can only exacerbate black anti-Semitism and make more credible the statements and charges of a relative handful of black extremists.

Despite talk of 'pogromist' and 'genocidal' tendencies and references to Hitler[26] it is important to keep the probable rise of black anti-Semitism and its causes in perspective. The most remarkable aspect of black anti-Semitism in the United States, a nation in which white anti-Semitism is still widespread, has been its very low level. Gary Marx, in his study *Protest and Prejudice*, found in 1964 that, on an index of anti-Semitism, 36 per cent of the black respondents were non-anti-Semitic and 40 per cent were 'low'.[27] Most blacks, 75 per cent, failed to make a distinction between Jewish and non-Jewish whites. By the 25 per cent that did make a distinction, Jews were seen in a more favourable light than other whites by a 4-1 ratio.[28] In another study, *What Americans Think About Jews*, by Gertrude Selznick and Stephen Sternberg, which was due to appear in the summer of 1969, it was found that, while blacks were more likely to accept negative stereotypes about Jews in the economic field than were whites, they were clearly less anti-Semitic in the action they would take with regard to discrimination against Jews; for example, almost all blacks, 91 per cent, stated that a private club has no right to exclude Jews — the comparable figure for whites was 69 per cent. Of the black population, 68 per cent would not be disturbed if their party nominated a Jew for President — the figure for whites was 51 per cent.[29] Selznick and Steinberg conclude that 'what seems to characterise anti-Semitism among Negroes is less an emotional than a *verbal* displacement of hostility'.[30] Their other major finding which reinforces the Marx data is that black anti-Semitism is part of a broader attitude toward whites. Gary Marx concluded that 'contrary to public opinion, much Negro anti-Semitism may be directed not at Jews as Jews, but at Jews as whites'.[31] In fact, he found that

> pure anti-Semitism, not accompanied by anti-white feelings, is to be found among only 4 per cent of the sample. Exactly the same proportion harboured anti-white sentiments unaccompanied by anti-Semitism. For the vast majority of Negroes, the two are relatively indistinguishable, and more than half of our respondents expressed very little hostility on either index.[32]

How can one account both for these 1964 findings and for the increase in anti-Semitism which seems now to be taking place? One important explanation appears to be related to the presence at the earlier period of an intervening variable which operated to minimise anti-Semitism. That variable was the fact that 'a sizeable percentage of the black population is aware of the support that Jews give to civil rights'.[33] In fact, Marx found that, among those blacks who had the highest degree of impersonal economic contact with Jews, with the latter in superior positions as shopkeepers, employers and landlords precisely the sort of contact which is most likely to produce high anti-Semitism — but who saw Jews as civil rights allies, only 21 per cent were high in anti-Semitism. On the other hand, 73 per cent of those with an equally high rate of contact but who did not see the Jews as allies were high in anti-Semitism.[34]

Given the situation, the declining relevance of this variable (that is, the growth of Northern Jewish, as indeed of Northern white, opposition to black demands in the fields of housing, education and employment) may account for a large part of the apparent increase in anti-Semitism. The resulting situation has involved conflict of interests between a large number of individuals who have a privileged position, and an increasingly active and vocal disadvantaged minority. The fact that among those whites with vested interests there are Jews must not blind us to the fact that the battle is not over their Jewishness — it is over their privileges. Thus in the fight over decentralisation the battle was fought in large part against Jewish teachers and Jewish administrators, not because they were

Jewish — despite the claims of the UFT on the one hand and some black militants on the other — but because of their position.

It is irrelevant and dangerous for these people who are fighting to retain their privileges to keep referring to the past when Jews were active in the civil rights movement and to then accuse the blacks of ingratitude. This is not to deny the presence of anti-Semitism, but it is to deny the centrality and extent which have been given to it by groups like the UFT. And it can only be increased by campaigns such as that run by the UFT which succeed in mobilising Jews as Jews to oppose institutional changes which are necessary if the blacks are to improve their position in American society.

The demonstration districts, even in the face of the chaos and disruption caused by the central Board of Education and the United Federation of Teachers, have made great strides towards improving the quality of education being provided as well as in improving the relationship between the schools and the community. I.F. Stone, after visiting Ocean Hill-Brownsville, commented: 'I found black and white teachers, Jewish and gentile, working together not just peacefully but with zest and comradeship .... The classes were orderly. There was none of that screaming, by teacher against pupil and among the children, which is common in most New York schools.'[35] Because of this commitment to improving education, the local board has encouraged experimentation and initiative, the sole test being how successful it is — not, as at present under the central Board, whether it fits into established programmes. One Ocean Hill-Brownsville teacher said, 'It's the first time in my eight years as a teacher that I have been allowed to use unconventional teaching methods.'[36] This factor has been responsible for the large number of New York teachers who have transferred into Ocean Hill-Brownsville and who are trying to do so: they want to teach and to use their initiative, and the present system does not allow this. For example, a major study of the city school system concluded that 'the greatest failing of the schools today is the failure to use the creative ability of teachers'.[37] The struggle over decentralisation has exacerbated racial and religious antagonism. It has brought the entire school system to a stop for the first three months of the 1968 school year and it has played a major role in the unification of the black community and in strengthening in them a sense of self-confidence and pride. As John O'Neill, who was fired by Shanker, said,

'Shanker has accomplished in five months what would have taken five years under normal conditions, in furthering the demands of community militants'.[38]

It is precisely this sense of unity and determination which will keep the fight for decentralisation going, despite the victory of the UFT and educational bureaucracy in the New York State Legislature. The State Legislature, after ten gruelling days, passed a decentralisation law on 1 May which gives the UFT virtually all that it asked for — one observer likened the law to a 'collective bargaining agreement' — and which will abolish the three demonstration districts. The law establishes thirty local districts under the supervision and judgement of a new Board of Education — one member to be elected by each of New York City's five boroughs and two to be appointed by the Mayor. Under the City's present political structure it is unlikely that a black or Puerto Rican will be elected. The Board and its Chancellor will have major powers of supervision as well as the final say on budgets; the Board of Examiners will be retained, as will the Civil Service list for appointments and promotions. The new decentralised districts are to be drawn up under an interim five-man Board, consisting of one member appointed by each Borough President. There are a few concessions given to supporters of decentralisation, but these do not compensate for the general pro-bureaucracy tenor of the law. Each district will be given $250,000 a year to spend on repairs, etc. and any district where children fall below 45 per cent on reading and arithmetic tests can appoint teachers from outside the Board of Examiners' list, provided that they have either a State or a National Teachers Certificate. This is fair but what happens if they succeed in raising the level of performance of the children? The district will then presumably go back under the Board of Examiners and be restricted in their choice of teachers and supervisors. The law has been bitterly attacked by the black community: Rhody McCoy called it a 'prelude to the destruction of public education'.[39] Charles Wilson, who is the Project Administrator of IS 201 in East Harlem, called the new law a 'disgrace' and declared:

> If you take away the hope of people who only have hope, you're on very dangerous ground .... After giving people a little taste of freedom and involvement, it is dangerous to put them back under the old order.[40]

The Rev. C.H. Oliver, Chairman of the Ocean Hill-Brownsville Board, indicated that one approach that they would take would be a law suit aimed at invalidating the part of the law calling for the election of one member from each borough, under the *Baker* v. *Carr* Supreme Court ruling. But beyond that, he indicated a quiet determination that the community's schools were not going to be put back under the control of the bureaucracy, regardless of what has to be done to prevent it.[41]

The blacks are determined to 'do their own thing' to control their own schools and, given the failure of the New York State Legislature to heed their legitimate demands, there is likely to be further disruption and violence because of this. Perhaps we can end with a quotation from a letter sent by David Spencer, Chairman of the IS 201 Complex Governing Board, in which he expresses the type of approach which may come to be seen in the black community as the only legitimate one, following their defeat in the legislature:

> We are convinced that the only language the city understands is disruption and turmoil. The Board of Education ignored our Governing Board until the UFT created a massive public crisis. Now we are discussing the necessary expansion of our powers with them. The city will continue to refuse to recognise local communities' rights to control their own schools until local uprisings *force* the Mayor to provide a voice in education for Black and Puerto Rican parents. It is still our firm belief that nobody is going to give us anything; the community is going to have to *take* it![42]

2 Race, Class and Civil Rights

The central thesis of this chapter is that, as far as the life conditions and chances of the mass of African-Americans were concerned, the attainments of the Civil Rights Movement (CRM) in the US were limited. For most blacks the removal of *de jure* segregation was a necessary, but insufficient, condition for fundamental changes.

In the US there is widespread structural inequality in the distribution of wealth, income and power. Institutional racism determines resource allocation: access to goods and services and opportunities including education, employment, health care and housing and assures that, compared with blacks, whites get privileged access to scarce resources. This version of equality in a *Herrenvolk* democracy maintains the class system by inculcating and reinforcing a race consciousness rather than a class consciousness among the white working class.[1] One has only to look at the history of 'race riots' — pogroms — against people of colour in times of economic and political crisis, for example, the race riots in Chicago and the current escalation of racial violence among unemployed and alienated whites.

White working-class racism represents an incorporation *of* the dominant ideology, as reproduced through the schools, the media and the political institutions of the society. This ideology serves the interests of the ruling class and is encouraged and reinforced both directly and indirectly.[2] While it is true that white working-class people are given psychic and, to a degree, material benefits from the racist system and, therefore, there is widespread acceptance of racism, it is important to note three points:

(a) racism is not a genetically determined, or human nature
   determined, set of beliefs and practices;
(b) the price white workers pay is very high indeed (as is the case for
   male workers and sexism); and
(c) working-class history contains many points at which the presence
   of an alternative ideology an alternative way of explaining the
   world and alternative conceptions about the ability to change
   reality lead to non- and anti-racist practice.

This threat fosters extensive political and ideological efforts on
the part of the ruling classes (and their allies in the media and
state institutions) to delegitimate these alternative ideologies. In
the US, in the post-Second World War period, for example, massive, state-led anti-Communist hysteria and purges played a
crucial role, not only in legitimating the Cold War but also in iso-
lating alternative visions about how US society itself should be
organised. Central to this was a determined effort to prevent any
linking of race and class in the black community and in black politics. Black people and their white allies have to overcome this
ideological assault, which aims at separating race from class,
intellectually and politically.

Civil Rights and the Cold War in the United States

In analysing the development of black politics in the period since
the Second World War, we must look at the following the interrelationship between political and economic spheres of life; the
interrelationship between domestic and foreign policies; demographic, economic and political changes in the US; the class
composition, ideology and hierarchies of the CRM; the incorporation of most industrial unions into the Cold War, anti-Communist
consensus; and the repression of those individuals and organisations that resisted. This attempt to place the CRM in a framework
of analysis is designed to enable us to understand its achievements
as well as its limitations and to understand the position of black
people in the US today. It is not intended in any way to deprecate
the courage, determination and creativity of those who struggled,
or the range of consequences which followed these struggles. It is
clear, for example, that we cannot understand the politics of the
1960s and beyond — including the development of the New Left,

the anti-war movement and, crucially, the second wave of feminism — without understanding the impact of the CRM.[3] But unless we situate the CRM in its appropriate framework, we are in danger of making a number of important and damaging mistakes. We would have to ignore (or fail to value) previous struggles of black people if we were unable to explain adequately why the CRM achieved what it did and why earlier struggles failed to achieve similar results. It is clear that African-Americans have struggled from the very beginning of their formation as a people — during slavery/resistance on the slave ships, through marronage and slave uprisings, and through their resistance to the re-establishment of the plantation economy, to Jim Crow (the system of *de jure* segregation) and to institutional racism. The outcome of the struggles of any people is determined not merely by their will and determination but also by the range and balance of forces against which they are struggling and the range and balance of forces on which they can call. A second and related danger in failing to place the CRM in its context, is that we may fall prey to the neo-conservative ideological campaign which purports to explain the position of the mass of black people at the bottom of the society in terms of their culture of poverty, or of the broken, pathological Negro family, or of other similar victim blaming explanations.

Bearing these caveats in mind, let us look at some of the fundamental shifts which were occurring in the US and which consequently altered the context within which black people struggled and achieved changes. The fight against Jim Crow's *de jure* segregation united all sections of the black community and reshaped social and political structures in the South. It also changed the nature of black leadership and of class relations. This legal form of racism denied fundamental rights to all blacks under its sway, irrespective of their class. It was a total system of racial humiliation designed not only to control blacks (then largely living in the former slave states), but also poor whites. By legislating in favour of racial supremacy the South's rulers gave poor whites a stake in a system which, in practice, kept them poor. Poor whites gave up their votes — when they had them — in return for this racial superiority and, consequently, their adherence to a highly unequal society was bought extremely cheaply. Whites in the South had lower wages, worse public services and fewer benefits than whites in the rest of the country. Any politician who dared to raise questions about this situation was defeated by demagogic appeals to racial superiority and unity.

It is important to see that, though *de jure* segregation was a powerful form of racial control, it was not the only one; Jim Crow did not embody all US racism and, therefore, its removal would not signal the end of racism. It was created to protect and reproduce the re-established plantation system of the South, in which 90 per cent of the nation's black people lived. The system depended on controlled (less than free) labour and terror and Jim Crow helped maintain the super-exploitation of a black rural proletariat for the benefit of Southern and northern capitalists. The system served the interests of all dominant financial and industrial capitalists — not merely the Southern white ones.[4]

The origins of the dismantling of Jim Crow can be traced back to the recruiting of black labour by Northern industry during the First World War. Despite the opposition of Southern political and economic elites, the imperatives of Northern capital proved too powerful to be resisted. This led to increased mechanisation of Southern agriculture, which was further encouraged by the New Deal, the Agricultural Adjustment Act (AAA) and other programmes which began the process of creating a capital — rather than a labour-intensive system of agriculture. This had the consequence of lessening the region's dependence on black labour and, therefore, its need to keep black people out of the national labour market and, thus, ultimately its need of Jim Crow itself. This is not to say, however, that there was not a strong determination on the part of large numbers of whites (or even of a majority of them) to maintain the system of petty apartheid. It is, however, to say that for the dominant section of large-scale Southern agriculture, Jim Crow was no longer necessary for its hegemony.

The South was also changing in terms of the mix of industry and agriculture. The Federal government played a crucial role during and after the Second World War in encouraging the industrialisation of the South and Southwest. This process increased the political and economic importance of industrialists (including Northern-based ones) in determining the future direction of the region. This dependence on outside capital provided a very important counter-pressure against Southern opponents of civil rights.

The experience of Northern industrialists throughout the twentieth century, but particularly since the First World War, proved to them that *de jure* segregation was unnecessary. When black labour was recruited for jobs in Chicago, Detroit, Pittsburgh and other industrial centres, it entered communities in which *de jure* segregation was not the norm and in which it was not created. Instead, the system of institutional racism was created through the efforts of local and federal government and the real-estate and financial institutions to contain and control black people, to facilitate their super-exploitation, to ration scarce resources so that the unequal system which had produced that scarcity in the first place could be maintained, and to separate white and black workers. It was, therefore, clear to industrialists that, however desirable, Jim Crow was unnecessary. Therefore, in a highly charged political atmosphere in which Jim Crow acted as the target, or lightening rod, of all black anger and political mobilisation, it was no longer clear that agribusiness and industrial leaders could, in the face of escalating disorder and instability, be counted on as steadfast allies of those determined to maintain Jim Crow.

As indicated earlier, black people were struggling in the years prior to the emergence of the CRM. In the post-First World War period, Marcus Garvey's UNIA (Universal Negro Improvement Association) became the largest mass movement of blacks in US history. The UNIA represented the nationalist strand of black struggle and its appeal is indicative of the massive anger against white racism felt by African-Americans.[5] During the late 1920s and 1930s, the Communist Party gave high priority to working with blacks and, though it never obtained great numbers of black members, it did put the concept of the links between race and class on the political agenda. It also was the most important white-led organisation to challenge white racism particularly in an era of unchallenged white supremacy. In 1945, Representative Adam Clayton Powell Jr said, 'There is no group in America, including the Christian Church, that practices racial brotherhood one-tenth as much as the Communist Party'.[6] The relationship between the CPUSA (Communist Party of the United States of America) and blacks, between race and class, was to be of growing importance and was a central target of the efforts of the US government and of white liberals and middle class black leaders.

Questions of who the leaders are and of who determines priorities are crucial to any discussion of black politics, as they are to the politics of any group. In his overview of black American politics,

Manning Marable[7] argues that:

> The central fact about black political culture from 1865 to 1985 is that only a small segment of the Afro-American social fraction, the petty bourgeoisie, has dominated the electoral machinery and patronage positions that regulate black life and perpetuate the exploitation of black labour. The buffer stratum has historically focused its energies on non economic issues, such as the abolition of legal segregation; and when it has developed explicitly economic agendas, more frequently than not it presumes the hegemony of capital over labour. Even during periods of black working-class insurgency within electoral politics, the Negro petty bourgeoisie tend to surface on the crest of such movements.

The system of white supremacy that had been created with the defeat of the First Reconstruction involved the *shaping* of the black community's leadership structures. As Bloom[8] has written:

> White power was able to reach into the black community itself and to shape it, to help determine the goals the black community sought, the means desired to seek these goals, the leadership the black community had, the kinds of personal options blacks often felt they had, and even the view that blacks had of themselves. As a result of the victory of white supremacy, blacks had few options. They were not in a position to confront the white-created social, political, and economic world in order to change its terms; rather, they had to find a way to survive in it, to adjust to it. Accommodation meant looking to powerful whites as benefactors, requesting favours, accepting paternalism and subordination. It meant that whites determined the black community's leaders by deciding with whom they would communicate and to whom they would grant their *largesse*.

Bloom[9] goes on to argue that, as a consequence,

> the dynamics of the old system had divided blacks along class lines. The divisions in the old system had a weak objective basis. Those considered of higher social rank often had a tenuous hold on their status. That was all the more reason for their subjective insistence upon an exaggerated social distance separating them from poorer and (in their view) less cultured blacks.

Emphasis on economic issues, especially for a socialist position, represented a threat to the interests of this petit bourgeois stratum. It challenged its class interests and the acceptability of its leaders acceptable, that is, to the white power structure. It is interesting and important to note that W.E.B. DuBois represented just such a threat and thus was removed twice from leadership in the National Association for the Advancement of Coloured People (NAACP). His writings were apt and prescient. During the Depression he 'urged the NAACP to develop a meaningful economic programme to assist African Americans. In May 1932, the Crisis reported that the "first job" of the Association was "to fight colour discrimination" but it also stated that "our fight for economic equality" must include economic co-operation and "socialisation of wealth".'[10] He went on to declare[11] that the NAACP had to devise 'a positive program rather than mere negative attempts to avoid segregation and discrimination .... The interests of the masses are the interests of this Association, and the masses have got to voice themselves through it.'

This emphasis on economic issues and on the masses having power continued to be stressed by Dr Dubois and continued to be denied by the established leadership. Yet the Second World War brought to the forefront the reality of the mass of black people's anger and sense of alienation from US institutions. The Office of War Information carried out a survey in Harlem in the Spring of 1942 to determine black attitudes towards the war. It concluded[12] that, 'resentment at Negro discrimination [was] fairly widespread throughout the Negro population.' Only 11 per cent said they expected conditions to improve if America won the war. Lee Finkle quotes Ollie Stewart, a reporter who had visited many army camps, reporting that 'black soldiers were ready to start the fight at home before the European war ended. He said that with some encouragement and ammunition they would head for Washington to end discrimination.' He also quotes Joel A. Rogers[13] reporting a letter from a hostile reader complaining about 'so called intelligent race leaders ... yapping all out for victory. I ask what victory? The white man feeds his jive to the race leaders and they take up the yapping and feed it to the ignorant masses .... Each week when I read how the whites do the race it cements me against them and their war.' George Schuyler reported, 'the masses of Negroes are far more ready to fight and die than their leaders and spokesmen' (i.e. for their rights at home rather than for the US abroad). E. Washington Rhodes of the *Philadelphia Tribune* reported[14] 'the mass of Negroes is more radical than ... those of us who publish

Negro newspapers. The less vocal Negro ... is thinking more radical thoughts than we are thinking.'

These concerns were central to Gunnar Myrdal's *An American Dilemma* (1962), a classic liberal statement on race relations, in which he lays out the liberal agenda for the post-war period, including a clear statement on the underlying assumptions of that agenda. Themes running through this statement include the need for white Americans to re-evaluate race relations; the need to contain black militancy; and the international implications of American race relations. He makes clear that reforms are a necessary consequence of the growing black militancy. As he put it[15] 'America can never more regard its Negroes as a patient, submissive minority.' He was also at pains to stress that Negroes in America could count on the 'glorious American ideals of democracy, liberty, and equality' and the adherence to these ideals by white Americans. Therefore, 'the Negroes do not need any other allies'.[16] Presumably included among those allies they did not need was the Communist Party. Given that it was *An American Dilemma* and would be solved by white Americans being true to the *American Creed*, blacks would not need Pan-Africanism either.

Myrdal[17] then elaborates on the new mood among the black people:

> Reading the Negro press and hearing all the reports from observers who have been out among common Negroes in the South and the North convinces me that there is much sullen scepticism, and even cynicism, and vague, tired, angry dissatisfaction among American Negroes today. The general bitterness is reflected in the stories that are circulating in the Negro communities: A young Negro, about to [be] inducted into the Army, said 'Just carve on my tombstone, Here lies a black man killed fighting a yellow man for the protection of a white man'. Another Negro boy expressed the same feeling when he said he was going to get his eyes slanted so that the next time a white man shoved him around he could fight back .... There is more money in circulation and some trickles down to the Negroes. With a little money in his pocket even the poor Negro day labourer or domestic worker feels that he can afford to stiffen himself. Many white housewives notice strange thoughts and behaviour on the part of their Negro servants these days.

He quotes the 'troubled view' of a black clergyman, Dr J.S. Nathaniel Tross: 'I am afraid for my people. They have grown restless. They are not happy. They no longer laugh. There is a new policy among them — something strange, perhaps terrible.[18] The international implications are dearly stated by Myrdal, who is worth quoting at length again: 'What has actually happened within the last few years is not only that the Negro problem has become national in scope after having been mainly a Southern worry'. The language is interesting: who has the problem and whose worry? It is also misleading in that it was always national in the obvious sense that blacks were American citizens denied their constitutional rights with the acquiescence of the national government and in the interests of the national economic system. Myrdal continues:

> It has also acquired tremendous international implications, and this is another and decisive reason why the white North is prevented from compromising with the white South regarding the Negro. The situation is actually such that any and all concessions to Negro rights in this phase of the history of the world will repay the nation many times, while any and all injustices inflicted upon him will be extremely costly.[19] The main international implication is ... that America, for its international prestige, power, and future security, needs to demonstrate to the world that American Negroes can be satisfactorily integrated into democracy .... The treatment of the Negro in America has not made good propaganda for America abroad and particularly not among coloured nations.[20]

And crucially in Myrdal's felicitous phrase:

> Particularly as Russia cannot be reckoned on to adhere to white supremacy, it is evident from the facts ... that within a short period the shrinking minority of white people in our Western lands will either have to succumb or to find ways of living on peaceful terms with coloured people.[21]

Thus, the stage was set. Fundamental economic and demographic forces had lessened the centrality of *de jure* segregation for the leaders of the New South. Blacks had become more urban and more Northern and, consequently, more important in terms of electoral politics and were, at the same time, being seen as potentially dangerous or possibly disloyal in future wars — particularly against coloured nations. The threat of renewed links between blacks and the CP red was worrying. Centrally for the politics of post-war America, Pax Americana was replacing Pax Britannica, with the US emerging from the war as the most powerful nation in the world, determined to organise the post-war world system for its benefit. This was to have implications for race relations within the US. Crucially, Southern blacks were increasingly prepared to resist racist intimidation and the domination of the white power structure and their own accommodationist leaders. The dynamics of a growing willingness to fight, the delegitimation of *de jure* segregation by the Supreme Court and other institutions, the rejection of leaders who refused to oppose segregation *per se* as opposed to negotiating marginal variations or concessions in its operation, the white Southern resistance to the 1954 Supreme Court decision, Brown v. the Board of Education of Topeka which declared the previous doctrine of 'separate but equal' which had legalised the system of *de jure* segregation, to be unconstitutional — all these led to what Jack Bloom has called, after the example of blacks in Harlem in the 1920s, the New Negro. This all took place in a world being reshaped by the development of television, ensuring regional, national, and world-wide coverage of the resistance, which in turn ensured that the uprisings of the post-Montgomery period unlike those of the earlier period became part of the public consciousness of blacks, North and South, of whites throughout the US and of people throughout the world.

The black-led coalition which reshaped Southern society included, in Bloom's analysis,[22] 'Southern business and middle classes, the Northern middle class, the national Democratic Party, and the federal government'. This coalition 'was the key to the victory of the civil rights movement'. The nature of this coalition was also the key to the limits of what the CRM could achieve. The essence of black politics was the understanding of the different goals of the various components of the coalition and of how to play one sector of the Southern elites off against the other and of how to put pressure on the various Northern components to act. The strategy was effective as long as the CRM's demands for freedom and equality were contained within the parameters of the dominant ideology, i.e. freedom from segregation and overt discrimination and equality of opportunity. These were the limits of the dominant ideology and the limits imposed by the structural interests of the white middle and business classes, North and South, of the national Democratic Party and of the federal government. These demands were also congruent with the class interests

of the black middle class. When, as a result of the greater involvement of the black masses in the South in the mass actions of the
CRM and in the North in the ghetto uprisings the meaning of freedom and equality was expanded to include an economic
dimension, a demand for structural change, the coalition broke
apart.

The range of political forces supporting the status quo are very
great. In the case of the status quo of *de jure* segregation these
included: the dominant ideology and popular culture of the US
which were racist; the effects on the legislative process of the combination of the Seniority system in Congress and the Solid South
(the one-party system dominating post-reconstruction Southern
politics — racist attitudes among decision-makers themselves; and,
generally, the weakness of those wanting change in terms of political and economic resources.

Therefore, for the CRM to succeed in overturning a system of
legalised segregation a range of pressures had to be brought to bear
on decision-makers so that these forces could be overcome. Among
these forces were, political pressure from Democratic politicians in
the urban centres of the North and Mid West (who were becoming
increasingly dependent upon the black vote); the moral delegitimation of overt racism as a result of the horrors of Nazism and the
moral imperatives of the Second World War (which placed the
defenders of Jim Crow and their allies on the defensive); threats to
the order and stability of the wider society (particularly after the
widening of support for the CRM in the non-South) through sympathetic boycotts and picketing; threats to order in the South,
which increasingly came to be seen as putting at risk new investment; and threats to the US position in the world from Soviet use
of Jim Crow and later of Bull Connor, Jim Clark and George
Wallace.

The removal of Jim Crow, therefore, had to be forced onto the
agenda of an unwilling political system. There were forces which
operated to limit the changes being made (under duress) to the
removal of *de jure* segregation and overt discrimination. Equality
of opportunity would require the removal of the latter so that
blacks could compete like everyone else. It might represent a threat
to particular whites or to particular institutions in terms of their
current practices, but the wider imperatives of the system would
work through these problems — as in the range of measures which

had been taken and which involved limitations in the absolute rights of property for the greater good. Factory safety, social security and child labour laws had all been opposed as interferences with freedom, but, in the face of greater threats, threats of more fundamental demands and radicalisation, concessions had been made. It is important to note that these concessions, as the ones made in response to the demands of black people and their allies, were limited, did not involve fundamental shifts in the distribution of wealth or power and would be secure only to the extent that the forces which extracted the concessions remained strong.

If we now look in detail at how these forces and processes were played out we can see the salience of Myrdal's international agenda in forming the liberal agenda within which the CRM developed and was shaped. The final report of President Truman's Committee on Civil Rights defined 'moral' and 'economic' reasons for ending discrimination and then defined the 'international' reasons.[23]

> Our position in the post-war world is so vital to the future that our smallest actions have far-reaching effects .... We cannot escape the fact that our civil rights record has been an issue in world politics. The world's press and radios are full of it .... Those with competing philosophies have stressed — and are shamelessly distorting — our shortcomings .... They have tried to prove our democracy an empty fraud, and our nation a consistent oppressor of under-privileged people. This may seem ludicrous to Americans [which Americans? Presumably Afro-Americans, Native Americans, Asian-Americans, Latino-Americans do now count] but it is sufficiently important to worry our friends. The United States is not so strong, the final triumph of the democratic ideal is not so inevitable that we can ignore what the world thinks of us or our record.

The centrality of the Cold War and of anti-Communism is crucial to our understanding of post-war US society and institutions. The Cold War provided the framework for the creation of a 'permanent wartime economy' — as had been called for by Charles E. Wilson, President of General Electric in 1944 — and for the opening up of the markets and economies of the 'free world' for US exports and investment as Dean Acheson had declared was necessary if the US were not to return to depression after the war.[24] The use by the Soviets and by nationalists in Third World countries of US apartheid to challenge US claims to leadership of the democratic, free world had to be limited. The records of the Truman,

Eisenhower and Kennedy administrations, for example, are full of indications of how sensitive was the US government. These concerns worked their way through into the decisions of the executive branch of the federal government and were instrumental in the Supreme Court's landmark decision in the Brown case, as in many others.

The international benefits to the US of removing petty apartheid would be reinforced by anti-Communist benefits at home for the federal government. Since the Communists were supposedly concerned to exploit Jim Crow for their own purposes of destabilising US society, the removal of Jim Crow would presumably end that threat. Despite the limited membership of blacks in the CPUSA, it is clear that decision-makers were conscious of the danger, in their terms, of black-white unity around class issues which a black-red alliance represented and, therefore, were determined to combine repression of the left with their anti-Jim Crow policies.

The anti-Communist hegemony, which was established, shaped the debate on black rights as it did all other debates. The determination to prevent the linking of black and red was central so central that the FBI and other agencies used as *prima facie* evidence of probable disloyalty the fact that a white person had black friends or invited black people for a meal. The purges of the Communists, fellow travellers, 'comsymps' and others unable to prove their loyalty became the dominant feature of life in the US. Most individuals and organisations succumbed and often tried to use the terms of the anti-Communist hysteria for their own purposes. In his book on W.E.B. DuBois, Gerald Horne (1986), reports that, after the firing of Dr DuBois, the NAACP 'strongly implied that those Euro-Americans most opposed to Jim Crow and racism were Communists and should be carefully watched in the branches'.

Naturally this heavy-handed approach caused a wail of protest and was 'corrected' in a subsequent editorial. But this episode was indicative of how far anti-Communism had gone, for apparently there was sentiment for routing out white members of the Association (who often were influential and sizeable financial contributors) in a spurious anti-Communist crusade.[25]

So central was anti-Communism that people in every walk of life identified as Communists were purged from public life. In this context Paul Robeson's prominence as a fighter for black rights in the US and for the freedom of the colonised peoples, his openly leftist position on questions about the political economy and his opposition to the Cold War, marked him out as a prime target. The US government took away his passport so that he could not travel abroad. This was accompanied by a massive propaganda campaign to label him a subversive, a false prophet who was misleading his people. The House Un-American Activities Committee (HUAC) and other committees not only regularly called him to testify but also had a succession of prominent black people appear before them to attack him. It was said at the time that a condition for employment for black actors (for what little work was available for blacks in Hollywood) was that they had to attack Paul Robeson publicly. This campaign succeeded in denying Paul Robeson work in the US threats of economic and/or physical retaliation were sufficient to prevent venues being made available to him.

The intimidation increased and there was violence against him and those who came to hear him sing. Listening to and applauding his songs were considered proof of being a Communist, at least by Adolph Menjou's testimony before the HUAC. The pressure to turn Robeson into a non-person continued unabated. Gerald Horne recounts[26] what happened when Dr DuBois received a copy of Langston Hughes's book, *Famous Negro Music Makers*, and discovered that Paul Robeson had been totally excluded. DuBois wrote to the publisher and received a 'remarkably candid' reply from Edward H. Dodd Jr, president of Dodd, Mead & Company, 'Hughes was told by experts of his acquaintance and probably also told by our library advisers that the inclusion of Robeson would probably eliminate the book from acceptance by a good many school libraries, state adoption lists, etc.'[27]

Other examples of the creation of a non-person in a democracy are provided by his son, Paul Robeson Jr, who quotes contemporary experts rating his father as one of the greatest football players of all time. He goes on[28] to declare that:

> In spite of these credentials, my father is the only two-time Walter Camp All-American who is not in the College Football Hall of Fame. Not only that, the Hall of Fame is located at Rutgers, and Paul Robeson was the first Rutgers player to win All-American honours. It is also a fact that the book *College Football*, published in 1950 by Muray & Co. and labelled 'the most complete record compiled on

college football,' listed a ten-man All-America team for 1918, the only ten-man team in All-America history. The missing man was an end named Paul Robeson.

The NAACP supported US foreign policy and tried to use that support as a way of obtaining federal government backing for its anti-discrimination agenda. The following statement to rank and file members by Alfred Baker, an NAACP board member, is an example of this approach: 'If there is ... a group interested in the discussion of foreign policy, they might take a speaker on the bad effect of racial discrimination on our foreign relations ... [they] should be able to answer questions about ... our exclusion of Communists and our support of anti-Communist foreign policy measures'.[29] Horne's conclusion is that 'the NAACP was trying to run with the hares and hunt with the hounds; attempting to tweak Uncle Sam, they hammered on the hypocrisy of foreign policy when it came to race while eagerly supporting the glue that held the policy together anti-Communism'.[30]

This anti-Communist campaign involved political elites on the national and local scene (governmental and non-governmental officials alike) and had an anti-union, anti-welfare state, pro-Cold War, pro military-industrial complex agenda. Racism was always part of this campaign either up front or *sub rosa*. The consequences included the retarding and weakening of black struggles for structural change, as well as channelling struggles into an anti-Jim Crow, anti-*de jure* segregation mode — and thus retarding the wider struggle for black rights and, even, as we shall see, distorting and retarding the limited, legitimate campaign. Victor Bernstein, writing prophetically in 1943[31] argued that:

> Since the Wagner Act made open union-busting illegal, race-baiting has become almost the chief weapon of the anti-labour storm troops. Certainly this is true in the South where the union man, himself torn by prejudice, is inclined to fall easy prey to the antiNegro mouthings of demagogues like [Eugene] Talmadge and ['Pappy'] O'Daniel ... and professional hate promoters like Vance Muste, who once described the non-existent Eleanor Clubs as a 'Red Radical scheme to organise Negro maids, cooks, and nurses in order to have a Communist informer in every Southern home'.

This link between black rights and Bolshevism has a long history in the US. President Truman's secretary of state, James F. Byrnes, had an equally long history of mouthing such hysteria and hate. In a speech on the floor of the House of Representatives in 1919[32] he attacked the *Messenger*, the socialist newspaper published by A. Philip Randolph and Chandler Owen, in the following terms:

> The material in the magazine would indicate that the source from which the support comes is antagonistic to the Government of the United States. It appeals for the establishment in this country of a Soviet Government .... It urges the negro to join the IWW's [sic], pays tribute to Eugene Debs and every other convicted enemy of the Government, and prays for the establishment of a Bolshevik Government in this land. It is evident that the IWFW's [sic] are financing it in an effort to have the negro of America join them in their revolutionary plans.

This anti-red, anti-black rhetoric was used by capitalists in their attempts to divide black and white workers and to destroy industrial unionism. Victor Bernstein gives a number of examples of this in the campaign by Humble Oil, a Standard Oil subsidiary in Beaumont, Texas in 1943 against the Oil Workers International (CIO) organising drive. He[33] quotes from two issues of the company union's publication:[34]

> The CIO is openly committed to a policy of complete elevation of the Negro to absolute social and economic equality with the white .... They want political power, and to have this power, they must have votes ... and a coloured vote unrestricted and unrestrained represents the greatest single block of solid voting power in America .... That is why they promise [the Negroes] white men's jobs, white men's houses and complete social equality with the white race on and off the job.

The CIO has come into our Southern State of Texas brandishing the torch of racial hatred, seeking to tear down the hundreds of years of good feeling and understanding which has always existed here between white and coloured races. The place to check them is here and now. Tomorrow may be too late.

There is widespread agreement among those who have looked at these developments that, in the words of Wayne Clark[35] 'race relations in the 1950s and early 1960s were shaped to a great extent by the pronouncements of those individual members of the political elite who assumed responsibility not only for preserving white supremacy but also for awakening the nation to what they considered the inherent dangers of international communism'.

Don Carleton[36] writing about Houston, found a similar pattern:

> After World War II, Houston's establishment began to perceive a threat to its wealth and power from the growing labour movement in Texas and an ever expanding Federal government. Houston's leaders faced a federal government they believed to be controlled by Socialists and left-wingers. They saw Washington attempting to make further incursions into sacred areas such as the oil-depletion allowance, labour relations, corporate tax reform, medicine, education and race relations.

They used the red scare to achieve ideological, political and economic hegemony. On the national scale this process was being encouraged and orchestrated by the Chamber of Commerce. Leslie Adler[37] writes that:

> Recovering from a serious decline in status, wealth and power suffered during the depression decade, business leaders were clearly making an all-out effort at the war's end to regain control over the domestic sector of the economy and to reorient national priorities away from social reform and toward the business foundation they believed to be central to the American way of life. Efforts to curb newly established labour union power were high on their own list of priorities, and given the long-standing link in business thinking between unionism and communism, it would seem natural that the communists-in-unions theme would appeal to businessmen.

Adler[38] then discusses how they accomplished their goals:

> Seeing themselves in the position to bring a great deal of influence and pressure to bear on American thinking, members of the Committee on Socialism and Communism did not take their self-appointed task lightly, and set about to research those who could best shape public opinion. 'Authorities who have studied this type of problem carefully,' [Emerson P.] Schmidt wrote to Committee members in early 1946, 'are convinced that approximately 8,000 American people are the genuine creators of public opinion the rest merely follow. If we can reach a goodly portion of these 8,000 with such a brochure, its influence will automatically tend to spread into the lives and homes of most of the people.' Careful planning such as this and a thorough knowledge of how to appeal to the American public marked the entire Chamber of Commerce crusade.

Along with the related activities of HUAC[39] this campaign led the Senate Internal Affairs Committee; President Truman's Loyalty Security Program, the Attorney-General's List of Subversive Organizations and the activities of the FBI and state and local 'red squads' succeeded in purging those who disagreed with the dominant ideology.[40] Clark[41] concludes that:

> There is little doubt that resistance activities hindered the organising efforts of the labour movement and protracted the civil rights struggle in the Deep South. The white leadership understood that picket lines, boycotts, marches, and other forms of organised protest could be used to fight segregation before these methods were actively used by civil rights activists. They instinctively associated those tactics with communists, labour militants, and agitators for integration. As a result, public opinion was strongly united against protest methods, particularly those involving direct action. The Cold War consensus contributed to this climate of hostility towards groups and individuals who exerted pressure for social change. It facilitated the development by anti-union and segregationist forces of a resistance to racial integration that was based, in part, on the knowledge that segregation was as effective in maintaining class barriers as it was in sustaining the colour line between whites and blacks.

In the South this campaign had the effect of thwarting unionisation and struggles for the tenant farmers. In his study of Southern radicalism in the 1929-59 period, Anthony Dunbar[42] wrote that:

> Though Southern plantations were still inhabited by poorly paid, educated, and housed workers, there were few fresh attempts to rekindle the union spirit of the 1930s. One of the reasons, of course, was the history of failure. But another was that there was no longer a Socialist party or a coherent progressive community willing to underwrite the cost of pressing the one demand that had traditionally rallied Southern farm workers: land for the landless.

The purge of leftists from CIO unions and of leftist unions from the CIO had particularly deleterious consequences for blacks. Sumner Rosen[43] argues that, 'to the extent that the unions expelled had been the more militant and devoted advocates of racial justice, the cause itself lost much of its meaning and appeal'. Boyer and Morais[44] write that

> The expelled unions were the soul of the CIO .... It was those unions

that had fought the hardest for Negro representation in trade union office. It was they that had led the fight for equal pay for equal work for women and it was they that had fought for the rights of such minorities as Puerto Ricans and Mexican miners. And what organisation had been accomplished in the South hat been done mostly by them.

The consequences were starkly summarised by Charles W. Cheng:[45]

> the drive to organise the unorganised in the South never fully materialised. Certainly a concerted effort by either the CIO or AFL would have increased the number of blacks in the labour movement. Instead, black workers in particular and large numbers of white workers, in general, continued to be economically exploited. The wall of white supremacy gained a new lease on life, and this wall would not be massively confronted until the 1960s. In any case, it seems probable that the expulsions, and thus the fragmentation of labour, were in part responsible for the failure of labour to organise in the South.

These purges, including those in Hollywood and in academic institutions at every level and in every area of the United States, reinforced the ideological hegemony of corporate America. In an interesting discussion of the issues dealt with (or avoided) by Hollywood in this period, Leslie Adler[46] has written:

> Though the changing composition of Hollywood films after 1947 cannot be attributed entirely to the impact of HUAC, a basic change did occur which oriented the industry further away from dealing with serious social themes and which seems clearly related to the investigations. The 1945-7 period had seen an increase in the film treatment of such themes, and as calculated by Dorothy B. Jones, approximately 28 per cent of the films in 1947 were of a serious social bent. From 1947-9, however, the trend was reversed, with only approximately 18 per cent of the films in 1949 qualifying. An even sharper break occurred from 1950-2 with an upswing in war films, pure entertainment films, escapist films, and a larger number of anti-Communist films. In 1950 only 11 per cent dealt with social questions and by 1953 that figure was further reduced to 9 per cent.

J. Fred MacDonald,[47] discussing similar developments in the newly emerging medium of television, reports:

The broadcast industry readily fell in with the government purgists. Entertainers adversely touched by the [HUAC] hearings found themselves blacklisted from radio and, more important, the burgeoning new medium, television. It made little difference to broadcasters if, in the jargon of the day, these political deviates were 'card carrying members' (actual dues-paying members of the CPUSA), 'dupes' (those fooled into supporting Red goals without realising the error of their ways), 'Pinkos' (those who were leftists, but not Red enough), or 'comsymps' or 'fellow travellers' (those who sympathised with Communist ends without joining the party). The CPUSA was considered to be an arm of the Soviet Union, not a legitimate political party springing from the fabric of American society. Those said to be associated with Communism, then, were considered anti-American conspirators. They were unwelcome in broadcasting. In this way the entertainment business became a political arena in which Cold War fears and ignorance became the basis for exclusionary professional policy. This was to be expected in a business that had been heavily politicised during the war .... In news and entertainment programmes television presented Americans a picture of world affairs in which the honest, selfless United States was forced to defend the Free World against the barbarous onslaught of Communism — with its godless ideologues and automaton commissars intent upon conquering the planet. Those not wholeheartedly in favour of the national crusade were often suspected of being at least tolerant of the evil empire. It was an over-simplified picture. But in the context of the United States at mid-century, it was widely perceived as genuine.

The Truman administration fully supported the development of this ideological strait-jacket and gave its highest priority to the pursuance of the Cold War and the creation of the national security state. Its tactical support for civil rights was always a lower priority, despite the periodic rhetorical emphasis on equal rights. Symbolic appointments and policy statements, combined with a limited number of executive actions (forced by pressure from blacks and from the foreign policy pressures of the Cold War) were the major aspects of the administration's practices. The red-baiting and purges, as has been discussed, actually adversely affected the struggle for black rights.

That struggle escalated in the 1950s, particularly after the Brown decision. The *Brown* v. *Board of Topeka* decision of 1954 overturned the 1896 *Plessy* v. *Ferguson* decision which had declared 'separate but equal' to be constitutional and held that *de jure* segregation was unconstitutional. *Brown II* was the 1955 enforcement decision which ordered implementation of the 1954 decision on the basis of 'all deliberate speed'. What should have been the crowning glory of the NAACP's elite dominated strategy of litigation and lobbying, in practice turned out to be the beginning of a new phase of black struggle. The reason for this apparent contradiction is that the Court in Brown II — its implementation decision — developed the unique concept of black children being granted their constitutional rights 'with all deliberate speed' and with the onus on black parents throughout the South having to go to court to obtain desegregation. Not surprisingly, this provided valuable breathing space for Southern racists determined to resist integration — especially as the president, Dwight D. Eisenhower, never supported the moral imperative of the decision and did not throw the weight of his tremendous popularity into the fray on behalf of the constitutional rights of black people.

Following the massive resistance to the Brown decision there was a growing disillusionment among blacks with the NAACP strategy and a receptivity to new forms of struggle. This disillusionment must be seen as being directed primarily at the NAACP on the national level. Local chapters and leaders were often in the vanguard of struggle, were subjected to local government and State repression, and often co-operated with other more activist groups. The most famous example of this new strategy developed in Montgomery, Alabama in 1955 when the black community carried out a year-long boycott of the bus company. This strategy of non-violent direct action became associated with the teachings of Dr Martin Luther King Jr and the Southern Christian Leadership Conference (SCLC), which emerged out of the Montgomery struggle and related struggles throughout the South. Dr King and non-violent direct action held centre stage for more than a decade. Following student sit-ins in 1960 and the formation of the Student Non-Violent Co-ordinating Committee (SNCC), there was mass mobilisation of Southern blacks and mobilisation of Northern support, among blacks and whites.[48]

These struggles received the attention of the print and visual media of the world, as they were intended to do. The strategy required the intervention of the federal government in all its forms, but to overcome the power of the Southern Committee Chairs in Congress, the lack of interest on the part of the FBI and other gov-

ernmental agencies, and the electoral interests of Kennedy, countervailing pressures had to be brought. For example, the pressures
on President Kennedy as a result of the Birmingham, Alabama
campaign were dramatic. Carl Brauer[49] writes that:

> The Birmingham crisis touched another sensitive Kennedy nerve when
> it attracted a great deal of publicity abroad .... In several countries,
> particularly in Ghana and Nigeria, the media poured out caustic
> denunciation of the racial outrage. Radio Moscow, after a hesitant
> beginning, was currently diverting a quarter of its output to
> Birmingham, much of it beamed to African audiences. Given
> Kennedy's expansionist view of his country's role in the world, the
> damage Birmingham had done to America's image undoubtedly
> concerned him.

This strategy clearly worked in terms of forcing President Kennedy
to introduce civil rights legislation. He told civil rights leaders that,
'the demonstrations in the streets had brought results, they had
made the executive branch act faster and were now forcing
Congress to entertain legislation which a few weeks before would
have had no chance'.[50] The problem black people and others
would face in the years following these victories, was what would
happen when the protesters' demands touched on structural racism
and the bases of inequality in the US political economy?

There were, however, important differences within the black
community about both strategies and goals. The major (moderate)
establishment groups defined the problem as that of blacks being
excluded from an otherwise fair, just and democratic system much
like the later bourgeois, mainstream feminists. The solution was to
allow blacks (or women) into that system on the same bases of
competition and individualism as was presumed to be the norm in
the US meritocratic system. These groups either supported US foreign policy or did not comment on it an implicit recognition that
the limits of assimilation, integration for blacks, meant that blacks
could speak on race questions but not on foreign policy or other
fundamental questions of the political economy. The radical black
groups challenged these positions across the board. They did not
accept the view that, apart from the exclusion of black people (or
women in the case of the socialist feminists), the US was a fair, just
and democratic society. Instead, they argued that the political
economy was a highly unequal, unjust system, not just for blacks

but for all. The solution, therefore, involved not the integration of individual blacks into that competitive system, but more collective responses designed to change the system as a whole. Increasingly these tendencies came to oppose US foreign policy, particularly in Africa and Vietnam. The established groups bitterly attacked these interventions on the grounds that they would put at risk the gains that had been made.

The political repression of Paul Robeson and W.E.B. DuBois — and the collaboration of the NAACP and other moderate groups in the repression focused very directly on their opposition to US foreign policy. As indicated above, Paul Robeson's passport had been taken away by the State Department. The government's reasoning is apparent in the following extract of the US State Department's deposition:[51]

> Furthermore even if the complaint had alleged ... that the passport
> was cancelled solely because of applicant's recognised status as
> spokesman for large sections of Negro Americans, we submit that this
> would not amount to an abuse of discretion in view of the applicant's
> frank admission that he has been for years extremely active politically
> on behalf of the colonial people of Africa.

If it appears surprising that the government of the US, which prides itself on being the leader of the free world and an anti-colonial nation, used as the basis of denying a passport to an American citizen the fact that he had frankly admitted to having worked on behalf of the colonial people of Africa, it is because of the widespread acceptance of US *bona fides*. It is important, therefore, to look behind the façade of US beneficence and anticolonialism. The *New York Times*, as much an establishment newspaper as one could wish for, wrote in its editorial on 22 November 1949 that, 'Africa is the continent of the future. We learned its strategic value in the Second World War. Its economic potentialities are the hope of Western Europe ... as well as the rest of the world .... The United States need not be afraid of the label of reactionary if [we] oppose too hasty independence.'[52]

Given the economic importance of Africa and the US government's acceptance of the advice of *New York Times* leader writers, it is not surprising to find the US expanding its economic and political role in Africa and acting as a leading anti-revolutionary power in conjunction with South Africa and Israel propping up an array of corrupt and brutal client regimes and destabilising nationalist and socialist governments. It is also not surprising to find W.E.B. DuBois a target of the US government alongside Paul Robeson. Dr DuBois had a long history of support for the 'colonial people of Africa' and for Pan-Africanism. Manning Marable and Gerald Horne have written about this aspect of DuBois's politics, which linked Pan-Africanism, the struggle for black rights and freedom inside the US to a critique of the reactionary role played by the petit bourgeois leaders of establishment-oriented moderate groups. Horne[53] writes:

> DuBois and the Council [on African Affairs] were rooting on a hasty independence for the continent and the fact that he was both black and influential was guaranteed to cause tensions. It was important that those of African ancestry in the United States be brought into line in support of US foreign policy, but DuBois and the Council were not cooperative .... The Council was not only sharply critical of the State Department and the United States-based transnational corporations but they also turned their microscope on potential friends and allies. They commended the NAACP for their resolution on colonialism in 1953 but criticised the use of the term 'natives' and the equating of the 'persecution' of Britons in South Africa with blacks; they questioned their lack of forthright support for specific organisations like the ANC and United States votes in the United Nations on Africa. A specific reference to East Africa by the Association — 'We view with alarm the terrorist methods of the Mau Mau in Kenya' — was strenuously attacked.

Marable[54] quotes DuBois saying that 'American Negroes freed of their baseless fear of Communism will again begin to turn their attention and aim their activity toward Africa.' They would soon recognise the role of American capitalism in the exploitation of African people. 'When once the blacks of the United States, the West Indies, and Africa work and think together,' DuBois concluded hopefully[55] 'the future of the black man in the modern world is safe.' DuBois's foreign policy activities were sufficiently threatening to US government and business interests that not only was his passport taken away but he was 'indicted for allegedly serving as an "agent of a foreign principal" in his work with the Peace Information Center in New York'.

The 82-year-old black man was handcuffed, fingerprinted and portrayed in the national media as a common criminal. Before his trial, the *New York Herald Tribune* convicted him in a prominent editorial: 'The DuBois outfit was set up to promote a tricky appeal of Soviet origin, poisonous in its surface innocence which made it appear that a signature against the use of atomic weapons would forthwith insure world peace. It was, in short, an attempt to disarm America and yet ignore every form of Communist aggression.'[56] The charges were dismissed but the government's determination to silence Dr DuBois was clear for all to see.

When Dr King came out in opposition to the war in Vietnam he was subjected to the same vitriol. Henry Darby and Margaret Rowley[57] studied these responses and have written:

> Well-known civil rights leaders and other prominent blacks such as James Farmer, director of the Congress of Racial Equality; Roy Wilkins of the National Association for the Advancement of Coloured People; Ralph Bunche, former United Nations under-secretary; Edward Brooke, senator from Massachusetts; Carl T. Rowan, newspaper columnist; Jackie Robinson, then special assistant on Community Affairs to Governor Rockefeller of New York; and some members of SCLC were fearful that King's opposition would result in a loss of support for the civil rights movement.

Charles Cheng[58] argues that, 'the NAACP's Roy Wilkins adopted the stance that the Vietnam War was not "a proper sphere for public analysis or criticism" at least not by a civil rights organisation.'

One of the most fundamental conflicts between the moderate and the radical black organisations was over anti-Communism. As the former had accepted the Cold War so had they accepted anti-Communism both were the price of admission into liberal America. The SNCC from the beginning had refused to accept the hegemony of Cold War liberalism, had refused to use the standard anti-Communist disclaimer as a condition for membership and had refused to follow the anti-Communist dictates about which organisations they could work with. This was particularly contentious in the run-up to Mississippi Freedom Summer in 1964. The SNCC had been working with the left-wing lawyers' association, the National Lawyers Guild (NLG). NLG lawyers had been providing desperately needed legal assistance and representation for the SNCC field workers in the face of massive Southern legal repression. There were few other lawyers available or willing to provide this assistance. The NAACP and other mainstream civil rights groups tried to put pressure on the co-ordinating committee to break with the Guild and when they failed the Justice Department joined the fray.

James Forman of the SNCC describes how he and two colleagues from the SNCC were called to a meeting with Burke Marshall of the Justice Department 'ostensibly to discuss the situation in the Third Congressional District [in delta Mississippi] .... But when it finally took place, the Lawyers Guild seemed to be the main subject on the minds of our hosts.' Describing the contribution of Cold War liberal historian and Presidential aide and hagiographer, Arthur Schlesinger Jr, Forman[59] goes on:

> Suddenly he spoke and when he did, we knew he spoke with the consent of the government officials present and the elder Bingham [Member of the House of Representatives]. 'There are many of us who have spent years fighting the communists,' he said as if he had made this speech many times. 'We worked hard during the thirties and the forties fighting forces such as the National Lawyers Guild. We find it unpardonable that you would work with them,' he concluded .... What blindness and arrogance, I thought. He knew nothing about the reality of our struggle in the South.

Forman[60] describes the fundamental re-evaluations that were taking place within the SNCC which were to lead to increasingly open challenges to the dominant ideology.

By the end of the summer, it was firmly established in the minds of the sisters and brothers that SNCC was like an underdeveloped nation, struggling for its own self-determination. We would take help from anyone, always insisting that no one who gave us help had the right to dictate our policies. We knew only too well that there were people who wanted us to 'fight Communism', to engage in their factional struggles. Whitney Young [of the NAACP] was not the first nor would Arthur Schlesinger be the last. These forces would continue to attack us, claiming that by allowing the guild to participate in the Summer Protest, SNCC was destroying years of hard work years of Red baiting, they should have said, and years of character assassination .... Therefore what SNCC had done was crucial. In effect, SNCC was breaking through the circle of fear that had been imposed on people by McCarthyism and which still lingered on. It deserves infinite praise, I believe, for its attitude on freedom of association, because SNCC fought not only for its own friends, but for the civil liberties of all.

This process of challenging the anti-Communist hegemony continued with the SNCC challenging Dr King's decision to fire Jack O'Dell from the SCLC because of pressure from the FBI and Kennedy administration over O'Dell's communist associations. Stokely Carmichael demanded that King and other established civil rights leaders 'stop taking a defensive stand on communism'.[61]

The challenge the SNCC presented to the status quo was reflected in the pressures Forman described above and in the conflicts between it and the other components of the CRM.[62] These were apparent over which priorities the movement should establish, over the seating of the Mississippi Freedom Democratic Party at the Democratic National Convention in Atlantic City in 1964 and in terms of the relationship between black organisations and liberal and labour organisations and in terms of whether civil rights organisations should be all-black, which then would form alliances with anti-racist whites. These divisions were heightened by the nature of the 1963 March of Washington (see discussion below), by the urban uprisings which raged through the US from the Summer of 1964 through 1968, and by differences over foreign policy (as discussed above). In these disputes over the direction and priorities of black struggle, access to and control of resources was an important variable affecting the outcomes of the conflicts. Herbert Haines made a detailed study of the funding of the CRM from 1957 to 1970 and found that the total amounts contributed to the seven groups he studied increased during the late 1950s and 1960s, and peaked in the late 1960s. He found that these increases primarily reflected increased funding for the moderate groups and an injection of new money. His conclusions are worth quoting at length.[63]

These findings suggest that positive radical flank effects contributed significantly to increases in the outside funding of moderate civil rights organisations in the 1960s. The increasing importance of corporations, foundations, and the federal government, moreover, suggests that a portion of the nation's corporate elite recognised that it had a crucial interest in pacifying the black population, particularly in the volatile cities, and in accommodating certain manageable black demands. It also suggests that many previously uninvolved groups were 'enlightened' by the glow of burning cities, after years of indifference to non-violent cajoling by the National Urban League and the NAACP. Some whites came to realise that the integration of blacks into the US mainstream was not such a bad idea after all, that it was in their own best interests given the more radical alternatives, and that it was something they ought to be encouraging with their resources. The prime beneficiaries of such changes of heart were the big moderate groups.

The conflict over the nature of the 1963 March on Washington was indicative of these growing splits. Malcolm X called it the 'Farce on Washington'. His description was rejected by liberals in all sections of US society as extremist though, as we shall see, it has been validated since then by the writings of those involved. Malcolm X speaking in Detroit two months after the March said[64]

The Negroes were out there in the streets. They were talking about how they were going to march on Washington .... That they were going to march on Washington, march on the Senate, march on the White House, march on the Congress, and tie it up, bring it to a halt, not let the government proceed. They even said they were going out to the airport and lay down on the runway and not let any airplanes land. I'm telling you what they said. That was revolution. That was revolution. That was the black revolution. It was the grass roots out there in the street. It scared the white man to death, scared the white power structure in Washington DC to death; X was there. When they found out that this black steam-roller was going to come down on the capital, they called in ... these national Negro leaders that you respect and told them, 'Call it off,' Kennedy said. 'Look you all are letting this thing go too far.' And Old Tom said, 'Boss, I can't stop it because I didn't start it.' I'm telling you what they said. They said, 'I'm not even in it, much less at the head of it.' They said, 'These Negroes are doing things on their own. They're running ahead of us.' And that old shrewd fox, he said, 'If you all aren't in it, I'll put you in it. I'll put you at head of it. I'll endorse it. I'll welcome it. I'll help it. I'll join it.' This is what they did with the march on Washington. They pined it ... became part of it, took it over. And as they took it over, it lost its militancy. It ceased to be angry, it ceased to be hot, it ceased to be uncompromising. Why, it even ceased to be a march. It became a picnic, a circus. Nothing but a circus, with clowns and all .... No, it was a sell out. It was a takeover .... They controlled it so tight, they told those Negroes what time to hit town, where to stop, what signs to carry, what song to sing, what speech they could make, and what speech they couldn't make, and then told them to get out of town by sundown.

In his glorified history of Kennedy's thousand days, Arthur Schlesinger Jr wrote:[65]

> The conference with the President did persuade the civil rights leaders that they should not lay siege to Capital Hill .... So in 1963 Kennedy moved to incorporate the Negro revolution into the democratic coalition.

Manning Marable's analysis[66] of the politics of the 1963 march also supports Malcolm X's contemporary analysis:

> Months before Kennedy announced his decision to obtain a new civil rights act, however, [A. Philip] Randolph proposed organising a second March on Washington DC, both as a means of dramatising the campaign for desegregation and as a method by which to place 'additional pressure on the Kennedy administration to support equal employment legislation.'... The response within the civil rights front was at best mixed. The CORE's [Congress of Racial Equality'] national steering committee 'eagerly agreed to act as a co-sponsor.' SNCC leaders, particularly chairman John Lewis, and theoretician James Forman, viewed the March as an opportunity to stage demonstrations at the US Justice Department against its abysmal failure to protect civil rights workers' lives. SCLC leaders Clarence Jones and Reverend George Latency projected 'massive, militant, monumental sit-ins on Congress .... We will tie up public transportation by laying our bodies prostrate on runways of airports, across railroad tracks, and in bus depots.' Such rhetoric threw a chill into the NAACP and Urban League bureaucrats. After learning that Kennedy objected to the march, [Roy] Wilkins [of the NAACP] contemptuously dismissed the mobilisation before reporters, stating, 'That little baby does not belong to me.' By late June, however, the call for a second march had acquired a life of its own, and it was too late for Randolph, Wilkins or anyone else to cancel.

Marable describes how the moderate leaders worked in conjunction with the Kennedy administration — as Schlesinger has written and Malcolm X stated — and hijacked the march and insured that it would not be confrontational. Randolph, playing the traditional role of the petit bourgeois leader, told Kennedy that blacks were now on the streets and it was 'very likely impossible to get them off. If they are bound to be in the streets in any case, is it not better that they be led by organisations dedicated to civil rights and disciplined by struggle than to leave them to other leaders who care neither about civil rights nor about non-violence?'[67]

Many radicals stayed away from the March — for example, Stokely Carmichael declared that the 'struggle for voting rights in Mississippi was more important than a showy display in Washington'.[68] John Lewis attended and prepared a speech which was so threatening in terms of the issues raised that the Catholic archbishop of Washington let it be known that he would boycott the March if it were delivered. After massive pressure, Lewis and Forman redrafted the speech which was still of a different order from the other speeches of the day:[69]

> We came here today with a great sense of misgiving ... It is true that we support the administration's Civil Rights Bill in the Congress. We support it with great reservations, however .... In its present form this Bill will not protect the citizens of Danville, Virginia who must live in constant fear of a police state. It will not protect the hundreds and thousands of people who have been arrested upon trumped charges .... It will not help the citizens of Mississippi, of Alabama and Georgia who are qualified to vote but lack a sixth grade education .... We must have legislation that will protect the Mississippi share-cropper who is put off his farm because he dares to register to vote. We need a bill that will provide for the homeless and starving people of this nation .... My friends, let us not forget that we are involved in a serious social revolution .... Where is our party? Where is the political party that will make it unnecessary to march on Washington? Where is the political party that will make it unnecessary to march in the streets of Birmingham?

The Civil Rights Act of 1964 and the Voting Rights Act of 1965 passed after the assassination of President Kennedy marked the apex of the achievements of the CRM. *De jure* segregation had been swept away and blacks could now enjoy the fruits of their class position middle class enjoying and the mass going hungry and could use the ballot box to achieve whatever was possible to achieve. The problems raised by Lewis in his speech, however, remained. The problems faced by blacks in the urban ghettos, for example, had not been created and were not being maintained by *de jure* segregation. The structures of the political economy have created the ghetto, have determined resource allocations which determine housing, education, health, employment and policing. None of these issues were addressed, or could be addressed, by the civil rights legislation. It was not surprising, therefore, that

Northern blacks whose pride had been raised by the CRM's bravery and dignity and whose interests were not being addressed were increasingly angry. The uprising in Harlem in the summer of 1964 began a chain of over 200 uprisings which raged through urban America for the next four years. The consequences of those uprisings were less clear-cut than the legislative victories of the CRM. There were a range of symbolic responses, an increase in welfare rolls, co-optation of activists, and an increase in training, equipping, and intelligence gathering by police forces at every level. What there wasn't was any fundamental change in the social, economic and political conditions which had produced the uprisings.[70]

The achievements of the CRM were real but limited. Spin-off from the movement led to increased and new types of political mobilisation in cities such as Chicago. The burden of Jim Crow was removed from the backs of black people in the South. But the class differences in the black community and the commitment to the capitalist economy of the black leadership, and the incorporation of large sections of the black middle class into various levels of the state bureaucracy, continued and increased the isolation of the mass of black people and their needs from the political agenda.

W.E.B. DuBois continued to raise such issues through the 1950s up to his death on the day of the march on Washington in 1963. In 1958 he received an honourary degree at Prague's Charles University and declared that:[71]

> [During the 1930s] I repudiated the idea that Negroes were in danger of inner-class division based on income and exploitation. Here again, I was wrong. Twenty years later, by 1950, it was clear that the great machine of big business was sweeping not only the mass of white Americans ... it had also and quite naturally swept Negroes in the same maelstrom.

In 1953 he had explored 'the economics of racism, he elaborated on the fight involving those fearless enough to go against the prevailing consensus, simultaneously, there was the potential Shangri-La facing those who wished to go along. He predicted the fall of segregation in public accommodation and schools, which would mean blacks 'will be divided into classes even more sharply than now'.[72] Marable[73] argues that:

> In early 1960, Dr DuBois argued that 'class divisions' within Negro

communities had so divided blacks 'that they are no longer [one] single body. They are different sets of people with different sets of interests.' At the University of Wisconsin, DuBois indicated that the civil rights movement's strategy of non-violent demonstrations and sit-ins 'does not reach the centre of the problem' confronting blacks. Nearly alone among major civil rights leaders, DuBois urged the proponents of desegregation to chart 'the next step' of their collective struggle. The abolition of Jim Crow meant little if Negroes were unemployed. Blacks must 'insist upon the legal rights which are already theirs, and add to that increasingly a Socialistic form of government, an insistence upon the welfare state'. The demand for civil rights must ultimately check the power 'of those corporations which monopolise wealth'. DuBois now recognised that full equality for Negroes was not possible beneath the capitalist system.

Dr Martin Luther King Jr made a similar progression in his politics. By the time of his murder he had moved not only to open opposition to the war in Vietnam but to a race/class politics. He was organising a Poor People's March at the time of his death. Fortunately for the US status quo, Dr King, like Malcolm X in 1965, was murdered and, as Paul Robeson, had been turned into a non-person in the Cold War period. David Garrow[74] has traced Dr King's trajectory in the following terms:

> By 1967 King was telling the SCLC staff, 'We must recognise that we can't solve our problems now until there is a radical redistribution of economic and political power', and by early 1968 he had taken the final step to the admission that issues of economic class were more crucial and troublesome and less susceptible to change, than issues of race. 'America,' he remarked to one interviewer, 'is deeply racist and its democracy is flawed both economically and socially.' He added that 'the black revolution is much more than a struggle for the rights of Negroes. It is forcing America to face all its interrelated flaws racism, poverty, militarism, and materialism. It is exposing evils that are rooted deeply in the whole structure of our society. It reveals systemic rather than superficial flaws and suggests that radical reconstruction of society itself is the real issue to be faced.'... by early 1968 he publicly was stating, 'We are engaged in the class struggle'. While his emphasis was not purely materialistic, redistribution of economic power was the central requirement. To one audience King stated, 'We're dealing in a sense with class issues, we're dealing with the problem of the gulf between the haves and the have nots'.

The position of the mass of black Americans at this time illustrates the validity of these perceptions of Drs DuBois and King. The deteriorating position of the large body of white Americans as capitalism is being restructured at the expense of the working class is further proof of the centrality of class in the US. The failure of the white working class to confront successfully the systemic causes of its predicament is largely a consequence of its failure to confront racism. The challenge facing progressive whites is to engage in a serious campaign to confront that failure. The challenge facing progressive blacks is to fight for control of black struggle against the traditional petit bourgeois leaders and to create space for the black masses to emerge into establishing their own agenda.

3 British Anti-discrimination Legislation

The Government and Race Issues

The British government has twice legislated against racial discrimination, in 1965 and in 1968. These Acts have been the most dramatic indications of Britain's new position as a multi-racial state. The path towards the acceptance of the implications of this new situation has not been smooth. There has been a marked reluctance on the part of many political leaders, as well as large portions of the population, to come to terms with the requirements imposed by this situation. These attitudes and expectations, as well as the political situation, have shaped the legislation, as they have shaped the nature of other governmental actions designed to deal with the problems related to the influx of large numbers of Afro-Caribbean and Asian people.

The initial response of most public officials to the large-scale immigration, which began in the mid-1950s, was basically, as Sheila Patterson has described, *laissez-faire*. They assumed that whatever problems emerged from this entry would largely solve themselves and, therefore, that no special government activity was needed. This approach continued until the early 1960s when it was partially eroded. It was replaced by a Conservative Party commitment to immigration control, culminating in the Commonwealth Immigrants Act of 1962. But this element of governmental interference was not accompanied by any comparable commitment to positive government action to deal with the social or racial problems associated with immigration. There has been more emphasis in recent years — mainly from the Labour Party, but also from some Conservatives — on more positive governmental activity, including the passage of anti-discrimination legislation. It is important to note, however, that the basic assumptions underlying the Labour government's commitment have led to the view that the level of activity needed was not very great.

The government has assumed that the problem was a small and easily manageable one, because of the size of the Black and Asian population, the relative recency of their arrival, and the fact that British people are basically law-abiding. There is an element of truth in each of these assumptions, but they are not completely accurate and the real advantages they bring are temporary. The fact that the Afro-Caribbean and Asian population of about one million is roughly only 2 per cent of the total population, is less significant than the fact that they are concentrated in certain areas. These areas are characterised by high job opportunities, but are also, unfortunately, noted for overcrowded housing and inadequate social services. Patterns of discrimination have formed despite the recency of the problem, as outlined in Chapters 4 to 7, and the extent to which British people are naturally law-abiding, can be overplayed. It is important to note that to a significant extent people obey the law because their value of so doing is not outweighed by a countervailing value. When it is, they will obey the law to the extent that the consequences of not doing so are both unattractive and likely. It is, therefore, important not only that legislation be passed to act as a guide-line for the population, but that such legislation be enforceable and enforced, if it is to be effective.

In a strange way, the relative newness of the problem made possible the passage of anti-discrimination legislation while militating against the passage of effective legislation. The newness meant that the opposition to any legislation at all was less intense than has been found, for example, in a country like the United States with its long history of racial conflict and its centuries of white vested interest in black suppression. This was reinforced by the nature of the British political system which limits the opportunities available to those who want to block completely government legislation.

Both factors, however, worked the other way as well when it came to ensuring effective legislation. The newness of the problem and its seemingly small size made it possible for political leaders to cling to their assumptions about the ease with which it could be dealt.

They saw the role of the government as largely declamatory. James Callaghan, who had responsibility for shepherding the 1968 Race Relations Bill through Parliament, expressed this point of view in his first interview as Home Secretary on 28 January 1968. The following statement is interesting not only because it was the basis on which he acted with regard to the 1968 Bill, but also because it had been made after the failure of previous government declarations to stem the tide of discrimination, and after both the PEP and Street reports, and was, therefore, seemingly immune to the large body of evidence about the nature of the problem and the required solutions. Mr Callaghan said in that interview:

> The race problem is as much a question of education as of legislation. I think the law can give comfort and protection to a lot of people who do not wish to discriminate but who might otherwise be forced by the intolerant opinions of their neighbours to discriminate. *Any legislation introduced, I think, will have less emphasis on the enforcement side than on the declaratory nature of the Act itself, which must show where we stand as a nation this issue of principle.*[1]

These assumptions, as we shall see, were largely responsible for the weaknesses in the 1968 Bill, as they were for those in the Race Relations Act 1965. Another factor which influenced the outcome of these legislative battles, and which affected the nature and extent of other governmental activity, was the political situation facing the Labour government. Although Labour won the 1964 general election its candidates lost a number of previously solid Labour seats. The most shocking of their outcomes was the defeat of Patrick Gordon-Walker, the shadow Foreign Secretary, in the West Midlands constituency of Smethwick. The general election was the culmination of an anti-immigration (that is, anti-Afro-Caribbean and Asian immigration) campaign which included the vicious slogan 'If you want "a nigger" for a neighbour, vote Liberal or Labour'. On 20 April 1968 Enoch Powell delivered his famous 'rivers of blood' race speech in Birmingham in which he warned of bloodshed and the destruction of the English way of life because of the influx of aliens. This speech was greeted with outrage by many and with enthusiasm by many, including a larger group of London dockers who marched on the House of Commons on 23 April, during the Second Reading of the Race Relations bill.

In 1968 there were few, if any, votes to be won by Labour

taking a clearly liberal line on this issue. In 1964, the government, with a majority of only three, had to be especially conscious of this fact and in 1968, despite their large majority, they felt it necessary to avoid Conservative opposition at Third Reading. These factors strengthened their reluctance to get far in advance of public opinion, which was based on their basic assumptions about the nature of the problem. It resulted in limiting positive government action and governmental leadership, and in weakening the enforcement side of the 1968 Bill.

This combination of forces has militated against a broad programme of positive governmental measures against prejudice and discrimination. To be effective, anti-discrimination legislation cannot operate in a vacuum. It must be accompanied by positive governmental programmes designed to eliminate the social problems which cause and exacerbate racial prejudice, which, in turn, justifies discrimination. This prejudice must also be countered by vigorous leadership from the political leaders of the land. Without these activities, the Black and Asian population will continue to be a ready scapegoat for whatever social and economic pressures, inadequacies, and frustrations are felt by the host population. If this happens, or is allowed to continue, then the assumed willingness to obey anti-discrimination laws upon which the government has been counting, will not be present; and the law will not be able to control and eliminate discrimination effectively. Despite this, and despite the availability of information about the nature of the social problems and prejudices of the white population, little in the way of positive programmes has been forthcoming until very recently. There has been a marked reluctance to provide special assistance to areas with special problems — assistance which would have benefited not only the Afro-Caribbean and Asian inhabitants but also the white residents who have suffered for decades because of the low priority successive governments have given to social programmes. It would have been politically risky to be seen giving special help to these people when 'our people' were in need. If political leaders were to risk this and educate the population about the truth of the situation, that is, that the Afro-Caribbean and Asian immigrants did not cause the social problems of overcrowded and inadequate housing, schools, and hospitals, they would have had to admit their responsibility for these shortcomings.

The Local government Act of 1966 made a tentative start in the direction of helping local authorities with special problems by authorising, in Section II, the Home Secretary to pay a proportion of the extra expenditure incurred by those local authorities who are required to make special provisions because of substantial numbers of Commonwealth immigrants but only in respect of the employment of staff. During his Second Reading speech on the 1968 Race Relations Bill, the Home Secretary said that £3 million had been spent in the 57 local authorities which had especially large concentrations of immigrants. This was hardly a magnificent sum and was hardly likely to make a significant impact on the problem. On 22 July 1968, the Home Secretary announced that subject to legislation in the forthcoming session of Parliament, the government would provide a further £20 to £25 million over the next four years. He indicated that priority would be given to nursery education and child care. While this is to be welcomed as an important step in the right direction, one may query whether the sum will be sufficient to make a major impact and whether housing might not have been a more important place to start. The government has hitherto been reluctant to use its powers to force local housing authorities to stop discriminating in the allocation of council housing. The consequence of this failure has been the development, and hardening, of inner-city incipient ghettos. This is a problem which should receive the highest priority, if the worst consequences of the American racial conflict are to be avoided.

There similarly needs to be a high degree of public education led by the political leaders of the country to counter prejudice and discrimination. The government has been content by and large to leave this to the National Committee for Commonwealth Immigrants a body which, incidentally, has received more money for its activities than has the Race Relations Board to enforce the anti-discrimination legislation. One would have expected, if the problem had the priority it deserved, that the political leaders of the country would have acted more expeditiously and courageously than they did to oppose Enoch Powell's race speech on 20 April 1968. Much of the public reaction to it was so frighteningly favourable that Britain can no longer go back to believing that racialism is not a major factor in British life. Despite this, government leaders were remarkably slow in mounting a counter-attack, and their leadership was very restrained, often accepting the legitimacy of some of Powell's points, for example, the relevance of voluntary repatriation. It took the Prime Minister two weeks to speak out and he did not follow it up with any further speeches. In a major television appearance, the Home Secretary talked in terms of 'our people' and 'them', and argued that it was unfair to accuse the government of not having a programme of voluntary repatriation by pointing to such a programme administered by the Ministry of Social Security. He did not, interestingly enough, challenge the relevance of such a programme for most immigrants and did not point out the dangers inherent in making repatriation a legitimate alternative to solving the problems of prejudice and discrimination in Britain.

In this situation, it is perhaps understandable that the political leaders did not give this problem the priority that is deserved, essential if their overall programme in this area were to be fully effective. For reasons of both attitudes and politics, they were reluctant to admit that the problem needed a major commitment of government time, energy, and money that it needed solutions that would seem to be almost revolutionary, entirely new and far in advance of anything that had been done before. They were reluctant to admit the relevance of much of the North American experience in this area. Here lies one of the most important aspects of the British experience in the fight against discrimination. If the political leaders are unwilling to be responsive information other countries' experiences, merely the availability of this information will not be sufficient to ensure that the same mistakes will not be made again.

The British government has dealt with this problem, as indeed, to be fair, they deal with most problems, in a piecemeal fashion. Each additional piece of government action is an important increment in the fight against discrimination. But each increment is not as effective as anticipated, for at each stage the problem becomes more difficult to deal with. Therefore, action which might have had a dramatic impact if taken in 1965 will tend to have a more marginal impact when taken in 1968 because patterns of behaviour have hardened in the intervening period.

The following discussion of the passage of the Race Relations Acts of 1965 and 1968 will highlight many of these points.

The Race Relations Act 1965

A History of the Act

The origins of the Race Relations Act 1965 can be found, in part, both in an ideological commitment to the principal of brotherhood and in political considerations. There always has been a strong ideological section of the Labour Party who felt that discrimination was morally wrong and that it should be outlawed by the government. There were a number of attempts to implement this view in the 1950s, starting with a Bill introduced by Reginald (now Lord) Sorenson in 1950 to make discrimination in public places a criminal offence. This attempt failed to obtain the support of the Labour government of the day, but was continued throughout the rest of the decade by Sorenson's long-time colleague Fenner (now Lord) Brockway, who introduced the first of his nine Private Member's Bills on the subject in 1956. The Brockway Bills kept the criminal aspect and provided that anyone found guilty of discriminating on the grounds of 'colour, race or religion' would be liable to a maximum fine of £25 and withdrawal of his licenses and registration, if any. The legislation was to apply to keepers of inns, lodging-houses, restaurants, public houses, and dance halls, as well as to employers of more than fifty people as regards hiring and firing. This exemption of employers of fewer than fifty employees was withdrawn from the 1958 Bill, and the whole field of employment was dropped in 1960, at the behest of trade-union-sponsored MPs. This was one of the first indications of trade-union attitudes towards legislation in this field, and the emphasis of the 1968 Bill on voluntary machinery was in part the price that had to be paid for Trades Union Congress (TUC) support or at least neutrality.

The Brockway Bills never achieved a Second Reading despite the fact that each successive Bill was supported by a wider spectrum of opinion, not only within the Labour Party, but from the other parties as well. The National Executive Committee of the Labour Party pledged in 1958 to 'introduce legislation to stop discrimination in public places', and Harold Wilson promised both in the Commons debate on the Expiring Laws Continuance Bill (on 27 November 1963) and at a Trafalgar Square meeting (on 17 March 1963), that if Parliament persisted in rejecting Fenner

Brockway's private member's Bill, 'when we have a Labour majority we will enact it as a government measure'.

This commitment to enact anti-discrimination legislation became even more important in terms of maintaining party unity when Labour came to power in 1964. Having experienced the Smethwick, Eton and Slough, and Leyton defeats on the race issue, the government decided to diffuse the race issue by strengthening the 1962 Commonwealth Immigrants Act despite their intense opposition to that measure when it was debated in Parliament in 1962. This strengthening, formalised in the White Paper of 1965 in *Immigration from the Commonwealth*, eliminated the 'C' vouchers, limited the number of Commonwealth immigrants to be admitted each year to 8,500 (with 1,000 reserved for Malta), limited the classes of dependants to be allowed free entry, and tightened controls on Commonwealth immigrants. It was bound to create a storm of opposition within the Labour Party. Given its tiny majority of three in the House of Commons, the government had to ensure party unity and this made the introduction of anti-discrimination bill even more important.

This commitment did not, however, involve the details of legislation, which were built around the Brockway formula of making discrimination a criminal offence. There was little consideration of the problem of discrimination outside public places or of the actual details of enforcement. The Labour Party appointed two committees to look into the question of detail in early 1964. One, chaired by Sir Frank Soskice, was made up of three members of the Shadow Cabinet (Soskice, Douglas Houghton, and Gilbert Mitchison). The other, set up by the Society of Labour Lawyers, was chaired by Andrew Martin. The Soskice Committee was much more restrictive in its approach, as was the government; and while basically accepting the Brockway approach, limited it by excluding discriminatory leases, the right of the complainant to bring civil suit, and Brockway's proposal that the discriminator should also be liable to the loss of license or registration, if any. They emphasised the difficulties of enforcement as justification for these omissions an argument which runs throughout the history of legislation in this area, The Martin Committee, which accepted the applicability of criminal penalties for discrimination in public places, went further than the Soskice Committee in wanting to include all places of public resort run by local authorities and by indicating that discrimination in other areas was more important and that, with reference to them, other methods might be more applicable — such as the American administrative machinery, based on conciliation.

Another group of outsiders who saw the importance of widening the scope of anti-discrimination legislation and of creating an administrative agency based on the conciliation process, was one led by Anthony Lester, a barrister familiar with the American experience. His group argued that the areas of employment, housing, credit and insurance, and government departments were of more importance than the restricted list of places of public resort which the government were considering and that a statutory commission, which had full powers of investigations and subpoena and authority to enforce its decisions through the courts, should be created. This commission could attempt to settle the complaint by conciliation in the first instance, but if that failed they would then use their statutory powers. The Lester group won over the Campaign Against Racial Discrimination (CARD), and other interested groups, and lobbied extensively on behalf of their proposals. They won over most of the interested Labour MPs who, unfortunately for the success of their attempt to get effective legislation, were all back-benchers and, therefore, not in a position to make the crucial decisions about the shape of the legislation.

Before moving on to a discussion of the legislation introduced by the government, it might be of interest to note that the Lester group talked of conciliation as merely one method of obtaining compliance. If it failed, the commission would use other methods. Unfortunately, in the debate both within Parliament and outside that followed Soskice's criminally based Bill, conciliation came to be seen as an end in itself, as the counterpoise to criminal sanctions, and almost, indeed, as the alternative to sanctions themselves. This misconception of the meaning of conciliation unfortunately continued and, as we shall see, was partly responsible for the weaknesses in the enforcement machinery of the 1968 Bill.

Unfortunately, the Lester group and their allies were not able to convince the government, and on 7 April 1965 Soskice introduced the Race Relations Bill 1965 which was restrictive in its scope, based on criminal penalties, and required the authorisation of the

Director of Public Prosecutions for legal action. In two other sections, it made illegal the incitement to race hatred in speech or writing and extended the scope of the Public Order Act. These later provisions are extraneous to the real purpose of the Bill, but were urged very strongly by such groups as the Jewish community who feared the revival of fascism and were part of the background to the Bill. This fear was related to the formation of Colin Jordan's National Socialist Movement and its slogan, 'Free Britain from Jewish Control'. The Jewish Defence Committees of the Board of Deputies of British Jews began its 1962 report with this revealing sentence: '1962 was without doubt one of the busiest years for the Jewish Defence Committee since its formation, and the events of the latter months of the years were in many respects, reminiscent of the situation provoked by the fascist activities of the late 1930s'. The Board, in co-operation with the Association of Jewish Ex-Servicemen and Women, the National Council for Civil Liberties, and the newly formed Yellow Star Movement, collected over 430,000 signatures on a national petition calling for legislation against racial incitement. In addition, a deputation led by the Chief Rabbi and the President of the Board met the Home Secretary, Henry Brooke, to ask for such legislation. While these efforts were unsuccessful in obtaining such legislation from the Conservative government, they did strengthen the Labour Party's resolve to link legislation against racial incitement with legislation against racial discrimination.

The Bill was attacked both by those who wanted no legislation and by those who wanted effective legislation. As happened again in 1968, this tended to lead the government to assume that since its policies were being attacked from both 'extremes', they must be correct. The Bill's criminal penalties drew most of the fire of those opposed to legislation and enabled them to appear to be in favour of more moderate legislation based on conciliation. *The Times* attacked the Bill's criminal provisions in the following terms:

> The trouble with the law making a criminal offence out of
> discrimination in place of public resort is that there is a risk of
> hardening attitudes and exacerbating prejudice in the few places
> where race relations are explosive, in return for some acceleration of
> full integration where things are proceeding in that direction anyway.
> Surely it would be better to try the effect of local machinery for
> conciliation and adjustment before dragging in the law.[2]

But those who were against legislation in this field were not the only ones to criticise the criminal penalties. It was argued that the North American experience clearly showed that few, if any, prosecutions would be brought and that it would be very difficult to prove beyond a reasonable doubt before a jury that discrimination had taken place. Also, as leading lawyer Louis Blom-Cooper argued: 'The criminal law is aimed at punishing the wrongdoer, it does nothing to correct the harm done to the victim'.[3] (This, incidentally, is a criticism which has been validly levelled against the 1968 Bill, i.e. that the Bill does not correct the harm done to the victim.)

Those opposed to legislation also centred their fire on the idea of a specially protected class, an attack which has continued throughout the years in which this problem has been discussed. This theme appeared in most of the leaders which opposed the Bill.[4] It also provided a large part of the Conservative opposition's arguments against the Bill in the Second Reading debate. Henry Brooke stated:

> I said in the House two years ago that I had no desire to be the Home Secretary who first introduced into our law the concept that some of my fellow citizens are to be singled out for special protection or distinction from others because of the race to which they belong. My successor appears to have committed this act of unwisdom.[5]

C.M. Woodhouse went even further, seeing such legislation as the beginning of the descent down the slippery slope of *apartheid*:

> However benevolent the original intention, once a dominant race starts deciding that it knows best what is needed for the well-being of other races living in the same geographical boundaries, it is only a matter of time before a still more paternalistic attitude creeps in, and then a big brotherly attitude, and, finally, *apartheid*. The lesson of this is, to my mind, simple, namely, that racial discrimination is just as bad when it is discrimination against minority and other races.[6]

Those who wanted effective legislation criticised not only the Bill's reliance on criminal penalties but also its narrow scope. They argued that the principles underlying this legislation were equally and more importantly applicable to those central areas of life excluded from the purview of the proposed law. David Ennals spoke for the critics when he argued this case:

I believe that the Bill is too limited. The net is not thrown wide enough. Clause 1 tackles the problem of theatres, cinemas, dance halls, and other places of public resort, but it does not deal with the problem of employment which is the most serious one. It does not deal with the problem of local authority and private housing. It does not deal with insurance ... with the granting of credit facilities. Admittedly, humiliation from exclusion in respect of restaurants and other public places is wounding and provocative, but in the long run, if we want to achieve equality, the right to fair employment practices is the most important right of all. It is a matter in which conciliation is more suitable than prosecution. Successful conciliation needs the force of law behind it. This is why I believe that we need the Bill, and a statutory commission.[7]

Aware of their lonely position supporting criminal penalties the government changed their mind in the month that elapsed between the publication of the Bill and its Second Reading. Indeed, Soskice began his speech with the significant phrase: 'We shall take note of what is proposed in that regard [about conciliation procedures] in argument in this debate'.[8] This was a sure indication of the government's intention to withdraw, especially when taken with the following statement:

We will listen most closely to the arguments advanced in favour of the introduction of a conciliation process. If we feel that it is practicable and in the public interest, we will, either before or during the Committee stage, amend the Bill to give such effect as we feel able to the general wish of the House.[9]

The narrowness of the government's legislative majority played a part in this decision.

The government's intentions vis-à-vis the Bill were very narrow, as can be seen in this quote from Soskice's speech: 'Basically, the Bill is concerned with public order'. This was true despite the wider problems of employment, housing, and education:

The Bill had, designedly, the more limited objectives which I have described. It is intended to implement the specific statement in the Labour manifesto of our intention to legislate with regard to discrimination in public places and to incitement.[10]

The Conservatives, led by Peter Thorneycroft, exploited the government's confusion to the hilt. They were able to play a number of different lines at the same time. They could criticise the criminal penalties, emphasise conciliation, and challenge the government for the narrowness of the Bill's scope, while at the same time questioning whether there really was as much discrimination as the government assumed and, thereby, question the necessity of such legislation. In 1965, they were not averse to using the North American experience in support of their arguments in favour of the conciliation process, something they shied away from later at the Committee stage and in 1968. Thorneycroft argued that:

> We have rather a good test case there, because some of the States have applied the criminal solution and others have adopted the conciliation method. Where they have adopted conciliation, it has, on the whole, worked not too badly; where they have tried the criminal approach, it has not worked at all, or practically not at all.

Taking a position from which the Conservatives backed away in practice, he then went on to state:

> He [Soskice] must choose between the two; either conciliation — supplied, if he thinks it necessary, with teeth through the civil proceedings, as has been attempted in a number of States in the United States of America — or the criminal law.[11]

The government won the day at Second Reading, with Liberal support, and Soskice introduced, as an amendment, a rewritten enforcement section, substituting conciliation machinery for criminal penalties. This machinery was based on a Race Relations Board in London which would create local conciliation committees around the country; these committees would receive and investigate complaints of discrimination on the grounds of race, colour, or ethnic or national origins, and if the complaints were found to be justified, the committees would attempt to conciliate. If they failed, the cases were to be sent to the Board who could merely decide whether conciliation had, in fact, failed and whether a course of conduct was likely to continue. If they decided both in the affirmative, they would then send the cases to the Attorney-General. Only the Attorney-General would be allowed to authorise court action. The local committees were not given any powers of subpoena and the Board was to be merely a post box once it had created the local committees.

And so the Bill remained limited in scope. The critics who wanted a stronger Bill were thus faced with the worst of both worlds: a Bill based on criminal penalties necessitated tight and narrow definition of its scope; and a Bill based on conciliation machinery did nothing to widen its scope.

This confusion was the basis of the first of the four main attempts to strengthen the Bill made by the seven Labour back-bench critics Donald Chapman, Ivor Richard, Paul Rose, David Ennals, Reginald Freeson, Shirley Williams, and Dr Maurice Miller supported by Norman St John Stevas and John Hunt from the Conservative side. This was an attempt to make the definition of places of public resort inclusive and, thus, to widen the scope of the Bill. However, the seven Labour back-benchers, including Chapman, who had moved the amendment, abstained on the vote. Presumably, they did so out of a desire not to embarrass the government and in the hope of finding the Home Secretary amenable to some of their proposed amendments. They were to be disappointed in this hope and were themselves embarrassed by the spectacle of only the two Conservatives, St John Stevas and Hunt, voting for an amendment proposed by a Labour critic. After this debacle and after they realised that Soskice was not going to accept their amendments, the Labour critics joined St John Stevas and Hunt in voting against the government. The government was able to beat off such attacks because of the consistent support provided by the rest of the Conservatives, who were similarly opposed to strengthening the Bill in any way. This alliance defeated attempts to include shops as places of public resort; to allow the Board to use the local conciliation committees for work on problems not actually outlined in the Bill; and to allow the complainant to bring civil actions in those cases in which the Attorney-General refused to act.

The Committee stage was marked by the government's unwillingness to go beyond the Bill in any meaningful way. It was also marked by the unwillingness of the Conservative front benches to see to it that the conciliation machinery was backed up by the terms Thorneycroft had suggested at Second Reading. The level of argument used by the government to justify their unwillingness to move beyond the Bill can only be explained by their basic assumption that the Bill was intended more to provide a lead than to be enforced and that one could not go too far, as this was new legislation. This alone could account for the argument used by Soskice against Chapman's amendment to include shops within the terms of the Act. Soskice argued that shops were different from places of public resort because the latter are places where; 'broadly speaking, a person goes to stay for a time and enjoy all the amenities which are provided in that place' and at, that therefore, discrimination in those places is more 'injurious and wounding to the feelings' than discrimination in shops. Secondly, he argued that the amendment would greatly enlarge the scope of the Bill. In opposing the amendment, he incorrectly assumed that it would include employment in shops and very revealingly used the sort of argument that many Conservatives were later to use against the 1968 Bill:

> There is also an enormous variety of offices. Many of them have almost the private quality which a club has. It is not quite the same but nevertheless an office is a place where people work closely together in the performance of a common task and in the carrying out of an enterprise whether of a business or other nature.[12]

He then went on to raise the spectre of the adverse consequences following from a Bill that could not be enforced, using as his example the proposed wording of the amendment which included the phrase 'Neglects to afford him access ... or facilities', and suggesting that a person who had been kept waiting in a crowded store could conceivably make a complaint. This, incidentally, was a technique used by the government in 1968 in defending their refusal to budge from their previously announced position.

The Labour critics were so disillusioned and angry as a result of the government's intransigence at Committee stage that the government made a concession in the form of a sentence in Soskice's concluding speech at the Third Reading to ensure their support. Soskice promised that 'the government will most certainly consider carefully what emerges in the coming months and years and will take such steps as may be dictated to suit the needs of the developing situation'.[13]

The shape of the Race Relations Act 1965 with its limited and very inadequate scope and its weak enforcement procedures, was a consequence of the government's minimalist expectations about the role of such legislation and of their very limited knowledge about the requirements of effective anti-discrimination legislation.

There was a marked reluctance on the part of the government to take any cognisance of the relevant North American experience. Such use as was made of this experience by most Conservatives, and certainly by the Conservative leadership, was only of a temporary tactical nature. Only those critics — both within and, mainly, outside Parliament — who wanted effective legislation understood and made use of this experience. But information by itself is not the most important variable in political decision-making. Without the will to act effectively, governments will not be receptive to the information, or they will use only that part of it which supports their limited measures.

The Race Relations Act 1965

Contents of the Act

The Act, passed on 8 November 1965, makes it unlawful for the proprietor or manager of a specified 'place of public resort' to practise discrimination on the grounds of colours race, or ethnic or national origins against persons seeking access to facilities or services at that place. The Act does not cover discrimination on religious grounds. It gives an exclusive and, therefore, restrictive definition of places of public resort. The Act covers public hotels, restaurants, cafés, public houses, theatres, cinemas, dance halls, and scheduled transportation services; but it does *not* cover private hotels, shops, offices, night-clubs, holiday camps, chartered transportation facilities, and, most importantly, the Crown. This leads to many anomalies: such as, discrimination by a hairdresser may be unlawful if his premises are inside a hotel, but not if they are outside it; discrimination in an off-licence is not against the law, but discrimination in a pub is unlawful. The Act establishes the Race Relations Board to obtain compliance with the law. The Board is required to create local conciliation committees which must receive and consider complaints of discrimination, make any necessary inquiries about the facts alleged in such complaints, and use their best endeavours to settle any differences between the parties and to obtain satisfactory assurances against further unlawful discrimination. One weakness in the law is that neither the Board nor the local conciliation committees are granted powers of subpoena and, thus, respondents can refuse to talk to members or staff of the Board's machinery. If a local committee is unable to secure such a settlement and assurance or if it appears to the committee that any such assurance is not being complied with, the committee must report to the Board to that effect. If the Board agrees that, on the basis of that report, a 'course of conduct' has taken place and is likely to continue, it must refer the matter to the Attorney-General. The Act empowers the Attorney-General, and only the Attorney-General, to bring civil proceedings in the county court to enjoin the defendant from practising unlawful discrimination. No other proceedings, whether civil or criminal, may be brought in respect of unlawful discrimination under the Act.

The Race Relations Act 1968

A History of the Act

The fight for wide and effective anti-discrimination legislation did not end with the passage of the token Act of 1965. In fact, soon after the enactment of that inadequate measure, it began anew with the replacement of Soskice (who was elevated to the House of Lords as Lord Stowhill) as Labour Home Secretary by Roy Jenkins. Seeing himself as a reformist Home Secretary, Jenkins had fewer compunctions about State action in the sphere than had his predecessor, and appointed Mark Bonham-Carter as Chairman of the Race Relations Board. Bonham-Carter, a long-time personal friend and intellectual colleague of Jenkins, was determined to get a better law, seeing the present Act as considerably inadequate; and there was a mutual understanding that this was a desirable goal. The Board, including Sir Learie Constantine and Alderman Bernard Langton, established this goal as its highest priority and devoted much of its time to building up the case for extended legislation.

Following the 1966 General Election, Jenkins began the process of public education necessary to make extension a legitimate exercise of government power and to ensure it a place in the government's legislation time-table. On 23 May 1966, in a speech before the National Co-ordinating Conference of Voluntary Liaison Committees, he defined integration 'not as a flattening process of assimilation but as equal opportunity accompanied by cultural diversity, in an atmosphere of mutual tolerance'. About the 1965 Act and the need for new legislation, he said:

> Some of you, I know, will think we have a better Race Relations Board than we have a Race Relations Act. I would say two things on this. First, I think a lot can be done under the present Act, and secondly, *as I have told the Board*, my mind is far from being closed about future changes to the Act .... By far the best way to get a wider Act is to work this one effectively and to show that this is a field in which legislation can help.

Many, I know, take the view that discrimination in employment and, indeed, in housing, should be covered by legislation. For the moment, I reserve judgement on the legislation point but I am in no doubt that the employment aspect of the matter in particular is rapidly becoming central to the whole future success of our integration policy. The problem is now developing with almost every month which goes by, because we are beginning to move from the era of the first generation immigrant to those [*sic*] of the second generation immigrant.[14]

In a major speech before the Institute of Race Relations on 10 October 1966, he went even further and indicated one of the main strategies of those in favour of extending the legislation to the important areas of employment, housing, and credit and insurance, i.e. making the case that discrimination was widespread. This involved the sponsoring of an objective study to show the extent of discrimination (the PEP report), alongside the Board's building up of a record of complaints outside the scope of the 1965 Act. Jenkins stated:

> It is not surprising that one should find what might be called mechanical faults in a wholly new type of legislation. I understand that the Board and the local committee are finding some. They find, for example, that the very process of conciliation which is central to the whole idea — is hindered by the lack of power to compel alleged discriminators even to talk to the local committees. It then becomes very difficult in certain circumstances to investigate complaints, much less to settle them by conciliation. The Board is finding other mechanical difficulties too, and I certainly do not exclude the possibility of the government amending the Act in due course to take account of experience.[15]

Before moving on to the Home Secretary's discussion of the possibility of widening the scope of the Act, it is interesting to note that this very essential power of compelling alleged discriminators to talk to the local committees was central in the Board's own recommendation in its first annual report, published in April 1967. The Board declared that:

> In some cases, persons against whom discrimination has been alleged have refused to meet representatives of the conciliation committee. This hampers their investigation and could, in certain circumstances, render them impossible. It should be considered whether, with appropriate safeguards, there should be power to compel attendance before the committee, or the disclosure of information to it.[16]

Despite the virtual unanimity of those experienced in administering the 1965 Act and those outside the government with knowledge of the North American experience, including the Street Committee, this provision was not included in the 1968 Bill through Parliament; James Callaghan, as we shall see, steadfastly refused to accept any such power for the Board, largely because of his assumptions about the nature of such legislation, which differed dramatically from those of his predecessor, and because of his misconception of the Board's role as 'conciliatory'. As indicated above, there has been a misconception of the meaning of the word conciliation, which sees it as an end in itself rather than as merely one method among many designed to achieve compliance with the law, which, to succeed, has to be supported by the force of law. In Mr Callaghan's eyes, giving the Board powers of subpoena would conflict with its role as a conciliator. One may hypothesise that had Mr Jenkins not changed positions with Mr Callaghan during the crucial phase of drafting the 1968 Bill, its enforcement provisions would have been very different.

In his speech to the Institute of Race Relations, Mr Jenkins went on to declare:

> When it came to amendment, the government will of course also consider matters of substance. We welcome the fact that, jointly with the National Committee for Commonwealth Immigrants, the Board is sponsoring an enquiry into the extent of racial discrimination in the fields of housing, employment, financial facilities and places of public resort not already covered by the Act [the PEP study]. This enquiry will report early next year. Along with this, the Board and the

National Committee are sponsoring a study of legal restraints on discrimination in other countries and their relevance to our own situation [the Street Committee study]. I look forward to reading these reports and needless to say, the government will not ignore them in considering any amendments to the Act.[17]

During this period, outside groups were equally active in their attempts to keep the issue before the public and to build up an overwhelming case in favour of extending the 1965 Act. The Race Relations Committee of the Society of Labour Lawyers published its third report in November 1966, which criticised the 1965 Act and made a case for new legislation, including detailed recommendations about the new Act. The Fabian Society held a conference on Policies for Racial Equality in November 1966, which was attended by Maurice Foley, then the member of the government with special responsibility for Commonwealth immigrants. This conference published papers in July 1967 in the Fabian Research Series (No. 262); edited by Anthony Lester and Nicholas Deakin, these papers made a very strong case for new legislation. During the period, CARD was active in encouraging victims of discrimination to send complaints to the Race Relations Board even, perhaps especially, if the cases were outside the Board's present jurisdiction. To keep up the pressure, Maurice Orbach, MP, introduced, as a Private Member's Bill in December 1966, a Bill to amend the 1965 Act and to extend its scope and strengthen its enforcement machinery. Drafted by CARD lawyers, led by Anthony Lester and Roger Warren Evans, and, with the assistance of Nicholas Deakin, this Bill had no chance of obtaining a Second Reading, but was designed to keep the pressure on the government and to continue making the case for such legislation. Mr Foley gave a lukewarm indication of the possible government attitude towards the findings of the PEP report, but added: 'Clearly, the extent of the comprehensiveness of the survey and the extent to which it can clearly demonstrate fields in which much needs to be done will have a decisive effect on the government in terms of their future attitude.'[18]

This build-up reached its peak in April 1967 when the PEP report on *Racial Discrimination* in England was published.[18] While its findings and conclusions were not a surprise either to the Black and Asian community or to those activists who had been working for better legislation, they did have a dramatic impact on the mass media and on public opinion. There was enormous coverage the report and newspaper leaders gave an overwhelming degree of support for new legislation. *The Times* shifted its position on the role of law as a result of the report, and *The Sunday Times* cogently declared:

> The first and indispensable step towards the provision of equal
> opportunities for all men is the enshrinement of equality in the statute
> book .... The message implicit in every line of the report was this: if the
> law does not guarantee a coloured immigrant's right to a job for which
> he is qualified and a home for which he can pay, no one else will. The
> gradualist myth was exploded by the facts. Left to the insidious
> guidance of their own fears and suspicions, too many employers, union
> leaders, landlords, estate agents and credit merchants do not and will
> not regard a coloured man as the equal of a white. As promoters of
> spontaneous integration they are simply not to be trusted.[20]

This report was followed by the publication of the Board's first annual report which reported that 238 of the 327 complaints received by the Board were outside the scope of the Act, with the largest single group of complaints (101) involving employment and with housing accounting for another 37 complaints. The Board recommended that the Act be amended to cover housing, employment, financial facilities, and places of public resort. It also recommended that certain mechanical deficiencies in the Act be improved: for example, a single act of discrimination should be sufficient to justify action, rather than the required 'course of conduct'; the Committee should have some form of subpoena power; the Act should bind the Crown; only communications made during the conciliation process should be exempted from admission in later proceedings; and, finally, the Attorney-General should be removed from the operation of the Act. It is interesting to note that except for the last of these enforcement recommendations, only those regarding scope were adopted by the government. Within a week of the publication of the PEP report, 106 Labour MPs signed a motion calling on the government to extend the Act to cover housing and employment.

The latter was to prove the major stumbling-block. Despite the Conference on Equality in Employment sponsored by the National Committee for Commonwealth Immigrants in February 1967, the Trades Union Congress (TUC) and the Confederation of British Industry (CBI) remained adamantly opposed to legislation in this area. They argued that there was at most only a minor problem and that it could best be dealt with by the traditional industrial machinery. The battle was fought with the government as well, with Ray Gunter and the Ministry of Labour taking a similar line. In order to carry the TUC and CBI along, the legislation was drafted to include voluntary machinery to be established by the unions and the employees, who would have first crack at complaints of discrimination in the employment field. This procedure has been criticised on the grounds that it is too cumbersome and time-consuming and that it is not directly under the Board. There is, as well, the danger of cosy arrangements to the detriment of the complainant. As *The Times* pointed out in an excellent leader:

> What is wrong here is not that the voluntary machinery is given the first opportunity but that a government department is to become involved at all. In principle it would be better to keep the government right out of the whole conciliation procedure ... it would be more reassuring for coloured people to feel that one independent body was in charge, even if it delegated its powers in certain fields to other bodies. It would be better for this new Department of Employment and Productivity which will have quite enough to do as it is, to be spared involvement in an area where discussions are very delicate and where it has little or no specialised experience. Above all, it would be advisable for industry's own arrangements to come under the scrutiny of a body that is dealing full-time with race relations — otherwise there is the very real danger that voluntary machinery could conceal a cosy agreement between management and workers to keep on discriminating.[21]

On 26 July 1967, the Home Secretary announced in the House of Commons that the government was going to extend the coverage of the Race Relations Act to include employment and housing. While many newspapers welcomed this announcement,[22] as did those groups outside Parliament that had been working so long and continuously for this announcement, there were many groups that continued their opposition unabated. The *Yorkshire Post* typified this latter group when it declared its opposition to the Home Secretary's announcement:

> The latest dose of well meaning foolishness from the Home Office would extend the Act to deal with discrimination on grounds of colour, race or ethnic or national origins in employment, housing,

insurance and credit facilities. Discrimination on those grounds alone in any of these fields is wicked and uncivilised but we doubt whether it happens as much as people are being led to imagine it does. The trouble is that immigrants are being encouraged to believe that the factors which discriminate against sections of the native population (such as lack of qualifications for the job, the absence of guarantees for credit facilities or housing, and the high fire risk in overcrowded houses) do not apply to them. They are being encouraged to believe that if they are asked to leave a first-class railway seat when they have only a second-class ticket it is because of their colour. Some immigrants may even take advantage of anti-racialism laws to get through subtle intimidation what they would not get through merit, or would not get, everything else being equal, if they were white.[23]

The details of the legislation had yet to be worked out, and the last part of the *scenario* in building up the case for legislation, and most particularly effective legislation, was yet to come: this was the Street report, published on 2 November 1967.[24] The report not only recommended the extension of legislation to include those important areas of life excluded from the 1965 Act, but also made detailed recommendation about the nature of the enforcement machinery required for effective legislation. Unfortunately, most of the Street Committee's valid proposals based on a perceptive analysis of the successes and failures of the North American agencies and made relevant for the British situation were ignored. The Board's recommendations and those of Equal Rights, the lobby group set up by those persons who in previous years had actively worked for new legislation, were similarly ignored.

The Bill introduced by the Home Secretary on 23 April 1968 was a courageous step forward in terms of its scope. The Bill included all the areas previously mentioned plus the field of education and closed the loop-holes in the 1965 Act. Yet its enforcement provisions seemed far too weak to ensure effective implementation of the legislation and apparently included a number of thoroughly obnoxious and dangerous loop-holes. One loop-hole exempted the merchant navy in instances where shared sleeping accommodation would be required. Another loop-hole would have exempted 'anything which is done in good faith for the benefit of a particular section of the public and which has the effect of promoting the integration of members of that section of the public into the community'. There was no definition of 'good faith', and this exemption could presumably have allowed separate but equal treatment, justifying the maintenance of segregated facilities on the grounds that it was being done in good faith for long-term integration.

The most important and controversial exemption is that for acts which are done 'in good faith' and designed to secure or preserve a 'racial balance' which is 'reasonable in all circumstances'. This allows discrimination against individuals if it is in the interests of 'racial balance'. Besides the obvious weaknesses of this exemption it neither defines 'good faith' nor does it state what constitutes a 'reasonable' racial balance there is an overwhelming objection in principle. This exemption violates the basic principles underlying the legislation, in that it authorises unequal treatment of individuals based on racial characteristics. In addition, there is the danger that once a pattern of discriminatory treatment of Afro-Caribbean and Asian people has become legitimised, it will be that much more difficult to combat later when the second generation of black British youngsters who are to be treated as white British youngsters as long as they were educated 'wholly or mainly' in Great Britain — is applying for jobs. There is also the danger of a disproportionate concentration of black and Asian employees in low-level, dead-end jobs, without adequate opportunities for promotion or training for new skills. This will establish a vested interest on the part of white employees in the maintenance of such a situation and will be infinitely more difficult to deal with at a later date. This provision was presumably put in to satisfy the TUC and CBI, to prevent the development of firms or departments with all-coloured work forces and to protect employers who wish to take action to prevent this happening.

The Bill's weaknesses in the enforcement sections spring from the two basic misconceptions outlined above: namely, the declaratory nature of the Bill, which is assigned greater importance than its enforcement procedure, and the meaning of conciliation. The government elevated conciliation to an end in itself and, consequently, opposed giving to the conciliating body the powers of either enforcement or subpoena. This ignored the Street report, the Board's own recommendations, and the lessons of the North American experience, all of which warned of the dangers of powerless enforcement agencies. Consequently, the Board was not given the power to subpoena witnesses or documents; there would conceivably be those occasions when the Board would have to face the choice of sending inadequately investigated cases to the courts and risking their dismissal, or not sending those cases that had not been fully investigated, which is likely to be most of the cases.

The operation of the legislation also embodied a basic misconception of the role of the complainant. He has been denied the right to go to court if he is dissatisfied with the Board's handling of the complaint; he has also been denied any meaningful appeal procedure within the terms of the Bill. He has been denied any satisfactory remedy because the courts, and, therefore, the Board, are not empowered to make positive orders requiring the provision of the job or accommodation in question or the next available ones. The only remedy provided is the payment of damages — of provable loss and of loss of opportunity, the latter being an entirely new concept which is likely to lead to a great deal of litigation and unlikely to be very relevant to the complainant. As the Home Secretary indicated in his speech at Second Reading: 'I do not expect that the amount of damages involved would normally be very large but there may be cases in which a claimant can demonstrate substantial loss as a result of discrimination, and I think that this should be payable in full if the case can be proved'.[25] The first part of the statement is likely to be the most relevant.

These weaknesses went against the Street Committee's conclusion that the aims of the implementing machinery were 'to secure a satisfactory settlement when there appears to be discrimination and to provide adequate enforcement against discriminators when conciliation has not been achieved'. The machinery certainly did not satisfy their three criteria of 'fairness, speed and effectiveness'.[26] These weaknesses did, however, bring the Bill closer to the Conservative leadership and, most particularly, Quintin Hogg's view of the role of such legislation. Under Hogg, their front bench Home Affairs spokesman, the Conservatives had moved away from the outright opposition to legislation that had been their position under Peter Thorneycroft. But despite the general support for the principle of legislation, the detailed positions taken by Mr Hogg were to weaken the Bill's enforcement provision and widen the exemptions, including the total exemption of financial facilities which would have the effect of largely negating the inclusion of housing, for most people would be unable to purchase a house without a mortgage or a loan. Hogg's position was based on the view that such legislation was intended for the public good, not for the benefit of any particular individual; and he was, therefore, unsympathetic to arguments urging more satisfactory individual remedies.

For internal party reasons, the Conservative leadership decided to table a reasoned amendment at the Second Reading. This decision was opposed by a group of liberal Conservatives led by Sir Edward Boyle who ostentatiously abstained on the division. The Conservative leaders were hard put to justify this decision intellectually, but the fear of a three-way split in the party, especially in the light of Enoch Powell's race speech on 20 April, won the day.

But following on from that vote, at Committee stage and at Third Reading, there was a determination on the part of both the government and the Conservative leadership to avoid Conservative opposition at Third Reading. This determination helped, in part, to define the nature of the Committee stage and shape the outcome of most of the divisions in the Committee. Of importance, too, was the tendency of the Home Secretary to see himself as the representative of common sense and the average 'Britisher', and to assume that because he was being attacked by 'extremists' on both sides, his middle course was of necessity the correct one. And, as the representative of the middle course, the Home Secretary was determined not to go too far ahead of public opinion. There was, in addition, the government's great reluctance to back down from a position to which they had publicly committed themselves a factor that was also found in the government's reaction to amendments to the 1965 Bill offered by Labour back-benchers. Both times there was an impatience with criticism, an almost contemptuous dismissal of detailed points about the enforcement machinery as 'lawyer's points', and, therefore, either irrelevant or damaging.

This was a marked characteristic of the entire legislative history of this Bill. The critics were predominantly lawyers, organised in Equal Rights; and they prepared briefing material and draft amendments for sympathetic Labour back-benchers and their Liberal and Conservative allies. Their campaign was hindered by their isolation both from the Afro-Caribbean and Asian communities, which were either unorganised or involved in militant organisation not particularly concerned with anti-discrimination legislation, and from a largely uninterested white community. This is not to say that they did not have any support in these communities, but such support as they did have, was not immediately or easily transferable to political action and, therefore, was not an important variable in the decision-making process. The critics were labelled as extremists by the government, who had successfully occupied the middle ground, arguing that they had introduced courageous and advanced legislation and yet some groups were still not satisfied and wanted even more. Additionally, there was an almost total lack of both trade-union or business support for the critics' amendments or pressure from sympathetic community and civic groups a very different situation from that found in the various American communities which have adopted such legislation. The legislative battles there were marked by a great deal of trade union activity and leadership on behalf of such legislation and political support provided by religious and civic groups.

The campaign, finally, was weakened by the decision of the Race Relations Board not to engage in public lobbying for a stronger Bill, despite the fact that virtually all its recommendations about the enforcement machinery needed for effective legislation, had been ignored. This decision seemed to follow from a number of factors, including the Board's fear that public lobbying would endanger its public position as a neutral, umpire-like, conciliation body. In addition, the split in the Conservative ranks complicated the issue from the Board's point of view, for it was essential not to be seen to be interfering in internal Conservative Party affairs and the Board felt, as did the government, great concern lest the government go too far out ahead of public opinion. It relied on contact and communication within the government, but was not as successful as it, perhaps, hoped to be. This was very largely due to the fact that the Board and its Chairman did not have the same, unusually close, ties that it had with Jenkins. In addition, the other factors mentioned above were obviously too strongly felt by the Home Secretary and the government to be challenged by the representations of the Board.

These factors led to an alliance of sorts between the two front benches, supported by most of the Conservative back-benchers on Standing Committee B and a handful of largely silent Labour back-benchers. Arrayed against them were most of the Labour back-benchers (ten out of fifteen), two Tories — Sir George Sinclair and Nicholas Scott — who showed extraordinary political courage in consistently voting against the rest of their colleagues, and the Liberal MP for Cheadle, Dr Michael Winstanley. The latter group wanted to strengthen the Bill's enforcement procedures, to close the loop-holes, and to limit the exemptions. The Conservatives, except for Sinclair and Scott, wanted to restrict the scope of the Bill to the larger employers and landlords, to provide greater exemptions in the fields of private housing and employment; and to exclude financial facilities altogether. The government was willing to make concessions on questions of scope, though it would not go as far as the Conservatives wanted. They were joined with their Conservative allies in a determination to resist attempts to strengthen the Bill's enforcement procedures.

This alliance was strong enough to dominate the Committee's voting on the enforcement provisions of the Bill, and the last weeks of the Committee's deliberations were marked by an increasing sense of frustration and despondency on the part of the Bill's critics, as amendment after amendment was voted down. This was despite the fact that, objectively, the critics had the better of the argument because they were following the logic of the reasoning behind such legislation in attempting to ensure that it was effective and inclusive. The government were forced to fall back on very naive and low-level arguments, knowing all the while that they had the votes to win the divisions. One such argument was used by the government against Nicholas Scott's motion that the courts be empowered to make positive orders so as to provide meaningful remedies for those who had been aggrieved. Speaking for the government, David Ennals declared that such remedies would not be desirable because it would be wrong to fire the innocent man who was hired in place of the complainant. This, surely, is not the point, for in a large operation men are being hired continuously and a suitable remedy would be to promise to offer the complainant the next attainable job for which he was qualified. The shocking aspect of this situation is that such a low-level argument could have been used at that late a date and after the government had had so much evidence about the North American experience.

The government's unwillingness to make concessions did not apply to Conservative attempts to limit the scope of the Bill and to increase the range of exemptions. In the early stages of the discussions, the government made a number of such concessions to the Conservatives: e.g. to increase the exemptions for small boardinghouses, lodging-houses, and hotels; to stagger the application of the Bill's housing provisions; to increase the size of firms to be granted exemptions for the first two years from those with 10 employees to those with 25, and in the second two years from 5 to 10; and to accept the so-called 'Colorado clause', which provided for the exemption of owner-occupiers who sell their houses privately and who do not use either an estate agent or public advertising. When the Conservatives wanted to go further, however, to exempt credit and insurance facilities from the Bill altogether, or to re-establish the 1965 Act's strict requirement of a course of conduct rather than the 1968 Bill's more liberal provision authorising action in the event of a single act of discrimination, or to remove damages from the Bill — which would have left the complainant with virtually no redress at all — the government, joined by the critics who wanted a stronger Bill, defeated the Conservatives. The concessions that were made, however, were sufficient to ensure Conservative abstention at Third Reading, especially when linked to the coalition's success in defeating attempts to strengthen the Bill.

After the critics' one major victory, the deletion of Clause 2, Subsection 3 — the 'separate but equal' clause — the government and Conservatives voted together to defeat all other attempts to strengthen the Bill: the government not only refused to remove the exemptions involving shared sleeping accommodations in the merchant navy — which represented defeat for the critics — but widened these exemptions to apply to discrimination on passenger ships and the shared mess and other common-room facilities on merchant ships. The critics' major defeat came over the racial balance clause when they failed, by a vote of 14-10, in their attempt to have it deleted. The critics who feared that in the absence of any criteria as to what constitutes a reasonable racial balance, employers who wanted to say 'no more coloureds' would be given the cover to legitimacy, seemed to have these fears confirmed when Eldon Griffiths, speaking for the CBI, said that it should be up to the employers and shop stewards to decide what constitutes a proper balance in their plants and departments.

When the Committee began its discussion of Part II of the Bill, dealing with the enforcement procedures, the differences in approach between the government and their critics became most apparent. The Home Secretary's position on the declaratory effect of the law and on the Board's role as a conciliator, linked with his need to avoid antagonising the Conservatives lest they vote against the Bill at Third Reading, meant that he and the government were not receptive to arguments pointing out the need for a law with teeth and for an administrative agency with adequate powers to carry out its function. He, therefore, responded negatively to an amendment moved by Nicholas Scott that would have empowered the Board to go to the county court to obtain the right to summon witnesses and order the production of documents. This was an attempt to get around the government's opposition to giving the Board that power directly — in spite of the Street report and the Board's own recommendations. It was widely assumed that the government would accept this compromise formula. But both Hogg and Callaghan felt that even this indirect power would interfere with the Board's performance of its conciliation function, and that, in any case, it was unnecessary; and both feared that such powers might violate the respondent's constitutional rights. This was a hard blow to the critics, which was only slightly softened by the government's concession empowering the Board to take a case to court on the basis of having 'formed an opinion' rather than having to 'determine' that discrimination had taken place.

The amendment designed to give the courts the power to make positive orders, which would provide satisfaction for the complainant and bring about changes in patterns of behaviour, was opposed and defeated by the government — Conservative coalition. As the 1968 legislation stands, therefore, the courts can only make a negative order or a restraining injunction, or order the payment of damages. The courts cannot order the affirmative action which has been found essential in North America.

These defeats helped to ensure Conservative abstention at Third Reading — despite the last minute revolt of a small group of right-wing Tories. From that point of view, one may characterise the government's strategy as a success.

The Bill completed its Parliamentary passage on 24 October and carne into effect on 27 November.

The Contents of the 1968 Act

The Act extends the areas in which discrimination on the grounds of colour, race, or ethnic or national origins is made unlawful, to include employment, housing, credit and insurance facilities, education and all places of public resort including shops and offices. The Crown is specifically included in the Act. The Act exempts discrimination in employment where such discrimination is done in good faith to maintain a racial balance that is reasonable in all the circumstances, but non-whites born in this country are not so exempted. It also exempts employment in private households and on merchant ships where the sharing of sleeping or mess facilities would follow from the ending of discrimination. It exempts for the first two years employers of 25 or fewer employees; in the second two years, employers of 10 or fewer employees will be exempted, after which time the Act will cover all employers except for those exempted by the provisions mentioned above.

In the housing field, there is an exemption for the private sale of property by the owner-occupier without the use of either estate agents or public advertising. In addition, there will be a phased implementation of the housing provisions, with shared accommodation involving fewer than 12 persons in addition to the landlord and his family being exempt for the first two years, and with a permanent exemption for shared accommodation involving six or fewer persons thereafter.

The size of the Race Relations Board is to be expanded to 12 persons and it will be empowered to initiate investigations where it has reason to suspect that discrimination has occurred. This is an improvement over the limited powers of the Board under the 1965 Act, but it is not matched by the granting of subpoena powers to the Board these have still been denied to the Board and its committees. There is a special procedure for the handling of employment cases involving the referral of all complaints to the Department of Employment and Productivity which will decide whether suitable voluntary machinery exists in the industry concerned. If it does, the Department will refer the case to that machinery for an initial period of four weeks, which is extendable. If the voluntary machinery is unable to settle the case satisfactorily, or if the settlement reached is unacceptable to the Department, advised by the Board, the case will go to the Board for investigation, but only if one of the parties informs the Board that he is aggrieved by the settlement. If the Board finds that discrimination has occurred they will attempt to obtain a settlement by means of conciliation. If they fail, they may take the case to one of the specially designated county courts to obtain injunctive relief (the Attorney-General has, thus, been removed from the proceedings completely). The courts can only issue negative orders — i.e. an injunction restraining the defendant from engaging in such conduct in the future but cannot order the hiring of the complainant or the provision of the next available accommodation, or the filing of compliance reports with the Board. It can order the payment of special damages, i.e. out-of-pocket expenses and damages for loss of opportunity.

Conclusion

Britain has legislated against discrimination much more quickly than most people in Britain could have predicted and more quickly than did any American community at a comparable period of the development of its racial problems. Britain's political leaders deserve credit for this. But when one looks at how they legislated and at the nature of the laws passed, it is hard to avoid the conclusion that they have not benefited from the availability of a great deal of information about the experience of various North American government bodies in enacting and enforcing similar laws. This meant that they had available information which, at the least, should have warned them about certain pitfalls. One of the most dramatic of these pitfalls has been the passage of unenforceable legislation, which not only fails to improve the situation but actually worsens it because both the discriminator and the victim come to have little or no confidence in the law and in the agency administering it. Another pitfall is that of overemphasising 'conciliation' as an end in itself rather than seeing it as part of compliance machinery, whose objective is 'compliance' not 'conciliation'. Kenneth MacDonald, Chairman of the Washington State Board Against Discrimination, addressed himself to this subject in a speech to the 1967 Conference of Commissions for Human Rights, a conference, incidentally, which was attended by the Minister with Special Responsibility for Commonwealth Immigrants, the

Chairman of the Race Relations Board, and a number of senior staff officials. MacDonald said:

> Statements by politicians, commissioners and staff members, and by enthusiasts for the legislation extolled the conciliative, educational and persuasive aspects of the law. For a long time the new agencies struggled to change attitudes, not regulate behaviour, and so not much was said then or now by public officers about the need to use 'law enforcement' or the 'coercive power' of the state to exert pressure for improving race relations. Thus words such as 'voluntarism', 'education', 'persuasion', 'conciliation', 'the necessity to change the hearts and minds of men' remained for years part of the jargon and litany under these new laws.

The North American experience also warns against weak enforcement agencies, with minimalist views of their role. As George Schwerner, a noted American practitioner, put it: 'A position of neutral, umpire-like disinterest by a commission has been demonstrated as only slightly more effective than no commission at all. A commission must make itself felt.'

Yet when we look at the legislation passed, so quickly in terms of the development of the problem, we find little or no awareness of these lessons. The 1965 Act seemed almost to be a result of an ignorance of the evidence. While unsatisfactory, it is somewhat understandable given the newness of the problem and of the assumptions with which government officials and political leaders approached it. That the 1968 Bill should have similarly evidenced a failure to take cognisance of the relevant experience of other societies, can only be deplored as wrong-headed. There is no immutable law which requires every country to make the same mistakes as others. Given the ease of communications and, especially in this case, the availability of information, one could have expected a greater awareness of the problems that have to be solved and the methods for their solution. This highlights the difficulties faced by those individuals and groups who are concerned about a problem and who are aware of relevant experience elsewhere. The political leaders must be receptive to the stimuli of this information. If they are not, then they may make the same mistakes as the pioneers who did not have this relevant experience to guide them.

It is, therefore, of great importance to see how Britain's anti-discrimination law will work in practice. The 1965 Act, with its restricted and largely irrelevant jurisdiction, does not provide a meaningful guide as to how this new law, dealing with important areas of life, is likely to be greeted by potential discriminators and their victims, and how effective it will be. In their first two years of operation, the Board, and its local conciliation committees, received a very small number of complaints, as was to be expected given its limited jurisdiction. In its first year of operation, the Board received 327 complaints, of which 89 were within the scope of the Act; and the corresponding figures for the second year were 690 and 108.

The actual case-handling of the small number of complaints falling within the Board's terms of reference again may not prove a very useful guide for the future. First of all, the new Act by-passes the local committee in the all-important area of employment and the voluntary machinery is likely to prove to be a delaying factor. This is something to be closely watched, given the absolute centrality of speed in handling complaints. Secondly, the Board's handling of many of the complaints was not as expeditious as it should have been, nor was the level of expertise and efficiency totally satisfactory. A number of obvious factors account for much of this, e.g. the inexperience of everyone concerned, inadequate staffing arrangements, and office procedure. There were also the Board's own priorities which placed working for new legislation as the top priority, followed by staffing the local committees and then actual case-handling. In terms of long-term improvement of race relations in Britain, this was in all probability the correct evaluation of priorities. We, therefore, cannot predict very accurately how well the Board will handle the increased and more complicated case-load that will follow from the 1968 Act, although the Board has built up a body of good staff, committees, and Board members. This is of absolutely crucial importance, for the attitudes and experience of the agency personnel have accounted for a great deal of the success (or failure) of the North American laws. This will be even more important in Britain, given the inadequate enforcement aspects of the 1968 law. These shortcomings will make the Board's inescapably taxing job that much more difficult because it lacks powers of subpoena; because it is necessary to use voluntary machinery; because it is impossible to issue positive orders; and, perhaps, because of the racial balance clause. Much will depend on the determination, skill, and ingenuity of the Board's personnel. They cannot operate in a vacuum, however, and much will also depend on other government programmes, such as major expenditures to remove the social problems in the twilight areas of the central cities which cause and exacerbate prejudice. Much will depend on the willingness of political leaders to provide leadership on this issue and on their willingness to use government resources to combat discrimination. Since 1966, the government have been giving urgent consideration to the question of including a non-discrimination clause in all government contracts. Such a clause, if properly enforced would strengthen the hand of the Board and would also foster the development of meaningful affirmative action programmes, for as the Street Committee concluded:

> The government are such huge customers of industry that they have a unique opportunity through the medium of their contracts to control racial discrimination .... We believe that through the medium of government contracts the opportunity should be taken of controlling discrimination by methods which would not at present be feasible in other areas of employment.[27]

Whether these programmes will be forthcoming, and whether such weaknesses as emerge in the operation of the 1968 law will be removed, only time will tell. On 22 October 1969 the government announced the introduction of a non-discrimination clause in all government contracts. The enforcement provisions, however, looked so weak that it is doubtful whether it will have much impact. One would have been more optimistic about the outcome and effectiveness of anti-discrimination legislation had there been a greater willingness to learn from the North American experience. Perhaps the British experience will demonstrate to the political leaders of other nations, the importance of receptivity to such information.

4 Parameters of British and North American Racism

The urban uprisings that have erupted in Britain's inner cities have raised fundamental questions about racism and the state in advanced capitalist societies. The urban ghetto uprisings in the United States in the 1960s and the responses engendered provide an important body of data which can illuminate the range of choices open to the British state and help predict which it will choose.

The US responses involved developments in police technology, tactics, training and command and control to pre-empt or put down future insurrections more expeditiously; efforts to relegitimise the system in the eyes of the black community; co-optation of sections of black leadership and repression of other sections, and an overall attempt to defuse the situation by de-emphasising the importance of race in American politics. But before we can analyse these responses, we need to look at the basic differences between Britain in the 1980s and the United States in the 1960s and the specific racial situation out of which the rebellions arose.

The US in the 1960s was in the midst of one of its longest unbroken periods of economic growth. The military-engendered boom was strengthened in the short run by the war in Vietnam. The economy functioned as it did on the basis of state intervention in two forms — massive military expenditure and huge investment in the creation and construction of the suburbs and the related infrastructure — generating growth in the construction, automobile and petroleum sectors of the economy. These provided the framework for the necessary political stability — based on the depoliticisation of large parts of the white, particularly male, unionised working class in the primary sector of the economy. In return for job security and wages in line with, and perhaps a bit ahead of, inflation, the unions provided a disciplined and reliable labour force. This facilitated the long-term planning that the monopoly corporations had to engage in. Blacks, as well as other racially oppressed groups, and most women and the white male poor, were left out of this cosy arrangement.

The key point was that, to maintain its profitability, monopoly capital, with and through its political allies, was willing to make material concessions to its labour force to ensure stability and growth. This meant that if the need arose there was already an economic and political framework within which concessions could be made to blacks to cool them out and reintegrate them into the system. As we shall see, however, this framework did not last out the decade of the 1960s and state strategies changed. The concessions were functional and when they were no longer necessary or could not be afforded, they were withdrawn.

In Britain in the 1980s, we find an economy under attack from competitors abroad and from the government at home. The government's monetarist strategy is predicated on cutting non-repressive state expenditure, relying on market forces to facilitate profitable economic activity — in Britain and outside — and cheapening labour within Britain by cutting the social wage and weakening or destroying working-class organisations. The ideological and material framework is thus very different from that of the New Frontier America of the 1960s, and the range and type of responses available to Britain are limited.

There are fundamental differences, besides, between Britain and the US in terms of their racial histories. Although racism emerged out of the creation and extension of capitalism as a world system, in which Britain played a leading part, and for whom the slave trade, the plantation economies and the conquest of India provided the major part of the surplus needed to fuel the creation of the industrial capitalist economy, Britain did not rely on black labour within its national boundaries for a major part of its work force. It used Irish labour and labour displaced from its own countryside. That is, until, starved of an adequate work force, it turned to its colonies for labour in the boom period of post-war reconstruction.[1]

The United States, on the other hand, virtually from its

inception as Britain's North American colony, has depended on black labour — and later, on that of the Hispanic peoples incorporated into the territory in the course of imperial expansion. Ideologically, therefore, the choices before white America have not included the repatriation of its black population.

A third and more striking point of difference follows from these distinctions. Because of its particular history of black employment and settlement, in Britain, unlike in the US, poor whites and poor blacks live cheek by jowl in many of the inner city areas and are subjected to the same deprivation, giving rise to the joint rebellion of blacks and whites against the system. These rebellions are not 'race riots' as such.

Background to the Uprisings

But there are common denominators between the uprisings in Britain and the ghetto riots of the US. Here I have concentrated on three key issues — the nature of policing, employment and education — which highlight the state practices that led to the rebellions.

Police

One central factor common to both Britain and the US has been the nature of policing in the inner cities. Not only have the police failed to protect the black communities of those areas, they have indulged in deliberate and sustained harassment of them, particularly of black youth. In the most run-down areas of Britain, 'this type of policing has also spilled over on to white working-class youth. There is a striking similarity in the nature of the 'special units' deployed in Britain and the US, and their use of deliberately aggressive tactics. In Britain, the Special Patrol Group and similar units are special squads deployed in large numbers, often without any preliminary warning, in the 'high crime' areas of the inner cities. Their concern is not, however, with major larceny, fraud or 'white-collar' crimes, but with 'policing' the inner city on the streets.

The Kerner Commission's[2] assessment of such practices in the ghettos of the US could equally well serve as a description of what takes place in Britain:

These practices, sometimes known as 'aggressive preventive patrol', take a number of forms, but invariably they involve a large number of police-citizen contacts initiated by police rather than in response to a call for help or service. One such practice utilises a roving task force which moves into high-crime districts without prior notice and conducts intensive, often indiscriminate, street stops and searches.[3]

The immediate trigger of the uprising in Brixton in the London borough of Lambeth in April 1981 was a police operation, felicitously named 'Swamp 81'. Margaret Thatcher had played the race card in the 1979 General Election by asserting that the British people had a legitimate fear of being swamped by an alien culture. Without warning, Brixton was flooded with plainclothes officers; in four days over 1,000 people were stopped and around one hundred arrested. This operation, which was pronounced a success by the officer in charge despite its consequences, was mounted even though only 4 per cent of black youth in Lambeth commit street crimes.[4]

This common pattern of harassment and invasion is reinforced in both societies by the criminalisation of large sections of the black communities — particularly the youth. In Britain, this has taken the specific form of what the Institute of Race Relations has called 'Sus 1' and 'Sus 2'. Sus 1, or the Sus law, is in fact a section of the 1824 Vagrancy Act,[5] under which an accused person can be brought to trial on no other evidence than that of acting suspiciously in the eyes of two police officers. The evidence of independent witnesses is hardly ever called. It is used primarily against Afro-Caribbean males — making parts of London, such as the West End, virtual 'no-go' areas for them. In 1977, for example, young Afro-Caribbean males, who made up only 2.8 per cent of the total population of London, accounted for 44 per cent of all Sus arrests.[6]

Sus 2, used mainly against the Asian population, is embodied in the 1971 Immigration Act, under which the police have 'the power to arrest anyone whom they suspect of being an illegal entrant'. And for suspected illegal entrants there is no right to a trial in open court — instead they are held indefinitely in detention until either removed or reprieved. 'Since all blacks are considered "immigrants" and some of them are illegal, the only way to tell an illegal black from a legal one is to suspect the lot.'[7] It is significant that this process of criminalisation and control has been accomplished by a combination of executive actions and judicial decisions, which have widened the scope of what is culpable under the Immigration Act — even including the failure to answer questions that were not asked in the first place. At the same time, basic common law protections have been eroded — habeas corpus is not available for people detained as suspected illegal entrants.

Sus 1, while specific to Britain in its details, is similar to police tactics used against young blacks in the US. It has been operated to increase fear and insecurity among the white public and to identify the source of that fear as young blacks. The creation of a scare about the new crime of 'mugging' in Britain is a case in point. There is, in fact, no such crime on the statute book, and if it means handbag-snatching or robbery with violence, it did not arrive with the coming to puberty of young Afro-Caribbean males. But mugging already had a meaning in Britain thanks to the media misreporting of events in the US and to the popularity of TV police series. Given this sensitivity, it did not take the British media, police and courts long to fasten the label mugger on young Afro-Caribbeans in general and create an atmosphere in which police invasions of black communities seemed reasonable and necessary for the common good. Sus 2 is similar to the experience of the Hispanic population in the US and, as the scapegoating of the so-called 'undocumented workers' increases, we will see an ever-increasing use of state power against them.

Police practices are further reinforced by the 'normal' racist functioning of the criminal justice systems in both societies — through the definition of crime itself, through selective, discretionary and discriminatory law enforcement, through differential access to bail and adequate legal representation, differential rates of plea bargaining and guilty pleas, differential conviction and sentencing rates — all adding up to a process which channels an increasingly significant portion of the black community into criminalisation and imprisonment. Blacks are grossly over-represented in America's prisons, and the same pattern is increasingly evident in Britain. Plea bargaining, with the threat of harsh sentencing if the accused exercise their legal rights and plead not guilty, thus 'wasting' the judge's time and the taxpayers' money, is widespread in both countries.[8] Legal representation and legal rights are commodities to be purchased — if you have the money. The Kerner Commission was forced to recognise this reality:

Some of our courts, moreover, have lost the confidence of the poor .... The belief is pervasive among ghetto residents that lower courts in our urban communities dispense 'assembly-line' justice; that from arrest to sentencing, the poor and uneducated are denied equal justice with the affluent, that procedures such as bail and fines have been perverted to perpetuate class inequities.[9]

If those are the characteristics of criminal 'justice' in normal times, what happens in times of insurrection? The Kerner Commission concluded that 'the massive influx of arrested persons resulted in serious deprivation of legal rights' and that 'judicial procedures became oriented to mass rather than individualised justice'.[10]

The Legal Action Group (LAG) in Britain, commenting on the operation of magistrates' courts after the 'riots' during the summer of 1981, described them as 'taking dangerous short cuts', in some cases simply assisting the police in 'street-clearing operations', and concluded that 'in many cases normal judicial principles and standards are being disregarded'. LAG sees calls by government ministers for quick justice, riot courts, new riot laws, heavy deterrent sentences and prison camps as 'inimical to the cool and orderly dispensation of justice'. It is afraid that sentencing will become 'punitive and arbitrary — as happened in many of the cases involving Southall defendants following the disturbances there in 1979'.[11]

The system has not only created the conditions for the oppression of black communities, but has also fuelled their anger and created the framework for a high degree of radicalisation of black prisoners. George Jackson and his colleagues were African-American prisoners in Soledad who were accused of killing a prison guard in retaliation for the death of a black prisoner. Jackson became a member of the Black Panther Party and published two books before being killed at St Quentin penitentiary. Jackson and the other Soledad Brothers were not alone in becoming politicised while in prison, and there is evidence that this process is taking place in Britain and feeding back into the communities and their struggles.[12]

There is another disturbing similarity in the police response to black rebellion. Tom Hayden, who observed the Newark, New Jersey, rebellion of 1967, wrote:

Thus it seems to many that the military, especially the Newark police, not only triggered the riot by beating a cab-driver but created a climate of opinion that supported the use of all necessary force to suppress the riot. The force used by the police was not in response to snipers, looting, and burning, but in retaliation against the successful uprising of Wednesday [12 July] and Thursday [13 July] nights.[13]

A similar pattern of violence and revenge by the police and/or the National Guard in other US cities, such as Watts, Los Angeles, and Detroit, has been reported.[14] In Britain, after the hit-and-run killing of David Moore, a crippled 22-year-old man, by a police Land Rover, in Toxeth, Liverpool, one journalist reported:

> It is no exaggeration to say that Toxteth believes Moore was deliberately run down and that his assailant will never be brought to book. It is also widely believed that, beginning last Sunday, Liverpool police set out on a deliberate vendetta, using the fresh riots as an opportunity to settle old scores.[15]

And in Brixton, some days after the latest street violence, there was a massive police raid on homes and businesses on the 'front line', Railton Road. Even toilets and televisions were smashed in what police claimed was a search for petrol bombs, but which was in fact consistent with their less publicised attempts — since the 'riots' of April 1981 — to reassert their control, teach the people of Brixton a lesson and get their revenge.

But of immediate and central importance as the police are, they are not the only racist institution that we need to look at for the background to the current wave of rebellion.

Employment

In both Britain and the US, blacks have been, and are, channelled into the dirtiest, lowest paid, lowest status and most insecure jobs, or into the reserve army of unemployed — or, today, into the never-to-be employed category. Changes in technology and investment have created the situation in which large parts of the black community, particularly the youth, are surplus to requirements.

In the US in the 1960s, even in the war-induced boom, black unemployment was double that of whites. In 1967, 26.5 per cent of non-white teenagers were unemployed, while the figure for white teenagers was 10.6 per cent — and these statistics understate the reality, based as they are on an extremely narrow definition of unemployment, which excludes all those not registered and those who can only take part-time work. A US Department of Labour analysis in 1966 found a sub-employment rate in the ghettos of 32.7 per cent — nearly nine times the national official unemployment rate.

The position of black people in Britain, particularly in Britain's cities, is shaped by a number of factors which make their current position similar to that of the urban blacks of the US. When the US southern blacks migrated to the older cities in the north and west, they became part of an urbanised, and often unionised, working class. But even as they did so, industry was moving out of the city centres — to non-city, non-union sites, indeed increasingly to Third World countries. The blacks were left stranded. In Britain, where black migrant labourers became a settler labour force, the massive process of deindustrialisation that occurred in the 1980s, to a significant extent as the result of government policies, is rebounding on the black communities. While there has been widespread discussion in the media — particularly since the uprisings — of black youth unemployment, it is important to note the growing level of unemployment among black men and women generally. The industries that they have been concentrated in (for example, textiles) have been hard hit in the current economic climate, and black workers are likely to get laid off first. Cuts in social and welfare services many of which have been major recruiters of Afro-Caribbean and Asian women — have also meant job losses.

Black teenagers attempting to enter a massively declining job market find it many times more difficult to find such work as exists — or even obtain places in government stop-gap schemes — than their white counterparts. In some areas there are black teenage unemployment levels of 50-60 per cent — comparable to the current situation in America's ghettos. In addition, young black people are vigorously resisting attempts to channel them into the jobs that their parents have done. The latter put up with the shit work of society on the understanding in the hope — that things would be better for their children. This clearly has not been so — indeed, as one black mother put it after the second round of battles in Brixton: 'These children are British, but they don't stand a chance. The police get after them, the employers won't give them a job and the teachers downgrade them.'[16]

Education

The educational system has been an important arena of struggle in both countries, central as it is not only to the reproduction of class relations but also to 'the web of urban racism', in which the various institutions of society interconnect to create, maintain and re-create racism.[17] Annie Stein, a courageous veteran campaigner and researcher, has analysed the functioning of the educational system in the US and has identified the 'strategies for failure' that have been developed and implemented by the state.

> The average child in eighty-five percent of the Black and Puerto Rican schools is functionally illiterate after eight years of schooling in the richest city in the world [New York].

This is a massive accomplishment.

> It took the effort of 63,000 teachers, thousands more administrators, scholars, and social scientists, and the expenditure of billions of dollars to achieve. Alone, however, the 'Professional' educators could not have done it. They needed the active support of all the forces of business, real estate interests, trade unions, willing politicians, city officials, the police and the courts.[18]

These schools have not 'failed' to educate black youngsters, they have succeeded in channelling them into failure, in blaming them and their parents for that failure and in channelling and training white youngsters, in class terms, to fill their appropriate places in the system. The whole range of processes, including low teacher expectations, which become self-fulfilling prophecies, racist or irrelevant curriculum materials, tracking/streaming, the use of IQ tests and segregation — *de jure* and *de facto* — have all worked to produce such an outcome. Malcolm X gives a painful — and by no means atypical — example of what happened when he told his favourite teacher that he wanted to be a lawyer.

> Mr Sostrowski looked surprised, I remember, and leaned back in his chair and clasped his hands behind his head. He kind of half-smiled and said, 'Malcolm, one of life's first needs is for us to be realistic.

Don't misunderstand me, now. We all here like you, you know that. But you've got to be realistic about being a nigger. A lawyer — that's no realistic goal for a nigger. You need to think about something you can be.'[19]

In the 1960s the language changed — from 'nigger' to 'cultural deprivation' and then back to genetic inferiority — but the processing of black children into failure, into shit work or unemployment continued. It was not accidental, therefore, that one of the most highly contested issues in the black struggles of the 1960s in the US was that of the miseducation of their children. These battles moved from demands for integration, through compensatory education programmes to struggles for community control of education.[20] There is not the space here to detail the outcome of these struggles — suffice it to say that, on the whole, they failed to gain control or to make the schools accountable to the black community.

In Britain in the 1980s we find a similar pattern of educational practice and black sense of betrayal and anger. The processing of black children into failure was noted as early as the late 1960s when black parents campaigned against the London borough of Haringey education authority for sending a disproportionate number of their children to schools for the educationally subnormal.[21] And throughout the 1970s black parents continued to campaign against the miseducation of their children, pushing for positive, non-racist teaching materials to counter the negative stereotypes and low teacher expectations and setting up nurseries, play groups and supplementary schools to counter the effects of state schools. Black children in Britain were being incorporated into a class-based educational system at the very lowest level. A recent committee set up by the government to investigate black 'under-achievement' concluded: 'we are convinced from the evidence that we have obtained that racism, both intentional and unintentional, has a direct and important bearing on the performance of West Indian children in our schools'.[22] It is perhaps not entirely coincidental that the chairman of that committee was subsequently persuaded to resign.

The range of processes, of acts of commission and omission, which the committee identified as contributing to the failure of West Indian children is directly comparable to those found in the US, ranging from low teacher expectations and racist curricula to the possibility that West Indian children were still being unfairly assessed and were over-represented among those suspended or excluded from school or sent to disruptive units. The similarity with ghetto miseducation in the US indicates that British schools are succeeding all too well in separating and channelling black youngsters into second-class status, clearly making education part of the contested terrain.

State Responses to Urban Rebellion

Public Order and Community Policing

What have been the US responses to urban rebellion? If we are to draw lessons from them as to possible courses of action for the British state, we must bear in mind the differences in the British and American political economies. It is also necessary to keep in mind the way in which some of the US state responses have changed in accord with changes in the political economy.

The first set of responses, which have continued to obtain since the 1960s, had to do with increasing the size and improving the efficiency of the state's repressive apparatus. One indication of the seriousness of purpose in this area is that the rate of increase in US government spending on criminal justice between 1966 and 1971 was five times as great as it was in the previous decade. In 1971 over $10.5 billion was spent in this area, and by 1974 the figure reached over $14 billion, with over $8 billion of that for the police alone.[23] Another indication of the seriousness of the state's determination to reassert control was that during the 1960s and early 1970s there were four separate federal commissions studying these questions, and several more set up by corporations and foundations.[24]

Of these, the Kerner Commission was of major importance for its recommendations, which can best be summed up in the old cliché of the iron fist in the velvet glove.[25] Its prime concern was to develop a more effective policy for the restoration of public order. Its apparently liberal, and more widely publicised, concern over the causes of the riots indeed its very composition and approach — can be seen as an attempt to re-legitimise and restore confidence in the system. But the heart and substance lay in making police methods more effective. What the Commission diagnosed was police 'over-reaction', bad or non-existent command and control and an inadequate range of weapons. What it recommended was improved control capabilities, improved discipline and command within police departments, improved tactics and sufficient personnel to implement these, and the development of a wide range of non-lethal weapons, including a specific recommendation in favour of the use of CS gas. The Commission specifically recommended federal funding of certain programmes — 'community service officers, development of portable communications equipment, a national clearing house for training, information and non-lethal weapons development', as well as increased support to 'pay for the large capital investment necessary for experimental programs or development of new equipment'.[26]

It was in this area that the Commission's recommendations were most enthusiastically and expeditiously implemented, in response not only to the urban insurrections, but also to the development of the New Left, the civil rights movement and the emerging anti-war movement. The Center for Research on Criminal Justice saw the initial government response as one whose 'overall thrust was toward reorganising the police as an effective combat organisation'.[27] Criminal justice information systems — police files — underwent a major computerisation programme, largely funded by the federal government's Law Enforcement Assistance Administration (LEAA). In addition, LEAA supplied money to police departments for the purchase of new guns, automobiles, riot control equipment, helicopters, computers and sophisticated intelligence-gathering systems.

It is here that we can see the clearest similarity with both existing and probable future British government policies. Indeed, since the Metropolitan Police first established the Special Patrol Group in London, most major cities have created their own special squads. This development, combined with the creation of Police Support Units (PSUs), involving an even wider group of police obtaining riot control training, clearly indicates the British state's approach. The Thatcher government's pledge — and its enthusiastic honouring of it — to increase police spending in real terms and to increase police pay (even, or especially, at a time of pay restraint for most of the rest of the public sector workers) is further indication of this approach.

The immediate reaction of Home Secretary William Whitelaw, police chiefs, police union officials and Tory backbenchers to the urban insurrections has been to call for new weaponry and training. Armoured cars, protective clothing, rubber bullets, CS gas and water cannons are all to be made available as police chiefs determine. The primary objective is to restore law and order and reassert police hegemony in black neighbourhoods.

But the adoption of harsher and more sophisticated measures of containment was not the only response of the US state. A necessary adjunct to them was a greater emphasis on community involvement. This not only served the function of acting as a sop to the black community, an attempt to deflect black resistance and legitimate the police in the eyes of blacks, it was also useful as a means of gathering information on the black community. As the Kerner Commission put it: 'Negro officers also can increase departmental insight into ghetto problems, and provide information necessary for early anticipation of the tensions and grievances that can lead to disorders'.[28] On the reasons for police involvement in community service, it was even franker:

> First, police, because of their 'front line position' in dealing with ghetto problems, will be better able to identify problems in the community that may lead to disorder. Second, they will be better able to handle incidents requiring police intervention .... Third, willing performance of such work can gain police the respect and support of the community. *Finally, development of non adversary contacts can provide the police with a vital source of information and intelligence concerning the communities they serve* .[emphasis added][29]

This approach has become an important part of federal government activities in the race field over the past decade. The Community Relations Service, originally established as an ally of the civil rights movement, has functioned since the late 1960s as an intelligence-gathering body for the state and has placed undercover operatives in ghettos throughout the US to provide early warning of tensions which might lead to disorder. The operatives cultivate local black elites and intervene to defuse struggles and isolate militants and activists.[30] The Kerner Commission has indeed borne fruit, and it is interesting that two Community Relations Service officials were brought to Toxteth for a Granada TV programme on 27 July 1981 to talk about the importance of having operatives in such communities. Community policing is important to the state in that:

it [is] useful to decentralise police functions without decentralising police *authority*, that is, the police should have close contact with the community, but the community should not be allowed to have any real influence on the police. The aim of this kind of decentralisation is to enable the police to integrate some citizens into the lower levels of the police system itself, on police terms, thus blurring the distinction between the police and the people they control.[31]

Repression and Concession

It is no coincidence that even as the community policing strategy was being developed, the US state was mounting a massive counter-insurgency programme (COINTELPRO) against black militants, the anti-war movement and other left groups. Patterned on previous campaigns against internal 'enemies', it involved the infiltration, destabilisation and disruption of organisations. Activists were arrested on trumped up charges and inordinately high bail prices were set, which, together with long pre-trial delays, ensured that the accused would be kept off the streets for up to two years. Frequent acquittals proved only that 'justice' still worked after all. There were, in addition, shoot-outs and the killings of activists, as in the murders of Mark Clark and Fred Hampton of the Black Panther Party in Chicago.

But this mix of outright repression and 'community policing' was still not considered sufficient. For by now, it was recognised that blacks could not be counted on to be quiescent. Their willingness to fight for 'freedom and democracy' in the future could no longer be assumed and the concessions of the early 1960s — civil and voting rights — were no longer enough. When Harlem exploded in 1964, soon after the passage of the Civil Rights Bill, it became clear that additional concessions — material concessions — would have to be made to cool out the ghettos, restore stability and provide the framework for a process of co-optation. Given the expanded economy of the time, such an argument had an appeal. New programmes needed personnel, and potential personnel were on the streets making trouble. Their incorporation into the system would help both to legitimate it and to defuse opposition to it. This was encouraged by foundations such as Ford, which provided large sums of money in the attempt to penetrate and buy off militant organisations (the internal struggles in CORE [Congress of

Racial Equality] exemplify the conflicts that such a strategy engendered).[32]

Before looking at the fate of these programmes and concessions and their implications for the political struggle of the black community it is important to reiterate that such an approach cannot automatically be reproduced in Britain in the 1980s. The level of US state expenditure, though totally inadequate, was on a scale that is extremely unlikely to be entered into by the monetarist Thatcher government. The US's expanding economy made the Keynesian approach appear as a reasonable way of ensuring social peace. Such an approach was also predicated upon the existence of a significantly large group of people who, if not co-opted, might become dangerous enemies. While it is clear, as Sivanandan cogently argued in *Race, Class and the State*,[33] that British policy towards the Asian population has, in part, been predicated on the possibility of utilising the existing class and age structures within that community to control the Asian working class and youth, such a strategy with regard to the Afro-Caribbeans, an overwhelmingly working-class community, has not been possible. Instead, part of the British state's strategy has been geared to creating a functionary stratum within that community through the race relations industry, for example, the Community Relations Commission, the Race Relations Board, the Commission for Racial Equality and the local community relations committees. But this stratum just does not appear large enough, nor does the pool of potential recruits, given the functioning of the racist British educational system. There is massive evidence that the entire strategy of dividing the Asian and the Afro-Caribbean communities, and using the divisions within each to maintain control, has come unstuck.

The crucial point to bear in mind is that the liberal, concessionary approach — allied, of course, to the repression — was not the only possible response of the American state and was dependent upon a particular set of political and economic circumstances. As these circumstances changed so did the ideological argument. And even in the mid-1960s we can see the forerunners of the rightist arguments that would come to dominate thinking and reflect government policy in the 1970s and 1980s. In 1965, for example, New York senator Daniel Moynihan, then working for the Johnson administration, prepared a report which blamed the structure of black families for their own situation.[34] The 'culture of poverty' approach was already widely used by social scientists and being popularised by people such as Edward Banfield, a professor at Harvard and major proponent of the cultural of poverty approach,[35] who saw crime and delinquency as stemming directly from the culture of the lower class. The poor lived in slums because they preferred it that way, having made the areas slums in the first place. It therefore made little sense to talk about slums, unemployment and poverty as causes of riots. The emphasis on moral decay and lack of parental discipline being offered by Whitelaw and others following the recent British uprisings is strikingly similar. In a recent issue of the *Daily Telegraph*, John O'Sullivan, editor of *Policy Review* (the journal of the far right-wing Heritage Foundation, a crucial organisational link between the neo-conservatives and the moral majority in the US), had this to say: 'all the youth employment schemes and social workers in the world will not reduce or eliminate rioting. That will only be done by enforcing the law and holding people responsible for their lawless actions.'[36] Or, put more succinctly by Mrs Thatcher recently: 'You can't buy your way out of the riots'.

Another strand of intellectual racism that re-emerged in the 1960s was that of scientific racism and its emphasis on the genetic inferiority of blacks.[37] Where Banfield and Moynihan and their ilk emphasised the blacks' pathological culture, the major proponents of the idea that intelligence was genetically determined, Shockley, Jensen, Herrnstein and their British ally Eysenck, emphasised the hereditarian basis of black inferiority.[38] Both positions postulated that the victim's position was due to his or her basic characteristics — a useful approach for a political system under attack for its racism.

Market Forces and Black Capitalism

By the end of the 1960s, the US political economy had moved and with it state strategies and ideological currents. The weakening competitive position of the economy, the inflationary pressure following the war in Indochina, the worsening profit position of capital, the growing indebtedness of American business and the development of what capitalist economists could label but not understand or cure, 'stagflation', all necessitated a counter-attack on the working class as a whole, and particularly against the material concessions which had increased the social wage and set some limits on the operations of the corporations and their ability to generate and realise profit. All such impediments would have to go, and go most of them did.[39]

This had disastrous consequences for the mass of blacks, and the new strategy also went hand-in-hand with the development of a neo-conservative movement that argued vigorously against the liberal interpretations of the 1960s, that attacked the gains won then and that claimed that the poor should be left to market forces, and to their own devices. Government strategy abandoned such reform efforts as had been attempted in the Johnson years; henceforth the market was to provide the basis for-individual black advance. Black capitalism became the rhetoric of the time. None of the reforms accomplished in the 1960s tackled the fundamental structures of the political economy. Consequently, the patterns of black un- and under-employment did not change; for even in the boom period new investment was capital- not labour-intensive, and was not made in the inner-city ghettos. The ratio of black/white incomes, the relative proportions of black and white poverty and the relative rates of infant mortality, for example, did not fundamentally change. And under the policies of benign neglect, the extent of deterioration is undeniable. As US economist William Tabb states:

> Even before the economic downturn in 1974-75 Black economic gains of the 1960s had vanished. Between 1970 and 1973 Black family income fell behind as inflation eroded monetary gains (White family income rose by over six per cent). The number of Black families living in poverty rose while the number of white poverty level families continued to decline.[40]

And these patterns continued for the remainder of the decade.

What has had a more lasting effect has been the co-optation strategy — resulting in the growth, small and insecure as it is, of a black middle class, in the state bureaucracy and in the major corporations.

> Growth of Black college enrolment, white-collar employment and entrepreneurship has gone hand in hand with continued high

unemployment. The rising Black bourgeoisie urges self-reliance on the Black poor and working classes, while it as a class has gradually abandoned the relative independence of self-employment for jobs as hired hands of government and big business.[41]

The goal of creating black capitalism has, however, not been achieved. All that is left from earlier initiatives is a residue of small, mostly family-owned shops and businesses, extremely vulnerable to the recession. Berkely G. Burrell, head of the black National Business League, put his finger on it: 'A banker is a banker is a banker and if the S.O.B. isn't going to make me a loan, he isn't going to make it with government money behind him either'.[42] The government backing did not last long in any event. Black capitalism as a slogan in Nixon's 1968 presidential campaign soon gave way to 'minority business enterprise' and to benign neglect and calls for corporate involvement, thus making it even less likely that the 'S.O.B.s' would make the loan. At the height of the appeals for corporate investment in the ghetto, a survey of 700 major corporations revealed that only 112 of them 'indicated a willingness to build new plants in or near slum areas'. In addition, not one of them would make the move unless certain conditions were met, including:

- A large and non-aggressive labour pool.
- Programs to train local workers with new and useful skills.
- Ample land at reasonable prices, roads and utilities, and new zoning codes.
- Pleasant environmental conditions, including quality housing in the immediate area and assurances that ghetto 'blight' would be removed.
- Lower real estate taxes.
- Adequate security and fire protection.
- Relations only with 'responsible community groups' not with militants.[43]

The British state and British finance capital are unlikely to be any more successful in the creation of black capitalism — particularly Afro-Caribbean capitalism. And no matter how many inner-city coach-tours Environment Minister Michael Heseltine organised for businessmen in 1982, it will be interesting to see how many of the conditions demanded by US corporations he will be able to deliver in monetarist Britain — even if there are any firms willing to take advantage of them. The free-enterprise zones mooted by government may be able to supply some of these requirements — but in their present watered-down form they are unlikely to attract significant investment.

Conclusion

The black uprisings of spring and summer of 1981 were increasingly joined by alienated, unemployed white youth who feel anger against the police and the system. Their experiences with the police, though not as severe or total as those of the blacks, have nonetheless given them cause for rage. In a racist and highly class stratified society, the struggle of the black community, essentially against the racism which permeates society, is also a struggle against the class system. For the white youth — and the white left — struggle against the class hierarchy cannot by itself lead to fundamental change — they need to confront and overcome the racism which has historically retarded and distorted white working-class consciousness.[44] It is also important that when looking at the British uprisings that began in St Paul's, Bristol, in 1980, blew up in Brixton in April 1981 and in city after city in July 1981, they are not isolated from the continuing struggles of black youth and the black community in general against escalating fascist/racist attacks.

The British state has begun the attempt to contain the uprisings as well as the more problematic task of preventing future ones. The media and the ideologues have entered the fray as well. The New Right from the US has been peddling its noxious doctrines of selfishness, black inferiority and repression alongside its British allies. The more sophisticated and liberal elements have raised the question of concessions of one sort or another — but not material ones, for after all, as Heseltine has said, there is 'no crock of gold'. More co-ordination of government activities has been proposed, as has an attempt to overcome racial disadvantage in housing and employment. As *The Times* put it: 'The more these disabilities can be removed, the easier it will be for black and Asian people to find satisfactory places for themselves in accordance with their individual abilities'.[45] A strategy to find 'satisfactory places' — at least for some — is made even more necessary because, as Sivanandan shows, changes in production related to micro-technology, and the investment decisions associated with those changes, are such as to make unemployment a permanent condition for a significant portion of the working class.[46] And we can be sure that blacks will be round in that group in large numbers. So central is this reality that even *The Times* had to acknowledge — albeit in muted fashion — that 'we have moved into a different economic climate in which jobs will be in short supply for years to come'.[47]

Meanwhile, the Labour Party and the trade unions have belatedly had to confront the consequences of their own racist policies and have proved unable to deal with them. The Labour Party, committed by both policy and practice to managing a capitalist economy (with some state ownership), will also have to give priority to capitalist requirements and capitalist economic activity — rather than to maintaining, let alone improving, social and welfare benefits. Given the massive and sustained erosion of Britain's economic and industrial base, and the lack of any Labour policies to deal with that, there is no way that it will be in any position to make the sort of material concessions made in the US in the mid-1960s by the Democrats. It is unlikely, therefore, that even with a change of government the conditions which give rise to the uprisings will be significantly altered. In the short run, there will be more repression, various symbolic gestures and increased attempts at co-optation.

This article began by looking at the US black insurrections of the 1960s, and the various state responses. We have seen that as the economy retrenched, capitalist imperatives required the clawing back of many of the material and procedural concessions made to the black community, in favour of repression allied to co-optation. It appeared throughout the 1970s that the strategy had worked. There were, however, a number of indicators that the ghetto blacks were not as quiescent as had been assumed. During a power failure in New York City in 1977 and during a blizzard in Baltimore — both of which put the police temporarily out of action — blacks engaged in widespread looting. In 1979 a black uprising in Miami followed the acquittal by an all-white jury of four white policemen who had beaten a black man to death.

The ideological disarray among liberals in the US, and the lack of concern about race — it is no longer an 'in' subject — has given the New Right allies of capital a dominant position. Their anti-black, anti-woman, anti-gay ideology provides the cover for a massive reallocation of state funds from the working class as a whole — with blacks and other racially oppressed groups bearing a disproportionate burden — in favour of capital.[48] On the whole, the co-opted black functionaries, at least those not being laid off as a result of cuts, can be counted upon to defend their new class position. But the danger from the state's perspective is that the mass of poor blacks will take matters into their own hands. US Attorney General William French Smith has stated that the possibility of racial violence erupting as a result of cuts in social programme budgets will be monitored by an 'early warning system' (he is referring to the Community Relations Service). But so far, 'we haven't had any great alarms that have gone off anywhere .... It's quite possible that the effect of these so-called budget cuts won't materialise at all in terms of causing temperatures to rise.'[49]

What this indicates — apart from the obvious propaganda element is a state on the attack, relying both on its domestic intelligence network and its agencies of force to contain trouble. At the same time, the ideological offensive against blacks and the poor is heightening, as evidenced in two recent major articles in the *Los Angeles Times*.[50] They are worth discussing in some detail because they exemplify current thinking, and give an alarming foretaste of future trends.

The articles argue that while twice as many whites as blacks are part of a new permanent underclass, the black underclass is more worrying because it is concentrated in America's major cities rather than being scattered in the Appalachias and other semi-rural areas. Structural factors in maintaining and creating this underclass are mentioned, but the overriding theme is that of its own responsibility for its position. And if statistics will not do to bring the message home to the reader, there is a case study of a day in the life of a South Side Chicago black welfare mother, with ten illegitimate children, five of whom are on welfare with her, and one of whom has just had an illegitimate child — under the invidious title 'The underclass, how one family copes'. These blacks are not only living off the rest of us because they cannot or will not work, but they also engage, we are told, in widespread criminal activity which also costs the rest of us. The experts quoted agree that not a great deal can be done, the economy is shrinking, and it's all the fault of the poor anyhow.

But more dangerous than the familiar 'blame the victim' structure of the debate is the way we are encouraged to fear and loathe
the victim. The second article, appearing one week later, drops all
pretence at social concern. Luridly titled 'Marauders from inner
city prey on LA's suburbs', it begins as follows: 'One by one and
in small bands, young men desperate for money are marauding
out of the heart of Los Angeles in a growing wave to prey upon
the suburban middle and upper classes sometimes with senseless
savagery'.[51] Robbery (with bloodcurdling violence) and the rape of
two white women is the stuff, we are informed, of one such 'raid'.
We are then returned to the ghetto with these savage marauders to
watch them showing off and spending their ill-gotten gains. We are
repeatedly told that the police do not have enough powers or man-
power and that the courts are too lenient.

The President of the Los Angeles Urban League, John Mack,
sees the solution lying with placing 'the major focus on the ones
who are still salvageable .... We are a race of people who are equal
to anyone else, but within that framework we have some winners,
and we have some losers. We have to go with the winners.' Mayor
Tom Bradley has a solution for the 'losers'.

> I think that there is a concept where you have a controlled
> environment, where you keep the child not just while he or she is in
> school but in the hours outside school, you have that child in a
> controlled environment. The kibbutz in Israel is one such concept ....
> It, of course, would not be a kibbutz, but it would be that kind of
> concept.[52]

Bradley's 'concept' — the twenty-four-hour a day controlled environment for the unco-opted members of the underclass — is the
frightening logic of the current US situation. Is that where
Whitelaw's army camps turned prisons for the rebellious youth of
Britain's inner cities will also lead?

5 The United States: The Revocation of Civil Rights

In the US today we are witnessing a reversal of many of the legal and political reforms stimulated by the civil rights movement of the 1950s and 1960s. This repeal of what may be termed the Second Reconstruction is proceeding in much the same manner as the reversal, a hundred years ago, of the First Reconstruction reforms that followed the American Civil War. In both cases, the executive and judicial branches of the federal government worked together in an increasingly racist, popular and intellectual culture to turn the clock back. In the last decades of the nineteenth and the twentieth centuries, black rights to equality in the economy were abrogated — as were their rights to be considered as 'real Americans'. In both cases, the 'counter-revolution' followed an incompletely conceptualised and implemented 'revolution' in which the economic basis of freedom was neglected by the political leadership of the African-American community and denied by the corporate political and economic elites.

First Reconstruction

In the case of the First Reconstruction, it was the denial of land to the freewomen and freemen which undermined their ability to protect their limited political rights. Radical Republican Congressman Thaddeus Stephens posed the challenge facing the victorious Union following the Civil War in stark and prophetic terms, when he stated that political democracy was impossible in a situation in which the majority were landless and most of the land was owned by a tiny group of 'nabobs'. So powerful was his insight that northern industrialists and their political representatives, the Republican Party, refused to confiscate the land and distribute it — '40 acres and a mule' — to the former slaves or to make it available at low prices with low rates of interest to poor whites. For, if political democracy in the South required a Jeffersonian economic democracy, would not political democracy in the industrialising North require a form of economic democracy as well?

What the industrialists and their allies wanted from the South was cheap cotton and that would be best produced by a re-established plantation economy. They also needed to keep control of the federal government to further their own economic and political interests. And, since only the enfranchisement of the former slaves would ensure the political dominance of the industrialists' party, the Republicans, in the immediate future, that also was key to the Reconstruction reforms.

Of these two aims, the re-established plantation system producing cheap cotton for export and for domestic mills remained inviolate until the First World War. The second goal was a more temporary one, for, as time went on, the black vote became less and less necessary to maintaining the new national political economy and the cost of protecting it became too high. Consequently, the political rights that had been extended to black men were swiftly eroded — by terrorism; lack of military protection for blacks in the South; the withdrawal of federal commitment to black rights as the price for Hayes's victory in the 1876 presidential election, and by a series of Supreme Court decisions. The latter overturned Reconstruction laws designed to protect the rights of the former slaves and overwhelmingly interpreted the Fourteenth Amendment, which guaranteed equal protection before the law, in such a way as, in fact, to deny it to black Americans — while at the same time providing protection for corporations against state regulation.[1]

The Supreme Court began the process of neutralising the gains blacks had made with the *Slaughterhouse Cases* of 1873. The Court argued that the adoption of the Thirteenth, Fourteenth and Fifteenth Amendments to the constitution — which formed the legal basis of Reconstruction — was not intended 'to destroy the main features of the general system' which gave the individual states primacy over their own affairs, including civil rights, 'and over the definition of the basic terms of citizenship within its boundaries'.[2] In 1876 the Court limited the rights of African-Americans further in the case of *United States* v. *Cruikshank* which

> established the principle that the Fourteenth Amendment guarantees the rights of citizens only against encroachments by the states, and not against ... private individuals. In addition, it held that the violation by a private person of the civil rights of another could only be a crime when it interfered with an act connected with national citizenship.[3]

In the *Civil Rights Cases*, decided in 1883, the Court overturned the Civil Rights Act of 1875, which had implemented the Thirteenth and Fourteenth Amendments by outlawing discrimination in places of public resort and transport facilities. This decision is crucial, not only because of the practical consequences following the repeal of the Act, but also because of the Court's rejection of the notion of 'special treatment':

> When a man has emerged from slavery ... there must be some stage in the progress of his elevation when he takes the rank of a mere citizen, and ceases to be the special favourite of the laws, and when his rights ... are to be protected in the ordinary modes by which other men's rights are protected. There were thousands of free coloured people in this country before the abolition of slavery ... yet no one, at that time, thought it was any invasion of his personal status as a freeman because he was not admitted to all their privileges enjoyed by white citizens, or because he was subjected to discriminations ...[4]

The Court had effectively equated the protection of equal rights for black Americans with 'special treatment' — thus placing them outside the category of American in the same way in which race-based chattel slavery served to exclude black from the Declaration of Independence's definition of men in its assertion that 'all men are created equal'.

The final stage in the legal process of creating an apartheid society in the South was reached in 1896 in the *Plessy* v. *Ferguson* decision. In this case the Court upheld a Louisiana statute establishing segregation of whites and blacks on railroad trains and held that the Fourteenth Amendment, 'in the nature of things could not have been intended to abolish distinctions based upon colour, or to enforce social, as distinguished from political, equality'.[5] Justice Harlan challenged the Court's majority decision in a vigorous and famous dissent, arguing that:

> The present decision ... will not only stimulate aggressions ... upon the admitted rights of coloured citizens, but will encourage the belief that it is possible, by means of state enactments, to defeat the beneficent purposes [of] the recent amendments of the Constitution, by one of which the blacks of this country were made citizens ... whose privileges and immunities, as citizens, the States are forbidden to abridge.[6]

This undermining of the First Reconstruction, with its consequent denial to African Americans of their political and economic rights, and the locking of most into debt peonage as tenant farmers in the South, followed on from the actions of the leaders of the former slaves as well as those of the white power structure. The black petit bourgeois leaders were committed to the capitalist political economy and thus failed to challenge its logic or to articulate the social class interests of the black majority. Frederick Douglass, an escaped slave who became a major figure in the abolitionist movement before the Civil War and key leader of African America in the post-Civil War period, said in 1880:

> Could the nation have been induced to listen to those stalwart Republicans, Thaddeus Stephens and Charles Sumner [who had favoured the confiscation of Confederate estates], some of the evils we now suffer would have been averted. The negro would not today be on his knees ... supplicating the master class to give him leave to toil .... He would not now be swindled out of his hard earnings ... because left by our emancipation measures at the mercy of the men who had robbed him all his life and his people for centuries.[7]

Indeed, this failure had even more deleterious consequences: it helped legitimate the repeal itself. Demands for justice and material compensation for blacks were transmuted into demands for 'special treatment' — clearly unacceptable in a society in which every individual was in competition with every other individual. Failing to challenge this stereotype, black leaders could not make the entirely valid case for group rights for those who had been enslaved for two centuries and then freed without compensation.

Second Reconstruction

Some hundred years later, a parallel process could be seen working to overturn the gains of the so-called 'Second Reconstruction' — brought about by the civil rights movement of the 1950s and 1960s. These gains were limited but real. The burden of Jim Crow — that is the system of *de jure* segregation which affected every aspect of a black person's daily life — was removed from the backs of black people in the South, and spin-off from the movement led to new types of political mobilisation in the cities of the North. But the class differences in the black community, the commitment to the capitalist economy by the black leadership and the incorporation of large sections of the black middle class into various levels of the state bureaucracy continued the isolation of the mass of black people and their needs from the political agenda.

Nonetheless, a liberal national agenda, combined with the changing economic and political situation in the South, facilitated a series of concessions which, fundamentally, overturned petty apartheid, *de jure* segregation, and provided for the incorporation of blacks into an existing, structurally unequal, political system on a (more or less) colour blind basis. The civil rights movement also acted as a catalyst for women, young people and other racially identified groups whose movements in the 1960s challenged a whole gamut of assumptions about what had been accepted as 'natural' in American society — for example, definitions of sexuality, the nature of the family, the truthfulness and significance of media representations, as well as institutional discrimination against blacks.

The Supreme Court, under Chief Justice Earl Warren, responded with a range of decisions which extended rights to groups in addition to blacks and in areas beyond the removal of de jure segregation. For example, establishing the right to counsel in *Gideon* v. *Wainwright* (1963); the right to remain silent in the face of police custodial interrogation in *Miranda* v. *Arizona* (1966); the right to be free from unreasonable searches and seizures in *Terry* v. *Ohio* (1968); the right to exclude illegally obtained evidence from trial in *Mapp* v. *Ohio* (1961). The liberal majority on the bench remained even after President Nixon appointed Warren Burger as Chief Justice, and the extension of rights continued in *Roe* v. *Wade* (1973), which legalised abortion, and in cases involving blacks, such as *Riggs* v. *Duke Power Co.* (1971) in which the Court unanimously placed the burden of proof in 'disparate impact' cases on the employer.[8]

The *Duke Power* case upheld affirmative action, which was one of the major concessions wrested from the system by the spreading of black struggle to the urban ghettos and by the urban uprisings of the 1960s. Another set of concessions involved the relaxation of some of the procedural barriers which had prevented many of those eligible for social benefits from obtaining them and the establishment of job training and creation programmes. These programmes did not, of course, address the fundamental inequalities of the society. Nor did they guarantee jobs. But they did provide an increased range of benefits to poor people.

Severely limited in terms of the continued structural inequalities though such reforms were, they were, nonetheless, vigorously opposed by those individuals and groups that came to be known as the New Right. Even symbolic measures of limited substance, designed to relegitimate the system, triggered visceral rage as the overthrow of the established order. This was seen, for example, in the New Right's defence of the patriarchal, nuclear family as the 'norm' and in its attempts to blame poverty, welfare dependency and other social problems on the supposed 'breakdown' of family values under the influence of the change-oriented movements.

Most importantly, whites were seen as threatened by black demands for equality in the labour market, in education and in other public spheres. The New Right built on Nixon's 'Southern Strategy', which set out to recruit white votes from the Democrats on the basis that they had become the party of blacks, 'women's libbers' and homosexuals, whereas the Republicans were a 'white man's party'. Nixon used the code-words 'law and order' to appeal to the white South and to white working-class voters in the rest of the country. And, once elected, he appointed as a special advisor Daniel Moynihan, author of the infamous Moynihan Report of 1965 and later a Democratic senator to New York, which argued that the 'pathological' black family was responsible for the poverty of blacks. Moynihan justified Nixon's confidence when he advocated a policy of 'benign neglect' towards the issue of race and argued, in effect, for the political isolation of the black underclass:

The Negro lower class must be dissolved .... It is the existence of this lower class, with its high rates of crime, dependency and general disorderliness, that causes nearby whites ... to fear Negroes and to seek by various ways to avoid and constrain them. It is this group that black extremists use to threaten white society with the prospect of mass arson and pillage. It is also this group that terrorises and plunders the stable elements of the Negro community ... forced to live cheek and jowl with a murderous slum population.[9]

The Repeal of the Second Reconstruction

Nixon set in train a process of changing the composition of the Supreme Court and other federal benches in order to get judicial repeal of large parts of the Second Reconstruction, a process that was continued under Presidents Reagan and Bush. All three Presidents used racism — and antagonism towards the gains made by women and gays — as central planks in their social agenda, which, in turn, has diverted attention from their economic goals.

These had basically to do with the necessity, given the decline in America's economic dominance, of rolling back a variety of concessions granted in the post-war period to a stratum of the working class — largely white, male, unionised and employed in the primary labour market. These concessions included relative job security, recognition of collective bargaining rights, pay levels linked to increases in inflation and company contributions to pensions and health care insurance. This augmented social wage bought for capital a disciplined work force, co-operative trade unions and political support for the Cold War and the permanent war-time economy. But loss of markets to the Japanese and Germans and higher labour costs than its international competitors eventually pushed American capital to seek a reconstruction of this Keynesian accommodation with labour. Capital required repeal of the high social wage and an increase in workers' output through speed-up, increasing the intensity of work and lessening, if not removing altogether, health and safety protection.

This economic strategy required a political framework, in which the attack on affirmative action was to play a central part. It scapegoated blacks and women as responsible for the deteriorating position of the white, male working class. One measure of the price now being paid by the working class is that the average

American family income, in real terms, is lower than it was in 1973, and it takes the paid labour of more family members to earn that income. The reorganisation of the economy has meant the replacement of higher paid working-class jobs with low-paid, non-unionised, temporary or part-time jobs. Two million Americans were poor in 1986 even though they worked full-time and year-round, and there were another 6.9 million people working part-time or part of the year and earning less than the poverty level. At the same time, job-training and job-subsidisation pro-grammes, among the benefits of the governmental response to black militancy in the 1960s, were cut by nearly 70 per cent. Spending on welfare also dropped and the real income of welfare recipients has fallen nationally by approximately one-third.[10]

The Reagan administration mounted a consistent attack on the enforcement of civil rights legislation, staffed enforcement agencies with opponents of the legislation and consistently encouraged legal challenges to past civil rights gains. Reagan's appointees to the Supreme Court were uniformly opponents of the rights of blacks, women and the working class. Reagan also appointed half of the lower federal judiciary in his eight years in office. Frank Deale, legal director of the Center for Constitutional Rights, sees this combination as particularly dangerous because lower court judges are now free to innovate in pursuit of their ideological goals with little fear that the Supreme Court will overturn their decisions.[11]

The Supreme Court's Assault on Black Rights

The Supreme Court, with its Reagan appointees giving it a reac-tionary majority, made a series of decisions in 1989 which set back significantly, if not repealed, the previous Court's decisions and legislative measures of the Second Reconstruction. In January 1989, in the case of *Richmond* v. *Croson*, the Court overturned the 1980 *Fullilove* v. *Klutznick* case when it declared unconstitutional a requirement in Richmond, Virginia, that construction firms must subcontract at least 30 per cent of their city contracts to minority-owned businesses. Despite the fact that prior to this requirement less than one per cent of contracts were awarded to minority-owned businesses in a city which is half black, the Court's decision, written by Justice Sandra Day O'Connor, held that: 'The 30 per cent quota cannot in any realistic sense be tied to any injury suffered by anyone .... Racial classifications are suspect, and that means that simple legislative assurances of good intention cannot suffice.' Justice Thurgood Marshall, in a strongly worded dissent (echoing Justice Harlan in 1896), said the decision marked a full-scale retreat from the commitment to equality of economic opportunity. He argued that:

> In concluding that remedial classifications warrant no different standard of review ... than the most brute and repugnant forms of state-sponsored racism, a majority of this Court signals that it regards racial discrimination as largely a phenomenon of the past, and that government bodies need no longer preoccupy themselves with rectifying racial injustice.[12]

In *Wards Cove Packing Co.* v. *Atonio*, the Court overturned the 1971 *Duke Power* decision, in which the Court unanimously placed the burden of proving that an employment practice is 'related to job performance' on the employer whose practice was being challenged. This decision had created the category of 'disparate-impact' cases that relied on statistical evidence to force employers to defend practices that had the effect of discriminating against blacks or women. In *Wards Cove*, the Court shifted that burden to employees, who must now prove that the challenged practices are not, in fact, necessary and employers need only show that what they did was a 'reasonable employment practice'. Justice Harry Blackmun, in a dissenting opinion, wrote: 'One wonders whether the majority still believes that race discrimination — or, more accurately, race discrimination against non-whites — is a problem in our society, or even remembers that it ever was'.[13]

In *Martin* v. *Wilks*, the Court overturned the 1979 *United Steelworkers* v. *Weber* decision in which the Court held that an affirmative action plan agreed in labour negotiations did not violate whites' civil rights. In *Martin*, the Court ruled that white fire-fighters in Birmingham, Alabama, could sue to reopen an affir-mative-action settlement, approved eight years earlier to remedy discrimination that had kept blacks out of all senior positions in the department. The Court held that a voluntary settlement in the form of a consent decree between one group of employees and their employer cannot possibly 'settle' the conflicting claims of employees who do not join in the agreement. It was felt by critics of the decision that this would lead to the reopening of many cases long closed.

In *Patterson* v. *McLean Credit Union*, the Court ruled that the Civil Rights Act of 1866 applied only to discrimination in hiring but not to discriminatory treatment on the job. A week later, on 22 June 1989, the Court, after suggesting this line of argument to the plaintiff, ruled again by a 5-4 majority in *Jett* v. *Dallas Independent School District* that the Civil Rights Act of 1866 cannot be used to bring damage suits against state or local governments for acts of racial discrimination. Under the ruling, plaintiffs can succeed only if they can show that the discrimination was not the random act of an individual public employee but resulted from an official 'policy or custom'. Justice Brennan, speaking for the minority, termed the ruling 'astonishing', adding that, 'Before today, no one had questioned that a person could sue a governmental official for damages due to a violation' of the 1866 law. By deciding as it did, the Court removed the benefits following use of that law, the obtaining of damages, and will force victims of discrimination in the future to use other legislation which does not provide for damages.[14] In the period between 15 June 1989 — when the Patterson decision was handed down — and 1 November 1989, there were ninety-six bias claims dismissed in federal courts without any substantive rulings on the claims themselves.[15]

In another decision, which, while ostensibly having nothing to do with race relations, will have disproportionate consequences racially because of a justice system which criminalises blacks and Latinos, the Court ruled in 1989 in *Murray* v. *Giarrantano* that indigent inmates on death row do not have a constitutional right to a lawyer to assist them in a second round of state court appeals. This has major implications because in capital cases these proceedings result in the death sentences being set aside in as many as two-thirds of all cases. In states which do not provide lawyers for such appeals, the supply of volunteer lawyers is drying up because of the costs in time and money involved.[16] This decision capped a series of decisions of the Reagan Court which overturned earlier decisions of the Warren Court equalising, to some degree, the rights of defendants in the criminal justice system with the powers of the police and prosecution.

Another crucial limitation on the right of blacks and other

victims of discrimination to use the courts to obtain redress is the recent application of Rule 11 of the judicial code. Under this rule, designed to prevent frivolous cases, a losing litigant who was deemed not to have a good faith argument for the 'extension, modification or reversal of existing law' could previously be penalised by having to pay his or her opponent's court fees. More recently, in an attempt to stop business-sponsored cases clogging up the courts, this penalty was extended to cover the other side's legal expenses as well. This rule is now being applied, by courts dominated by Reagan-appointees, to civil rights cases. Thus, lawyers and organisations defending black rights now run the risk of heavy financial penalties if they lose cases. The NAACP Legal and Defence Fund was hit by a $90,000 penalty.

The cumulative effect of these Supreme Court decisions was summed up by Justice Thurgood Marshall in an address to federal judges on 8 September 1989. They 'put at risk', he declared, 'not only the civil rights of minorities but the civil rights of all citizens .... It is difficult to characterise last term's decisions as the product of anything other than a deliberate retrenchment of the civil rights agenda .... Thirty-five years after the Supreme Court ended the era of legal segregation with the decision in *Brown* v. *Board of Education*, we have come full circle. We are back where we started.'[17]

6 Racism, the National Health Service, and the Health of Black People

Racism has been and is central to an understanding of the health of black people in Britain. Black people have played and are playing a central role in the National Health Service (NHS). Their role is, however, shaped by racism. Their experiences as consumers of the NHS are also shaped by racism — in terms of their treatment for both physical and mental health problems. In addition, their specific health problems such as sickle cell anaemia have not received the attention they deserve. The NHS has become part of the internal control system of the British racist immigration system. The cuts in the NHS, and in other areas of the welfare state, since 1979 have created the conditions for increasing racial conflict on the one hand and for interracial class-based resistance on the other.

> Good health is not merely the absence of illness and disease; it is a
> state of complete physical, mental and social well-being. Whether we
> are healthy, therefore, is determined almost exclusively by our
> working conditions, the standard of our housing, our access to health
> and welfare services and the treatment we receive from them.[1]

Black people have been involved with the National Health Service (NHS) from its inception. As in other areas of British life, their contribution has been great, but structured within the framework of racial stratification. Their role as consumers within the health service has also had the characteristics we have seen elsewhere and has to be seen in the wider context of racism, which creates special or augmented health problems as well as limiting or distorting the responses to those needs. Racism has structured the ways in which black people's experiences have been interpreted — or ignored. For example, *The Black Report*, which is regarded as the most detailed study of health in Britain, devotes less than three pages to the discussion of the health of Britain's black population, which it describes in terms of immigration. There is little or no discussion of racial inequalities in health care.[2] Much of the research that has looked at the health of black people has been based on ethnocentric assumptions, and has identified ethnicity and the cultures of black people as the key questions and as problems whose solution lies in the changing of those cultures. The training based on such assumptions has, not surprisingly, been misleading, often dangerous, and has diverted attention away from institutional racism.[3]

By 1948 when the NHS was established, local selection committees were established in 16 British colonies, including Nigeria, Sierra Leone, British Guyana, Mauritius, and Trinidad and Tobago, to recruit nurses and midwives; 63 hospitals agreed to accept colonial recruits. This process, like the associated recruitment of overseas-born doctors and ancillary workers, represented a solution to labour shortages similar to that adopted by other sectors of the British economy and by other Western European and North Atlantic countries. In these cases, labour from former colonies or from poorer, underdeveloped regions was channelled into the richer, developed countries thus continuing the historical processes accompanying development in the first instance and represented a form of foreign aid, i.e., the transfer of human capital from the poorer to the richer regions and countries.[4]

In the case of the British health service, the structure of employment of black people, at all levels, paralleled the often more obvious patterns found in other sectors. The lower the status, the less desirable the position, and the dirtier the job, the greater the proportion of black workers. Although the presence of large numbers of professionals may have given a misleading impression of equity, the reality of racial stratification within the medical and nursing professions was similar to that found in the divisions between the clerical and non-clerical ancillary sectors in the health service. In the case of both doctors and nurses, overseas-born professionals are disproportionately recruited to lower status and lower prestige hospitals and specialities. For example, one recent study found that although overseas-born doctors account for 30 per cent of all hospital doctors, only 19 per cent are in the prestigious teaching districts, and those in general practice are concentrated in areas of high Asian settlement. In 1983 a Commission for Racial Equality (CRE) study documented the failure of the NHS to promote Asian and other overseas-born doctors. The study identified the maldistribution of overseas-born doctors not only in terms of status but also in terms of specialities. The CRE found that while overseas doctors accounted for 8.6 per cent of consultants in general surgery, they constituted 24.3 per cent of consultants in mental illness and 43.4 per cent of those in geriatrics.[5]

The CRE, in a study of two of the 14 Regional Health Authorities in England (the North-Western and the Merseyside Authorities) published in January 1987, found this pattern continuing. The study found that 'one in three of the overseas doctors who were not in their first choice of speciality had to change because they could not get a job in the speciality they had hoped for. This was true of only 12 per cent of the white British trained doctors.'[6] It also found that 'overseas doctors were over-represented in locum posts and that they held these posts for longer periods with fewer prospects of promotion' and that they were 'under-represented in the Teaching Authorities';[7] and 'four out of ten white doctors and five out of ten ethnic minority doctors felt that there was discrimination in the Health Service'.[8]

Sir Raymond Hoffenberg,[9] President of the Royal College of Physicians, delivered the Centre for Contemporary Studies 1985 Winter Lecture, 'The Health Service and Race', in which he noted this evidence. He argued that these patterns were more the result of 'a not-unexpected tendency to favour graduates of one's own medical schools' than of racial discrimination. He interpreted the meaning of an anecdote about the fate of a graduate of his own medical school who was of Indian descent and had great difficulty in obtaining admission into a training scheme for general practitioners (GPs) until Sir Raymond wrote indicating that although the doctor was of Indian origin he had been educated in Britain. Sir Raymond states that this example 'might be construed to support my feeling that ethnicity is a less important factor than the stable in which the young doctor was trained'.[10]

Other experts, however, locate the cause of these patterns firmly in racism within the medical profession and the NHS. Steve Watkins,[11] Senior Registrar in Community Medicine in Manchester, quotes the Medical Practitioners Union evidence to the parliamentary Social Services Committee in which the Union declared that 'overseas doctors have been shunted by the processes of medical racialism into the least attractive and least educational posts where they have been systematically exploited by employing authorities and ignored by their professional colleagues'. Dr Watkins concludes that:[12]

> Health workers at all grades suffer from both overt and covert racialism. The medical profession clearly uses black doctors as pairs of hands to do the work which white doctors do not want to do. It measures the status of a hospital by the proportion of its staff who are white, the status of a speciality by the extent to which it can fill its posts without resorting to the use of black doctors, and the status of a job by the number of white applicants it receives. It barely conceals its use of these criteria for judgement.

A similar pattern has been found in the types of hospitals and specialities in which black nurses are employed and in their under-representation in the posts of senior nursing officer (sister) or principal nursing officer (matron). New entrants into the nursing profession are finding a similar pattern of racial discrimination. Young black British people have been channelled into becoming pupil nurses, leading to the less prestigious SEN (State Enroled Nurse) qualification, rather than student nurses, leading to the SRN (State Registered Nurse) qualification. Recent evidence shows that as separate categories of nurse training are being phased out, black youngsters are being denied entry altogether on the grounds of unsuitability, even after meeting the objective requirements.

Sir Raymond Hoffenberg sees this pattern as 'more complex' for nurses than for doctors since relatively few nurses have been trained overseas.[13] Other commentators, including black health workers and patients, are quite clear about the nature of the racism that produces these outcomes. A black nurse working in 1981 at St Ann's Hospital in London described her treatment and the treatment of other black health workers in the health service as a whole and in St Ann's Hospital thus:

> In the last 30 years, black people, mainly women, have been cleaning up the mess in NHS hospitals as nurses, cleaners, laundry assistants, kitchen maids, etc. in some places working in the most archaic environments. In many hospitals, for example, the laundry area, where some of the least desirable work is done, has not improved

since the period when it was a work house. Apart from bad working environment, many of the jobs which black workers are channelled into are extremely low paid and they are the most degrading jobs in the hospitals. So what you have is an apartheid system of job division between black and white workers in NHS hospitals — you find black women cleaning up the shit and the whites telling them how to do it .... What actually occurs is that ward domestic and black staff nurse both find themselves in the same position for ten or 15 years, neither even being considered for promotion and if they do leave, they'll only get a similar position in another hospital.[14]

The ambulance service is known as a virtual 'no-go' area for black people. As in the emerging situation for those who want to become nurses, potential ambulance service employees have to satisfy white personnel officers of their suitability and respectability, and are obviously failing. A number of detailed studies of particular hospitals[15] or of a health authority[16] have validated the general observation that black people are concentrated in the ancillary services, catering and portering and cleaning rather than clerical, and, as McNaught[17] has found, 'in those units providing geriatric, psychiatric and community health services'. The Greater London Council (GLC) Health Panel found 'the concentration of black people in the most unpopular jobs and the least favourable working conditions'. These patterns have been noted for a number of years and little or nothing has been done.[18]

Before discussing the amount and nature of health care that black people receive as users of the NHS, and consequently, analysing the character of that service, we will look at the forces shaping the health status of Britain's black population. As *The Black Report* and other studies have demonstrated, social and economic factors are major determinants of health.[19]

In March 1987 the Health Education Council published *The Health Divide: Inequalities in Health in the 1980s*, which updated *The Black Report*. They concluded that:

Serious social inequalities in health have persisted into the 1980s. Whether social position is measured by occupational class, or by assets such as house and car-ownership, or by employment status, a similar picture emerges. Those at the bottom of the social scale have much higher death rates than those at the top. This applies at every stage of life from birth, through to adulthood and well into old age. Neither is it just a few specific conditions which account for these higher death rates. All the major killer diseases now affect the poor more than the rich (and so do most of the less common ones too). The less favoured occupational classes also experience higher rates of chronic sickness and their children tend to have lower birthweight, shorter stature and other indicators suggesting poorer health status.[20]

In a racist society, racism that shapes the life conditions of black people therefore crucially affects their health — either directly or indirectly. The general picture, as summarised by Allan McNaught, is that:

> While there are a handful of health conditions with a strong racial link, the bulk of mortality and morbidity of black and ethnic minority groups are from diseases and conditions which affect the whole population. However, black and ethnic minority group members seem to experience worse levels of mortality and morbidity, with some exceptions.[21]

The unemployment rates, low pay, and poverty rates of Britain's black population are clearly worse than those for white Britons. When in work, black workers are concentrated in unskilled or semi-skilled occupations, in jobs with awkward or unsocial hours, with an unpleasant or dangerous working environment, and with relatively low earnings. Some or all of these characteristics are the norm for black workers. Among the health consequences that follow from these characteristics are inadequate diet because of low income, which leads in extreme cases to deficiency diseases or in the case of pregnant women to low birth-weight children, and to debilitation and lower resistance to illness. Unemployment, as a number of recent studies have shown, leads to a variety of stress-related illnesses and medical consequences including increases in mental illness, suicides and attempted suicides, and increased use of the health service. A recent study carried out by Dr Norman Beale and Ms Susan Nethercott for the Royal College of General Practitioners has shown a 20 per cent increase in consultations with family doctors and a 60 per cent increase in visits to hospital outpatient departments connected with unemployment.[22] The Health Education Council concluded that 'It is now also beyond question that unemployment causes a deterioration in mental health and there is increasing evidence that the same is true of physical health'.[23] Poverty and low income in contemporary society similarly create stress and stress-related illnesses. The dirty, dangerous jobs in which blacks are concentrated have health consequences; for example, brick works, textile mills, and foundries are industries associated with long-term industrial diseases as well as with industrial accidents. There have been a number of recent studies showing the health consequences of shift work, and one of the characteristics of black employment is a high degree of shift work.

Black people are disproportionately found in worse housing, in the least desirable accommodation, with more overcrowding and lack of amenities, and with a larger proportion of the population lacking sole use of amenities. Among the illnesses associated with such housing are respiratory and rheumatic complaints, stress-related illnesses, and tuberculosis. As the GLC Health Panel concluded: 'Asians are at particularly high risk from tuberculosis and while there is little doubt that some of the disease experienced here results from infection originating overseas, there can equally be little doubt that its spread and re-emergence is helped by unsatisfactory housing conditions and overcrowding experienced in this country'.[24] The comparable tuberculosis rates per 100,000 are 9.4 for whites, 354 for Indians, and 353 for Pakistanis and Bangladeshis.

The concentration of black people in run-down inner city areas has consequences for the primary health care received by black people. Studies in Liverpool and London have documented 'the broad correlation between the areas where ethnic minority communities have settled and the areas where primary health care problems are at their most intense: single-handed GPs working from inadequate premises, often without the support of a primary health care team'.[25] Ntombenhle Protasia Khotie Torkington[26] in her study, *The Racial Politics of Health — A Liverpool Profile*, extends the discussion by pointing to the right of individual GPs as independent contractors to refuse to accept individuals or groups of people onto their lists, so that black people can and are denied service because of the prejudices of GPs.[27]

The health consequences of the high level of racial violence experienced by black people are marked. In 1981 the Home Office calculated roughly and in a manner likely to underestimate the reality of racial violence — that West Indians were 36 times more likely to be the victims of an interracial attack than were whites and that Asians were 50 times more likely to be victims. The lack of police protection has been so marked that the Policy Studies

Institute has calculated that to get the true figure, these rates would have to be multiplied by a factor of 10.[28] Under such conditions, where, for example, sections of the black community are living under siege conditions (as is the case for Bangladeshis in London's East End) and the rest of the black community never knows when it will be attacked, the stress caused by this terrorism is enormous. The implications for the mental as well as the physical health of black people are severe and reinforce the related strains of coping with life in a racist society.

In the case of mental health and mental illness we come up against not only the illness-causing forces of a racist society but the racism within the particular institutions of that society under consideration, in this case the health service itself. In a study of Mental Health Services in London, the GLC Health Panel has identified a number of trends that are indicative of this problem. Among them are the following:[29]

· Black people are more likely to be mental patients than whites.
· Black patients are four times more likely than white patients to reach a mental hospital through the involvement of the police; twice as likely to have been sent to hospital from prison; and twice as likely to be detained in hospital under the mental health legislation.
· Black mental patients are more likely to be diagnosed as schizophrenic — and twice as likely as white British patients to have their diagnosis changed during treatment. At the same time depression is more likely to be missed in black than in white patients.
· There is a greater reliance on physical treatment — major tranquillisers and electro-convulsive treatment (ECT) for black patients; while scarce psychotherapy resources are more likely to go to white patients.

These patterns are the result of the operations of a racist system. Black patients are diagnosed, or misdiagnosed, by professionals who may not speak their language, who may not understand or value their culture, who may not understand the reality of racism and its consequences, and who are overwhelmingly white males from middle- and upper-class backgrounds. The recent increase in the proportion of women in medical schools has not redressed the class and racial stratification characteristic of the student body, which is still being trained within a scientific and ethnocentric framework. An example of the consequences of such an array of forces was the committal of a Rastafarian prisoner, Steven

Thompson, to Rampton Mental Hospital under Section 72 of the Mental Health Act days before he was due to be released from prison, on the grounds that his belief in the tenets of his religion constituted evidence of mental illness. He was only released three months later after a campaign and a review by an independent group of psychiatrists, one of whom was a West Indian, challenged the original diagnosis.

This ignorance of, and disrespect for, black culture has been present throughout the health service. For example, the campaign against rickets established by the Department of Health and Social Security (DHSS), the Stop Rickets Campaign, has placed its primary emphasis on health education. Rickets, a vitamin D deficiency disease, now affecting primarily Asian children, had previously been so widespread in working-class areas of British cities that in the rest of Europe it was known as the English disease. It is a disease of poverty and was eliminated, not by changing the culture of the working class but by fortifying basic foods such as margarine with vitamin D. Sir Raymond Hoffenberg, after analysing the various explanations for the outbreak of rickets in the Asian community, is clear about the solution: 'the disease may be prevented and cured by supplementing the diet with vitamin D'.[30] The government has refused to follow such advice and to do for the Asian community what it had done for the white working class. Instead, emphasis has been placed on changing the Asian diet, thus transferring responsibility on to the culture of Asians. This approach also has the danger of exposing Asians to the health dangers of changing from a pulse-based, high-fibre diet to a Western high-fat, meat-based diet and thus to a range of diseases such as cancers of the stomach, colon, and rectum.

Distortion of black culture, blaming the culture for medical problems, and placing priority on changing that culture rather than changing the practices of existing institutions have become important characteristics of the operations of medical institutions. The Brent Community Health Council in 1981 published a report entitled *Black People and the Health Service* in which this process is discussed. The authors quote the statement of a group of GPs in Brent that 'the pain threshold for Asians is half that of Caucasians they complain twice as much for half the reasons they come with minor symptoms'.[31] A related 'truth' that medical professionals are being taught about Asian culture is that to justify sympathy and support an Asian who is ill 'should go to bed and stay there until he gets better. It is considered natural for the sick to express anxiety and suffering. Asian patients may cry and moan in a way that upsets the other patients in a British hospital. They are unlikely to realise that they are disturbing other people.' This version of Asian culture is from Alix Henley's Asian Patients in Hospital and at Home,[32] which is widely used in training medical professionals. The Brent Community Health Council rejects this interpretation of Asian culture on the grounds that 'there is absolutely no truth in any of this'.[33] (The author was told by a nurse of a situation she witnessed that illustrates the implications of such views. When she was in hospital having a child, an Asian woman in the next bed was having a very prolonged and obviously very painful labour. Understanding professional etiquette the nurse/patient did not interfere, but after a time she felt that she had to intervene. When she suggested to the ward sister that the doctor should be called she was informed that it was not necessary, because 'these people' have a low pain threshold and cry out disproportionately. The finale of the story was that the Asian woman's baby was born dead. The point is not that there is evidence that earlier medical intervention would necessarily have saved the child, but that such 'truths' about black people's cultural characteristics have profound professional behavioural implications.)

Black people — patients and health workers — have identified a similar disrespect for black culture by white professionals in the areas of family relationships, child-rearing, and birth control. The Brent group found that Asian women who desired the presence of female relatives at the birth of their children and their participation in the rearing of the children came up against disapproval from professionals who presumed that such desires were unhealthy because they differed from current theories about the role of husbands and about mother-child bonding. Health education material addressed to black people has been primarily about diet, antenatal care, and birth control. We have already discussed this professional concern with diet in the context of the Stop Rickets Campaign. The concentration by professionals on educating black women about the necessity of using antenatal provisions assumes that it is the ignorance of these women about such facilities that leads to under-utilisation and that the solution lies in health education.

There are, however, important questions to be raised about the nature of the existing antenatal provisions before we accept such assumptions. It is necessary to note, for example, that white working-class women also have a low utilisation rate of such services. If services are not used or are under-used by both working-class white women and by black women and are most used by white middle-class women, perhaps it is necessary to examine the organisation of the services rather than to assume that the under-users are ignorant. If, for example, Muslim women wish to be examined by a female doctor but the antenatal service provided fails to respect that desire, then we should not be surprised if the take-up level by those women is lower. The question to be asked is why that option is not made available as a right rather than how to change the Muslim women's culture. If interpreters are not routinely made available in antenatal clinics in areas inhabited by women whose first language is not English, then we must question the suitability of the service not the intelligence of the women. If the clinic is located not in the neighbourhood with easy access but in a central hospital some distance from the homes of the women and requires expensive and time-consuming travel, then we should expect lower take-up levels.

Torkington challenges the mainstream professional view and argues that 'In a racist patriarchal society black women are at the bottom of the hierarchical ladder and in consequence among their children there are higher than average rates of mortality and morbidity'.[34] She quotes the study of Oakley and MacFarlane,[35] which shows the limitations of antenatal care in dealing with the problems of low birth-weight children (who in 1977 accounted for two-thirds of perinatal deaths) through dietary advice during pregnancy. The key to reducing perinatal mortality lies in improving the environmental conditions of the mother and the woman's nutrition throughout the whole of her life rather than in a compensatory diet during pregnancy. (The perinatal mortality rate in manual worker families is five times higher than that in professional families.) There is the slight problem, in addition, of how poor women are to afford such a compensatory diet, and black women are disproportionately located in that category. Oakley and MacFarlane also point out that traditional antenatal care is stress producing and may actually be counterproductive for some women since it gives rise to 'precisely those problems it is designed to avoid',[36] and therefore, in this area as in many others, the experience of black women exposes the class as well as the racial and sex biases of the system.

Given the centrality of the numbers game in all discussions of race, the centrality of racism in the government's immigration policies, and constant legitimisation of racism by the actions of the government and the effusions of the media, it is not surprising that more leaflets about birth control are translated into Asian languages than about any other topic. Birth control has been a central theme of health education directed toward both the Afro-Caribbean community and the Asian community. The widespread assumption that the number of black people in the society is a determinant of good race relations and, in Margaret Thatcher's felicitous phrasing, that there is a danger of black people 'swamping' British people (note the exclusion of black people from the category of British), it is not surprising to find this emphasis. The numbers game and the ignorance of black people and their cultures have combined in the use of Depo-Provera (DP), an injectable progesterone-based contraceptive with many unpleasant side effects, in black women. There are great doubts that informed consent has been obtained from the women, and the GLC Health Panel concluded that racism is a fundamental factor in its use:[37]

> There are indications that DP is given primarily to black and working-class women in this country. The panel of experts appointed to hear the evidence for and against the use of DP in this country has admitted that it will be difficult for many women to give informed consent to receiving the drug because of the lack of time available for explanation and counselling by medical and nursing staff, and the lack of training and skills in such counselling among doctors not specialising in family planning. This is particularly worrying for women whose first language is not English and who will be in an extremely disadvantaged position in terms of being fully informed of the side effects of the drug and the lack of data on its long-term safety.

Black women testifying before the GLC Women's Committee clearly stated that there should be 'less attention and pressure on birth control and more attention on services for mothers and babies, on mental health, and on services and policies which support women caring for others in the community'.[38]

The Brent Community Health Council identified the central

themes underlying the white health professional approach to black people:

> What is perhaps most interesting is the similarity between the stereotypes being generated within the health service and those in other parts of the state. In the NHS the mythology is that Afro-Caribbean women are feckless and irresponsible, while Asian women are compliant but stupid. West Indian women are dubbed as having no culture, the problem for Asians is their culture. Either way black people's diets, child rearing practices, family relationships, highly established medical systems are seen as either inadequate or downright harmful. Meanwhile the SUS law has helped create the stereotype of Afro-Caribbeans as reckless, irresponsible and criminal,[39] while the immigration law has encouraged white people to see Asians as law abiding perhaps, but only because they have no legitimate reason for being in Britain in the first place. The similarity between the two sets of stereotypes is not remarkable, but it reminds us just how much what goes on in the health service reflects, is reinforced by and itself reinforces values which serve the interests of the state.[40]

Just as damning and damaging has been the NHS's refusal to respond to the specific health problems of Britain's black population. Sickle cell disease is a common inherited disorder that affects mainly people of African descent. It is estimated that at least 50 babies are born in London every year with the disease and that there are at least 4000 sufferers in Britain yet until recently there were no central guidelines or resources provided by the NHS. In contrast, phenylketonuria with an estimated incidence of about 10-12 cases in London every year is covered by a central new-born screening and follow-up program, and haemophilia with about four to five thousand sufferers in Britain is well provided for by the NHS. The GLC Health Panel concluded about this disparity in NHS response (or lack of response): 'the signal failure by the NHS so far to produce an effective response to the problem which deeply concerns large numbers of black people, can only be attributed to racism'.[41]

Faced by this lack of concern, black communities, assisted by dedicated medical and nursing staff, organised and demanded the establishment of sickle cell screening and counselling services. A number of centres have been created in response to these pressures, five in London and one each in Liverpool and Manchester. Most of these, however, are on short-term funding and have not succeeded in obtaining long-term funds. This creates major difficulties in terms of future planning, long-term development work, and training. The authors of the most comprehensive survey of sickle cell disease and the NHS reported that the only course for sickle cell counsellors (when they published their study in July 1985) was that offered by the Brent Sickle Cell Centre. The Centre had repeatedly failed to obtain recognition, validation, or funding.[42]

Racism has also functioned to use black people as scapegoats for shortcomings in services and provisions available to the white working class. Such shortcomings, whether in housing, education, social benefits, or employment as well as in health, have little to do with black people, who receive even less of the provisions. But the centrality of a racist ideology constantly being legitimated and reinforced by state action makes such claims newsworthy and believable. These claims also lay the groundwork for additional state racism and controls imposed on black people and for continued deterioration of services for the working class as a whole; it is interesting, therefore, to note the use of such tactics in the field of health. The demands for immigration control in the late 1950s and in the early 1960s, i.e., control of black immigrants, used scare tactics concentrating on the supposed dangers of leprosy, tuberculosis, and various 'tropical' diseases being brought in by black people. Black women already in Britain were accused of overloading the NHS maternity services and preventing 'our' women from obtaining maternity beds. The numbers game was thus combined with using black people as scapegoats for shortages in NHS provisions.

Examples of such scapegoating include the declaration by right-wing Labour MP, Harry Hynd, on 3 April 1958, in support of a special motion on immigration, that 'The immigrants [from the Commonwealth] are undoubtedly adding difficulties to our health authorities. When these people arrive in our country, they immediately become eligible for National Assistance. We know the financial difficulties which the Government have had in that connection and it is something which cannot be ignored'.[43] On 29 October 1958, the extreme right-wing Conservative MP, Cyril Osborne, who had been pushing for immigration control of black people since 1950, declared in Parliament that he would deny access on the grounds of ill health, and using what he assumed to be a clinching argument asked, 'What would happen if a shipload of lepers came here from West Africa? Would there be any power to refuse them admission?'[44]

Such stereotypes and antagonism to black people not only contributed to the passage of racist immigration legislation but has
also continued to be a determinant of its enforcement. Dr Peter
Cooper, head of the health control unit at Terminal Three at
Heathrow Airport, expressed similar views in an interview with
the medical magazine *Pulse*. The interviewer indicated that Dr
Cooper evidenced 'strong feeling beside the calm reasonableness of
his views'. Cooper declared: 'The health system is too open to
abuse .... A Moslem immigrant might bring in four tubercular
wives, eight spastic children and an aged grandmother. Now you
tell me' — he goes on aggressively — 'is that right?' One might
assume that the possession of such views may have had some effect
on his role in the administration of virginity tests on Asians'
fiancées. When asked about this barbarous practice he said, it
'makes you think' and 'no comment .... In any case I don't remember anything about it. I've got a shocking memory.'[45]

In the Thatcher years the deterioration of the NHS, despite
promises that it would be safe in her hands, has been accompanied
by scares of foreigners swamping the service and leaving less for
those of us who were entitled to its use. Despite the absence of any
evidence of misuse, the DHSS in 1979 issued a circular entitled
'Gatecrashers' to all health authorities in the London area,
instructing staff to ensure that only eligible people received service.
Within a month there were reports of black people being challenged to prove their eligibility, including a black member of the
Commission for Racial Equality. The *Guardian* quoted an administrator at St Stephen's Hospital as saying: 'It is just a matter of
common sense, whether we go on their being foreign, or their
colour or whatever. All we can do is ask someone politely if they
can show their passport and if they do, then this immediately clar-
ifies the matter. It is a practice that is well established, a lot of
London hospitals do it'.[46] In 1981, citing 'fairly widespread abuse'
but no evidence, the government announced the introduction of
charges for certain people from overseas using the NHS, and
although it was forced to modify certain features of the scheme,
the measure came into operation in October 1982. Organisations
ranging from the Commission for Racial Equality (which said that
the proposals were 'damaging to race relations and ... inevitably
discriminatory') to the Confederation of Health Service Unions,
the Trades Union Congress, and the Joint Council for the Welfare

of Immigrants condemned the measure as divisive and racist. The measure was clearly going to be directed against black people, would reinforce the view of black people as somehow having less right to be here and use services than the rest of us, and would be another step toward a 'pass law society' for black people.[47]

This state racism legitimated racialist ideas on the streets and in the hospitals. In 1981 when lawyers acting for Ibrahim Khan, who had been thrown out of a window by three youths, wrote to St Mary's Hospital in London to request a letter from the hospital so that a claim for criminal compensation could be made on his behalf, they received the following reply:[48]

> No one here is prepared to write a report for you about this patient ... Mr Khan has been extremely fortunate to receive treatment that exceeds the cost of a heart transplant. There is absolutely no reason why this patient should receive preferential treatment or become a burden on the tax-payers here. I find it immoral to use public money allowing Mr Khan to become a burden on their dwindling resources. Signed: Orthopaedic secretary and over-burdened taxpayer.

The increasingly widespread demand that black people produce their passports to prove eligibility for health care, for the education of their children, for social security benefits, and for housing illustrates the development of the system of internal controls of black people. The hospitals, schools, housing offices, and welfare offices become outposts of the Home Office and adjuncts of the immigration service. These controls are directed at black people, black people as immigrants, black people as suspected illegal immigrants, black people as abusers of Britain's welfare state all views legitimated by racist immigration laws and by the media and politicians. Therefore, if the immigration laws are themselves racist (and the state makes no attempt to deny that fact), then it is logical that black people would be the targets of the extension of immigration controls into the community. Given the need to explain away inadequate services available to the white working class worse housing, worse medical care, lower levels of unemployment benefits and lower pensions than are available in other industrialised countries, and lower wages and higher levels of unemployment the attack on black people as illegal immigrants and abusers of the various services diverts attention from those responsible and from those who benefit from the present system of resource allocation. These attacks and controls make black people less likely to claim benefits to which they are entitled. They may be fearful that if they claim benefits they will get into trouble and be deported, a not imaginary fear given the links between DHSS and the Home Office and the large number of highly publicised cases of deportation proceedings being taken by the Home Office against black people who had gone to DHSS offices to claim benefits. This fear and consequent reluctance to claim in the face of government's implementing racist immigration laws and consciously keeping black families apart is but one part of a process that makes black people second-class claimants in a system that already stigmatises claimants as 'scroungers, spongers and lead swingers'. The social security system denies claimants information and stacks the deck against them by purposely creating excessively complicated claims forms, using different criteria for different benefits and maintaining secrecy and discretion as key characteristics of implementation. It is not surprising, therefore, to find massive underclaiming as the norm in the British welfare system.

In conclusion, to quote again from *The Heart of the Race*:

> The combined effects of racism, discrimination against women workers and the steady loss of health services for working-class people generally have been more apparent to us than to any other group of hospital workers because we have experienced them simultaneously, on all three levels, for some time.[49]

These experiences, described so painfully by the authors and the other black women who contributed to this book, have located black people at the centre of resistance to both the destruction of large parts of the welfare state and the dehumanising practices that have been such a major characteristic of that system. The racist disrespect for black people was built on a system that disrespected women and the working class generally. The hierarchical structures that oppressed lower status workers and distorted the services delivered to all clients disproportionately but not exclusively oppressed black people. The cuts that have already affected the ability of these institutions even to offer the services they had hitherto offered have most affected black people both as workers and clients.

The greater burden borne by black people has had the effect of masking the full scale of what has been happening from the white community. If black people were not really part of 'us' anyway and if they were 'gatecrashing' and 'abusing' the services provided for us, then their exclusion from benefits or services was only right and proper and did not have anything to do with us. If jobs had to be lost, surely 'our people' had the right to the remaining jobs. If the old, decrepit hospitals that got older and more decrepit, and subsequently had to be closed, were in inner city areas largely populated by black people and by the white poor, who would notice or care? Privatisation would save money and was therefore necessary, and anyway, who were disproportionately working in the hospital laundries and kitchens? If costs had to be cut in the provision of nursing services and by the worsening of career prospects and job satisfaction, the worst consequences could be hidden by the use of agency nurses, and who were disproportionately on the agency books?

In each case the working class as a whole, and women in particular, as workers and clients have suffered, are suffering, and unless these policies are reversed, will suffer the consequences of these so-called radical reforms in the welfare state. In each case black workers and black women in particular have paid an even higher price. In each case black people as a whole have been the most aware and the most militant in their resistance, as consumers and as workers. Their resistance in the 1972 ancillary workers' strikes and in the long and bitter health workers' struggles of 1982-3 has been central in the development of a new consciousness among health workers, including nurses. The organisation of the health service, the nature of services provided, and the need to take militant action to resist cuts and to improve services have been placed firmly on the agenda.

Black people as clients in the welfare system have struggled against the racist ideology and practices that have taken their children into care and into white foster homes. It was their resistance that forced adoption agencies and social service departments to recognise the need for black children to have an authentic and appropriate environment in which to grow and mature. It is their resistance that is forcing many social workers to reconsider their assumptions about the black family. Perhaps those professionals who are forced to question their previous 'common sense' and professionally legitimated assumptions about black people and their culture might understand the necessity to re-evaluate their class- and sex-biased assumptions. It is clear that without such black struggles, such revaluation is highly unlikely.

7 The Political Economy of White Racism in Great Britain

The plight of the white working class throughout the world today is directly traceable to Negro slavery in America, on which modern commerce and industry was founded, and which persisted to threaten free labour until it was partially overthrown in 1863. The resulting colour caste founded and retained by capitalism was adopted, forwarded and approved by white labour, and resulted in subordination of coloured labour to white profits the world over. Thus the majority of the world's labourers, by the insistence of white labour, became the basis of a system of industry which ruined democracy and showed its perfect fruit in World War and Depression.[1]

Racism has blighted the lives of millions of people of colour all over the world and has functioned to maintain class-stratified societies. Racism has been contested for its entire history. Whites and people of colour, as both individuals and groups, have resisted the imposition of racist ideology and the racialised organisation of society. Given the continued influence of racism, it is important to understand the conditions within which some whites have opted for a more inclusive definition of 'us'.

In this chapter I shall trace the development of white racism accompanying, and engendered by, the development of the British capitalist system during the eighteenth and nineteenth centuries. I will analyse the institutionalisation of racism in British society, particularly against people of colour, and the implications of that institutionalisation — for the distortion and limitation of working-class consciousness and organisation. I will also review the contemporary position of the British working class, the crisis in the capitalist system, and British workers' abilities to challenge the destruction of much of the social wage and welfare state protections they had previously extracted from the state and capital. The paper concludes with a discussion on the resistance to such racism and the need to construct alternative visions and practices.

Slavery, Early Capitalism and the Origins of Racism

Plantation economies based on slavery in the New World underwrote the development of manufacturing in Britain in the eighteenth and nineteenth centuries. Triangular trade between Africa, the West Indies and Britain's North American colonies, and Great Britain was a stimulus for British manufacturers and for economic development in the British settler colonies of North America. Africans were bought in exchange for British manufactured goods. Those slaves who survived the middle passage in British ships had to be clothed and fed by British firms. The crops that Africans produced on the plantations provided both the raw materials for industry and capital for investment in new plant and equipment in other words, providing crucial funding for the industrial revolution.[2]

The importance of the slave trade can be gauged by the following quote from a Liverpudlian authority writing in 1797:

> This great annual return of wealth may be said to pervade the whole town, increasing the fortunes of the principal adventurers, and contributing to the support of the majority of the inhabitants; almost every man in Liverpool is a merchant, and he who cannot send a bale will send a bandbox. It will therefore create little astonishment that the attractive African meteor has from time to time so dazzled their ideas that almost every order of people is interested in a Guinea cargo.[3]

Professor H. Merrivale delivered a series of lectures in 1840 at Oxford on the theme 'Colonisation and Colonies' and asked:

> What raised Liverpool and Manchester from provincial towns to gigantic cities? What maintains now heir ever active industry and their rapid accumulation of wealth? .... Their present opulence is as really wing to the toil and suffering of the Negro as if his hands had excavated their docks and fabricated heir steam engines.[4]

These material acts were reflected in the ideological sphere and produced the ideological contradictions inherent in an economic system based on human slavery. In the first instance, this dependence on slavery posed a moral question. Equiano, an ex-slave and one of the leaders of the anti-slavery movement in eighteenth-century Britain, posed the problem as follows: 'Can any man be a Christian who asserts that one part of the human race were ordained to be in perpetual bondage to another?'[5] Interestingly enough, on the other side of the English Channel the French philosopher Montesquieu articulated the problem in similar terms when he wrote: 'It is impossible for us to suppose these creatures to be men because, allowing them to be men, a suspicion would follow that we ourselves are not Christians'.[6] Thus, British society was being faced with a moral and political challenge. To continue on the path of economic development based upon the enslavement and dehumanisation of people of African descent and become progressively dehumanised and desensitised in the process, or build an alternative society based on an inclusive definition of humanity. The choice, of course, would have fundamental consequences not only for Africa and Africans, but for the indigenous population of Britain itself in terms of the reproduction of class inequality and the development of associated ideologies justifying such inequalities in terms similar to the permanent inferiority's of the poor.

The triumph of capitalism as the dominant economic system was accompanied, and validated, by the triumph of classical liberalism as the dominant political ideology. Both systems of thought emphasised the individual as the key actor with the fundamental value of private property being seen as central to the political and economic systems. Individual transactions in the free market were seen as the basis of economic activity and social progress; each individual was 'free' to sell her or his labour to any would-be purchaser. People were to be 'freed' from feudal ties to the land and, of course, landowners would be 'free' to displace labour no longer required to maximise profitable use of the land as a commodity.

Individual freedom and equality, however, had to be constrained in terms of political power and responsibility because of the need to protect private property as the core value of liberalism. Therefore, the political system constructed to provide representation and to hold the executive accountable had to be based upon property — that is, only those with property could be trusted to participate in their own governance. Thus, there were fundamental class contradictions in this new political economic system. There were even greater racialised contradictions in building a new social system theoretically dedicated to individual equality and freedom on the backs of slaves. One crucial solution to the latter contradiction, which also functioned to mask the former, was the adoption of a racist ideology of white supremacy.

This rationalisation was very similar to that adopted earlier by the British *vis-à-vis* the Irish Catholics. Irish land and freedom had been stolen by England, and justified by defining the victims of these processes as apelike, less than human, and savage.[7] Moreover, there was also an ideological congruity between stereotypes of the British white working class who were exploited in the mills, mines and factories, and the slaves. For example, it was argued that the white poor were lazy, lived from hand to mouth, and seldom thought of the future, and that poverty was the necessary goad to their participation in the labour market. Therefore, the argument went, increasing their pay and removing the threat of hunger would only make things worse for them and for society as a whole.

The fact that there was this congruity in the ideology was, however, not the whole story. There was also the racist ideology which posited the particular inferiority of the Irish and of the peoples of the conquered periphery. The white and English poor were encouraged to adopt racism in order to have a feeling of superiority over another group of people in a hierarchical society. But, the property-owning minority in a liberal democracy no matter how limited the democracy cannot rely solely upon assertions of class superiority and authority to rule the propertyless majority. Because the latter are seen as a potential threat to order and property and, in fact, periodically rise up in riots or other disturbances; the ruling forces must find ways of dividing the majority. Indeed this was the tactic employed by Great Britain as a means of ruling the Empire. But it was no less necessary or effective in ruling the metropole.

It is important at this juncture to point out that the construction of a racialised identity as an essential part of the divide and conquer strategy did not reflect a natural racism of the white, British working class. Indeed, the history of class struggle in Britain is the history of attempts by major sections of the working class to develop its own consciousness and development of class consciousness among nineteenth-century workers, John Foster found that militants in Oldham Lancashire, were very conscious of the need for solidarity with the Irish working class:

> In 1834, a mass meeting demanded the elimination of wage differentials and the levelling up of labourers' pay. The year before there had been a call for an end to coercion in Ireland and throughout the period a predominantly English population was willing to accept Irishmen among its leaders. The very fact of class formation meant that the controlling spell of the ruling-class had been broken, and with it the subgroup system by which people accommodated 'unfairness'.[8]

The defeat of Chartists and other reform movements weakened the ability of working-class individuals to construct their own, more inclusive identities and weakened their confidence in alternatives to the 'subgroup system.' As Foster noted,

> ... In the 1850s ... there was a rapid expansion of Orange Lodges; in 1861 serious Anglo-Irish riots; and from then on mass politics in Oldham largely hinged on the existence of two racial communities.[9]

But, within a decade, it became clear that many state policies underpinned a racist ideology which was being constructed to limit the consequences of the dislocations, tensions and conflicts which accompanied the rise of the new order. For instance, the state implemented policies in Britain physically to separate the Irish and the English working class, and ideologically to separate the white European working class from the people of colour in the periphery. As we shall see in the next section the development of racialised identities was actively pursued by state officials, particularly, but not exclusively, in the educational arena.

Racism in the Post-Slavery Period

> ... I wonder the working people are to quiet under taunts and insults offered to them. Have they no Spartacus among them to lead a revolt of the slave class against their political tormentors?[10]

> ... it was 'our ignorance of society and of government our prejudices, our disunion and distrust' which was one of the biggest obstacles to the dissolution of the 'unholy compact of despotism'.[11]

Prejudices, disunion, and distrust were all characteristics of the response of the majority of the working class in Britain to the triumph of capitalism. This response involved the acceptance of the hierarchy, and the placement of oneself and one's group into hierarchies based on skill, job status, ethnicity, gender, and race. These divisions were further reinforced by the distribution of material resources. State action directly and indirectly maintained this social order which made possible the continued functioning of the system to control the production and distribution of the material resources. Politics based on an inclusive class consciousness had to confront these ideological and material forces. It is not surprising, therefore, that alternative political projects typically failed.

Prior to World War I, Britain was the world's leading manufacturing, trading and investing nation.[12] While Britain led the world in colonisation, foreign trade, manufacturing, railroads and shipbuilding, many scholars have identified several problems inherent in British imperialist policies due to the burden of the costs of maintaining the Empire, the falling rates of profit abroad, and the fact that 'The British as a whole ... did not benefit economically from the Empire ... [while] individual investors did.'[13]

Moreover, in late nineteenth-century Britain, 40 per cent of the population were living in poverty. Two-thirds of those in poverty were likely to be reduced to abject pauperism at some point in their lives.[14] Less than 11 per cent of the manual labour class led what could be called comfortable lives. At the other end of the spectrum, only six per cent of the population left any property worth mention, with only four per cent leaving more than 300 pounds. The social consequences were grave. Eleven- to twelve-year-old boys from private schools were, on average, five inches taller than boys from industrial schools. Teenage boys from private schools averaged a three-inch height advantage over the sons of artisans. During the Boer War, three out of every five Manchester volunteers were turned down as medically unfit. Of all the young men called up for military service in Britain in 1917, 10 per cent were rejected as unfit, 41.5 per cent had 'marked disabilities', and 22 per cent had 'partial disabilities'.[15]

While organisations such as the International Working Man's Association, founded by British, French and German workers in London in 1864, attempted to offer an alternative vision of the nature of the working class and of society, the British working class did not want to accept these social conditions. However, there was occasional support for colonised peoples in some part of Great Britain. For example, Lancashire textile workers supported the anti-slavery struggle in the United States and the Union in the US Civil War.[16] Irish employees of Scotland Yard helped Indian nationalists smuggle their political literature into England. But the British working class remained oblivious to the plight of the workers in the periphery.[17]

This indifference, or ignorance, was not only found among the working class of Britain. This racism served not only to reinforce the *class hierarchy* at home, but also the *racial hierarchy* at home and abroad. It became an element of the dominant culture of Britain in part through conscious efforts by the state to keep the have-nots in a constant state of repression. Horn has noted that, 'As early as 1878, Her Majesty's Inspectors of Schools were directed by the Education Department to encourage the study of "the Colonial and Foreign Possessions of the British Crown" ... '[18] Furthermore, in the Code of 1890, the 'acquisition and growth of the colonies and foreign possessions of Great Britain' was to be part of the history syllabus. The purpose of such an educational system was clearly articulated by Edmund Holmes in 1899. Holmes, later to be chief inspector for elementary schools, stressed that even the village school had an imperial role to play. 'Its business is to turn out youthful citizens rather than hedgers and ditchers; ... preparing children for the battle of life ... which will be fought in all parts of the British Empire.'[19] Historian J.A. Mangan has observed that,

> A major purpose of this education was to inculcate in the children of the British Empire appropriate attitudes of dominance and deference. There was an education in imperial schools to shape the ruled into patterns of proper subservience and 'legitimate' inferiority, and one ... to develop in the rulers convictions about the certain benevolence and 'legitimate' superiority of their rule.[20]

In 1911, one pioneer of the 'Empire Day'[21] movement, the Twelfth Earl of Meath wrote:

> In former ages the burdens of Empire or of the State fell on the shoulders of a few; now the humblest child to be found on the benches of a primary school will in a few years be called on to

influence the destinies not only of fifty-four millions of white, but of three hundred and fifty millions of coloured men and women, his fellow subjects, scattered throughout the five continents of the worlds.[22]

Another example of how imperialist ideology became accepted as common sense is Roberts' recollection of the educational system in early twentieth-century Salford. He noted that pupils gazed

> with pride as they were told that 'This, and this, and this' belonged to Britain. It was difficult to see what the 'underclass' gained from the Empire, but once instructed they remained staunchly patriotic. 'They didn't know,' it was said, 'whether trade was good for the Empire, or the Empire was good for trade, but they knew the Empire was theirs and they were going to support it.'[23]

Imperialist culture was reproduced in newspapers, music halls, juvenile fiction, and melodrama. MacKenzie identified the move from class to racial tensions in melodrama during the nineteenth-century as follows:

> Some plays from the early nineteenth century did display class tensions. By the end of the century such class antagonism had disappeared from melodrama. By then imperial subjects offered a perfect opportunity to externalise the villain, who increasingly became the corrupt rajah, the ludicrous Chinese or Japanese nobleman, the barbarous 'fuzzy-wuzzy' or black, facing a cross-class brotherhood of heroism, British officer and ranker together. Thus imperialism was depicted as a great struggle with dark and evil forces, in which white heroes and heroines could triumph over black barbarism, and the moral stereotyping of melodrama was given a powerful racial twist.[24]

> Thus, the acceptance of the inevitability of hierarchy by most of the working class weakened their ability to resist the ideological and cultural hegemony of the ruling class. The inability of the British working class and its allies to create alternatives was a major factor in the continued domination of the working class. As Karl Marx indicated in his letter to Engels about anti-Irish racism,

The antagonism is artificially kept alive and intensified by the press, the pulpit, the comic papers, in short by all the means at the disposal of the ruling classes. This antagonism is the secret of the impotence of the English working class despite their organisation.

It is the secret by which the capitalist class maintains its power. And that class is fully aware of it.[25]

Racism in Modern Britain

Britain acquired a black population not out of spirit of highmindedness nor in a fit of absence of mind as some liberals have argued, but because of the need for cheap labour.[26] Black workers were first brought to Britain during World War I. In 1919, several riots were reported in centres of black population, such as Liverpool and Cardiff. Faced with demobilisation and job insecurity, white seamen responded with vicious attacks against non-whites.[27] In South Shields, attacks on Arab workers were encouraged by the leadership of the National Union of Seamen.[28] Overall, there was a rise of support for fascism and racism. For instance, MP David Logan asked in the House of Commons:

> Is it a nice sight, as I walked through the south end of the city of Liverpool to find a black settlement, a black body of men I am not saying a word about their colour all doing well, and a white body of men who face the horrors of war walking the streets unemployed? .... To see Chinamen ... in the affluence that men of sea are able to get by constant employment while Britishers are going to public assistance committee?[29]

The British Government responded to these events by institutionalising racism. The major instrument of British policy aimed at the black population was the Alien's Restriction Order (Coloured Seamen) of 1925. As Neil Evans has put it:

> This was a solution very much in the imperial tradition of legislation which was racist in intent but not in the letter .... There was no formal challenge to the right of imperial subjects to enter the motherland. That would have been too embarrassing in the wider world and fired a thousand empire nationalists. Instead, coloured sailors were required to have an identity card with a thumb print (because they all looked the same!) in order to go about their business.[30]

The turning point for Britain's becoming a multiracial society, however, occurred in the 1950s. Between the end of World War II and 1957, there was a high demand for cheap labour to rebuild the economy, to staff the public service, and to cheapen indigenous labour. The British state responded to these demands by allowing over 350,000 Europeans into Britain under a variety of programmes. Since this move was insufficient to meet labour requirements, Britain then turned to the colonies which had a surplus of labour, and blacks were recruited into British industries as cheap labour.

Immigrants typically did the jobs that indigenous workers were unwilling to take. For example, the textile industry in Lancashire introduced new technology which required the continuous operation of a night shift. Even the weak unions in this industry would not accept capital's demand that there be no night-shift differential for white male workers. Women were 'protected' by law from working the night shift. The union leaders and rank and file, however, were ready to agree to a solution which satisfied almost everyone. Asian male workers were hired to work a permanent night shift at single rates of pay. Other jobs performed by blacks had similar wage differentials. Immigrant workers from India were recruited into the foundries of the West Midlands. These cases exemplify the role that immigrant workers were expected to play namely, occupying the dirtiest, lowest paid, lowest status and most dangerous jobs — a pattern found still to be prevalent in the 1990s by the Policy Studies Institute.[31]

During this period, Afro-Caribbean and Asian migrants entered a racist political culture where the white working class had largely accepted the dominant racist ideology. It was this acceptance which helped maintain the context within which these people were treated as cheap labour. There was, obviously, nothing inherent in them which made them cheap. It was the unwillingness of white-dominated institutions, even those supposedly serving the interests of the working class, (e.g., the Labour Party), to challenge structural and ideological racism which channelled Afro-Caribbean and Asian migrants into these disadvantageous positions. However, this acceptance was not irrevocable. While British political leaders found the British public insufficiently racist,[32] it was the leadership of the Labour Government after 1945 which acted on the basis of their own racist attitudes to create the post-war racist ideologicaland structural context.[33] There were other voices in the Labour Party and the wider labour movement. For example, Fenner

Brockway, MP, combined opposition to colonialism with opposition to racism within Britain and introduced a number of private member's bills throughout the 1950s to outlaw racial discrimination.[34] Tom Driberg, MP, who had opposed the colour bar associated with US forces in Britain during World War II raised, as Chairman of the Labour Party in 1961, a crucial question in a speech to the Trades Union Congress:

> People talk about a colour problem arising in Britain. How can there be a colour problem here? Even after all the immigration of the past few years, there are only 190,000 coloured people in our population of over 50 million that is, only four out of every 1,000. The real problem is not black skins, but white prejudice.[35]

Although the system of welfare capitalism constructed after World War II was a major reform of capitalism, it did not mark the shift of all power to the working class. Despite overall improvements in the health and education of the working class, class inequality remained.[36] But, as social conditions deteriorated, the racial scapegoating took on a turn for the worst. Many racist politicians used immigrants as scapegoats for the social problems facing the country. Blacks were blamed for housing shortages, for the failure of the educational system to provide high quality education for white working-class children, and for shortages in health care provision.[37] This racial scapegoating legitimised, and was legitimised by, a series of racist immigration laws that emerged in the 1960s and 1970s. One such law was the 1962 Conservative Government's Commonwealth Immigration Act which marked the institutionalisation of racism and the transition in labour recruitment from those with no citizenship rights to contract workers to those who did hold such rights.

Following the 1964 general election won by the Labour Party, the Labour Government's 1965 Immigration White Paper established a quota of 7,500 for the New Commonwealth and 1,000 for Malta, and abolished the 'C' entry voucher for unskilled workers without a specific job. The 1968 Kenya Asians Act abolished the right of entry for non-white holders of British passports. The Conservative Government's 1971 Immigration Act ended the right of entry for non-white Commonwealth citizens as primary immigrants. As a result, many families were kept apart, and attempts at reuniting family members were portrayed as an invasion into

Britain by a flood of illegal immigrants. Women and children were subjected to indignities, humiliations and doses of radiation.[38] These laws exemplify how institutional racism underpinned and legitimated popular racism by strengthening the racist belief that immigrants were the sole cause of existing social problems in the country.

Racist scapegoating has always served to reinforce the operation of a system based on the reproduction of class inequality. Since racism can be utilised to provide the means for business together with conservative politicians to bring about the restructuring of the relationship between capital, labour, and the state, the race card was introduced to ensure sufficient support for destroying the old social contract from sections of society whose interests would be harmed by the restructuring. This political manipulation was facilitated and maintained by the vigorous and vicious racism of the British press.[39]

The Race Card and the Triumph of Thatcherism: Racism, Politics and the Media

Margaret Thatcher first played the race card in 1978 during her infamous 'swamping' speech in which she declared that the British people had a legitimate fear of being swamped by people of an 'alien culture'.[40] Playing the race card was an effective strategy primarily because year in and year out there was a constant reiteration of an appeal to Britain's identity as a white, civilised European country with a history of bringing civilisation to the backward peoples of the world, whose identity was being threatened by floods of violent, criminal and culturally inassimilable *immigrants, refugees, bogus asylum-seekers*, and *alien wedges*.[41]

The *Daily Mail* published a three-part series in October 1991 on 'The Invasion of Europe' with headlines such as: 'Out of Africa onto our Doorstep', 'Swamped ... by the New Underclass', and 'Dark Shadows over the New Germany'.[42] The author of the articles wrote that the invaders represented a 'tidal wave' of immigrants who came armed not with weapons of war, but with passports and tourist visas, and sought to remain by 'utterly fraudulent' claims for asylum.[43] The *Daily Star*, a tabloid, ran a campaign in 1991 to 'halt the influx of foreigners who end up living off the state'.[44] The writers claimed to have uncovered illegal immigration rackets and falsely charged that a family of nine arriving from Bangladesh only knew one word in English, 'House', which they repeated 'parrot-style' until they were given a 'rent-free council flat'.[45]

Having produced what writer and educator Chris Searle calls, 'Your Daily Dose of Racism',[46] the media was then able to tie these doses directly to support for the Conservative Party during elections. In 1992, for example, the *Daily Express* produced nine articles during a three-week campaign, warning of the threat of Britain being swamped by undesirables, i.e., nonwhites.[47] A taste of these stories can be obtained from the following sample: 'Let Bogus Migrants Stay' (election day, 9 April 1992); 'Baker's Migrant Flood Warning' (7 April 1992, front page); 'Open Door to Chaos' (2 April 1992); 'Fake Immigrants: An Explosive Problem' (2 April 1992).

Among the five stories published in the *Daily Mail* during the campaign dealing with immigration was the only story targeting the Liberal Democrats for failing to protect (white) Britain from mass immigration of nonwhites — 'Paddy Puts Out the Welcome Mat for 4m from Hong Kong'.[48] Additionally, the *Daily Mail* used the image of black criminality and violence to delegitimate Labour: 'Race and the Rapist: Cultural Differences are Behind Some Sex Attacks, says Expert'.[49] On 7 April a story was published entitled, 'Rapist "Boasted of Taking Revenge on White People"'.[50]

The ending of primary black immigration did not, as its proponents asserted, lead to the end of the immigration issue in British politics and the production of good race relations. In fact, immigrants were continuously portrayed as outsiders who did not belong in Britain. Right-wing politicians continued to raise the spectre of 'swamping' and the replacement of church bells with calls to worship at the mosque. In 1993, right-wing Tory MP Winston Churchill asserted,

> We must call a halt to the relentless flow of immigrants to this country, especially from the Indian subcontinent .... The population of many of our northern cities is now well over 50 per cent immigrant, and Moslems claim there are now more than two million of their co-religionists in Britain .... With this government continuing to bring in immigrants each year at a scale, in Mrs Thatcher's immortal phrase of 15 years ago 'equivalent to a town the size of Grantham' a halt must

be called — and urgently — if the British way of life is to be preserved.[51]

Right-wing newspapers, columnists, and politicians played the 'race card' to its fullest. Writing in the newspaper of 'Little England', *Daily Mail*, right-wing columnist, Paul Johnson described what he perceived to be the problem as follows:

> The smouldering anger among the British people reflects the fact that they believe they have been lied to twice. The first time was when a flood of Commonwealth immigrants arrived without anyone asking the British electorate if they were welcome. Within a generation, fundamental changes had taken place in the composition of the nation and we had become a multi-cultural, multi-racial society without any of us being given the smallest choice in the matter.[52]

The 'Triumph of Thatcherism' — greatly influenced by the race card played by British politicians as well as the media — has had some significant impact on the social and economic climate of the country. It has meant a fall in real wages, massive cuts in the social wage, and increasing insecurity for workers. These depressed social and economic conditions have created a situation ripe for racial violence.[53] In 1981, the Home Office calculated that West Indians and Asians were 36 and 50 times more likely to be the victims of a racial attack than were whites, respectively.[54] The Policy Studies Institute has calculated that the incidence of racial harassment was probably ten times that estimated in the 1981 Home Office survey.[55] The Institute study also found that of those who had experienced racial harassment, 60 per cent had not reported these cases to the police.

In 1984, the Greater London Council concluded that 'racial harassment in London is an increasingly serious problem'.[56] A poll commissioned by London Weekend Television's London Programme in 1985 found that one in four Asians in the Boroughs of Redbridge, Waltham Forest, Tower Hamlets and Newham had been attacked due to their ethnicity.[57] A report commissioned jointly by the Sheffield City Council and the Commission for Racial Equality concluded that, 'No black person, male or female, young or old, from any ethnic group, is safe from harassment and violence'.[58] A survey by the Leeds Community Relations Council found 305 cases of harassment over an 18-month period in a pop-

ulation of about 4,000 which suggested a level ten times that estimated by the 1981 Home Office survey.[59] A 1986 survey found
that one in four of Newham's black and ethnic minority residents
were victims of racial harassment in the 12 months prior to the
survey, and that two out of every three victims had been victimised
on more than one occasion. Interestingly enough, only one in 20 of
the 1,550 incidents recorded by the survey had been reported to
the police. Eight per cent of the black and ethnic minority victims
reported being dissatisfied with the way in which the police handled their case. Indeed, the Scottish Ethnic Minorities Research
Unit of Glasgow has found that in 1987, 44 per cent of racial incidents were not reported to the police.[60]

The European Parliament's Committee of Inquiry into Racism
and Xenophobia indicted Britain for its 'intolerably high level of
racial harassment and violence', and estimated that there was a
racist attack every 26 minutes in Britain.[61] A special report in the
Guardian documented the massive rise in racial attacks in Britain,
which the *Guardian* saw as more widespread than in Germany. In
1992, eight people were killed as a result of racist attacks and
Home Office figures indicated that there were nearly 9,000 racial
attacks in 1993 alone.[62]

The Government has been faced with the reality that the situation may be even worse than is estimated. Peter Lloyd, Minister of
State in the Home Office, told the Home Affairs Select Committee
of the House of Commons in July that racial attacks could be as
much as 20 times the reported level.[63] Although the British Crime
Survey reported 7,793 attacks a year, nearly double the 1988 figure, the true figure has been estimated to be as high as 140,000.[64]
The level of racial violence in Britain during the last decade has
been the worst in the European community. The reported deaths of
at least 17 people in racist attacks in 1993 and 1994, and the high
rates of racial violence and harassment in Britain are indications of
the effects of popular racism fostered by the activities of the state
and the media.

Unfortunately, the Conservative Government, suffering the
worst public opinion standing in decades, has begun once again to
play the race card. Michael Howard, the Home Secretary,
announced in 1995 that the government was considering legislation to 'crack down on illegal immigrants'.[65] The proposed
measures would further restrict the rights of asylum-seekers fol-

lowing the passage and implementation of restrictive legislation in 1993.[66] A report in the *Guardian* reported the Home Secretary's decision in the following terms:

> Mr Howard's decision to prepare legislation to be published this summer and introduced this autumn indicates that the government sees a need to placate the demands from the Tory right for further tough action. Immigration welfare groups have voiced concern that Ministers were prepared to play the 'race card' in an attempt to reverse the spiralling decline in party fortunes.[67]

According to the *Financial Times*,

> A vision of a UK swamped by immigrants was revived by a Department of the Environment report on Monday. It forecasts a net inflow of 50,000 people a year for the next two decades, whereas a 1991 report had predicted no net immigration. Indeed, for the year to June 1993, the last period for which figures were available, there was an outflow of 11,000 people and tougher checks and the unreliability of figures may mean that the projected flood of migrants few of them the 'benefit tourists' or low-skilled workers of Mr Wardle's vision could never materialise. If they do not, the forecast of 4.4m new households in England over the next 20 years an increase of nearly a quarter begins to sound dubious too.[68]

The Home Secretary's proposals of further restrictions on the rights of asylum-seekers and those of Peter Lilley, the Secretary of State for Social Security, to deny social security benefits to those who have applied for political asylum after entering Britain or who are waiting for their appeals to be heard, have been seen as blatantly playing the race card in anticipation of the next general election. This tactic has been so obvious that *The Times* has condemned the proposals by stating that,

> The covert racism in these proposals must be apparent to Conservative Central Office; otherwise it could surely not have felt the need to prepare the defensive guidance notes to Tory MPs which were leaked this week. These are ugly cards for ministers to be playing and will be seen as such by a majority of the British public.[69]

The combination of racist state policies legitimating popular racism and the destruction of working class jobs have created a collapse of hope and a sense of community in Britain's cities. This process has been exacerbated by the failure of the Labour Party and trade unions to defend these communities. The racism of the white working class has left the immigrant community susceptible to the appeals of the far-right racist and fascist movements.[70] The Labour Party had not only passed two of the four key restrictive, racist immigration laws of the 1960s, but had failed to challenge the increasing stereotyping of blacks and other ethnic groups as criminals and illegal immigrants whose sole purpose is to live off the welfare system.

The playing of the race card by politicians and the press continues to encourage popular racist attitudes. An ICM poll conducted for the *Guardian* in March 1995 found that 79 per cent of white Britons polled think there is prejudice towards black people, defined as those whose families originally came from the West Indies or Africa.[71]

Conclusion

In sum, this paper has traced the development of the dominant racist ideology and of current state policy which have defined blacks and other migrants as outsiders. These factors have been of central importance historically in preventing the development of an inclusive working-class consciousness and of an inclusive working-class politics. Thus, although the British working class had been able to obtain concessions from the state and capital, particularly following the shift in the moral imperative resulting from the coalition politics of fighting the good war — World War II — its ability to gain power or to defend those concessions was weakened by its acceptance of the dominant racist ideology. This weakness has both facilitated the electoral victory of Margaret Thatcher and maintained social order as Thatcherism fundamentally restructured the British social and economic systems. The triumph of Thatcherism has meant the cheapening of labour, massive cuts in the social wage and increasing labour flexibility namely, increasing insecurity, stress and dislocation. The challenge that the capital and its political allies face in liberal democracies such as Britain is how to obtain the acquiescence of the majority of the population whose interests are being sacrificed as the price of this restructuring. Racism has played a central role in ensuring the necessary divisions and hatreds and fears among the majority to ensure the support on racial grounds of a significant enough portion of the white working class.[72] Thus, despite massively increased economic insecurity, large sections of the white working class voted for Thatcher and continued to buy into the racist scapegoating which she and her colleagues had provided. There was no massive increase in class mobilisation during this period.

The increasing inequality in income and wealth, which characterised the years of Conservative rule from 1979 to 1997, was accompanied by cuts in the welfare-support systems leading to greater insecurity for the majority of society dependent upon collective provision for health, education and support for the elderly or for periods of unemployment. The inability of the political and economic systems to meet the needs of the bottom 30 per cent of the population and the increasing insecurity of the next 30 per cent of the population create a real challenge for progressive anti-racist forces. The willingness of the state and capital to buy acquiescence from the white working class by material concessions has clearly diminished. In the absence of such concessions, those in power are relying ever more centrally upon scapegoating and division. Such is the crisis facing large parts of the displaced and insecure populations that an opportunity is present to challenge the fundamental myths of the system and to expose its class nature and create an alternative, more humane democratic system. But, such an outcome depends largely upon the willingness of the white working class to reject that identity and the limited, illusory privileges based on racism. Failure to develop an inclusive and democratic politics will lead to acceptance of an increasingly polarised, impoverished and imprisoned society with the politics of racism and division establishing the limits of democratic involvement and participation.

8 Racism and Anti-Racism in Western Europe

There is mounting fear for the safety and future of Europe's estimated 15 million people of black, Third World, and peripheral country origin. This fear is based on an increasing level of racial violence and murders in Western Europe and the increasing share of votes received by far-right political parties such as France's Front National and Germany's Republikaner Partei. Fears have also increased due to the increasingly unaccountable and undemocratic nature of decision making with regard to 'racial' populations within what has been called 'Fortress Europe'.

Races do not exist biologically or genetically, but are defined by physical categories and from geographic locations.[1] At different points in European history, groups have been defined in racial terms without having different skin colour. For example, the Irish were defined as a race by the English in the seventeenth century during the conquest of Ireland and displacement of the Irish Catholic peasants from their land.[2] Although skin colour has been used to determine racial hierarchy in white settler societies such as the United States, Australia, and South Africa, racial dominance does not depend on different skin colour. The potential for 'racial' conflict exists among people with few physical distinctions, but who differ in culture, religion, and national origin.

In most European countries, a variety of identifiable groups are defined racially and treated differently: Polish miners in France and Belgium; recently settled migrant workers from the colonial empires, such as Surinamese and Indonesians in the Netherlands; Afro-Caribbeans and Asians in Great Britain; North Africans and

Africans from sub-Saharan Africa in France; and recently settled migrant workers from peripheral countries, such as Turks in Germany. Then there are settled minority populations like the Roma people in various European countries, as well as various refugees and asylum-seekers.[3] How these groups are defined, what subordinate roles they play in Great Britain, France, Germany, and other Western European countries, and how they are controlled come out of historic racial practices. This process, now under way in Western Europe, is the subject of this chapter.

Race and the European Community

Europe, particularly the countries of the European Community (EC), has been constructing a new European identity while it has been constructing the barriers of Fortress Europe. This new identity is a racialised identity. Europe is being defined in terms of its imperialist past, with its civilising mission in opposition to the Third World and the countries of the periphery, and in terms of Christianity in opposition to Islam. In doing so, Western Europe has excluded what has been called the EC's thirteenth nation, the 15 million or so descendants of other nations.[4] This racist ideological construction has been paralleled by racial discrimination in terms of immigration policy, policing and criminal justice policies, education, and health and housing policies state racism. This is a common, European racism with a common view, which defines all Third World people as immigrants and refugees, and all immigrants and refugees as terrorists and drug-runners, [which] will not be able to tell a citizen from an immigrant or an immigrant from a refugee, let alone one black from another. They all carry their passports on their faces.[5]

It is important to analyse the root causes of these developments and to attempt to identify their ramifications for Europe and its people. It is essential to challenge the media and politicians, who place the responsibility for the rise of racism on the victims of it — migrants, settler workers, asylum-seekers, and refugees. For example, the Conservative government in Britain and most of the British media have blamed the rise of neo-Nazi violence in Germany and the rise of neo-Nazi groups in continental Europe on the invasion of bogus asylum-seekers. In March 1992, Douglas Hurd, the

British Foreign Secretary, linked 'feeble immigration laws' with the rise of Europe's neo-Nazi right and asserted 'There is no sign that the Labour Party understands it [the tenfold increase in asylum applications in the past three years] or can be trusted to deal with it. On past form they will handle it with slogans and ambiguities.'[6]

The debate in Germany over racist violence has been structured by the government as a debate over Germany's constitutional obligation to receive asylum-seekers. There has been an attempt to 'explain' German violence as a result of the economic and social dislocations associated with reunification, particularly unemployment in the former East Germany. The newly unemployed, especially the young, facing the collapse of the old order and lacking the skills, psychological orientation, and competitive values necessary to survive in the new capitalist environment, have turned on guest workers and asylum-seekers as scapegoats. It is their view that these 'foreigners' are getting everything, whereas they, good Germans, are getting nothing. This explanation is not adequate and does not explain the rise of neo-Nazi violence and political activity in the former West Germany, as well as in France, which has not gone through unification.

Roots of the New European Racism

European racism was an integral part of the historical processes of nation-building and economic development, which involved the conquest of large parts of the rest of the world and the construction of a world system based on slavery, plantation production, and superexploitation. Instead of being isolated in the colonies, racism and superexploitation continued after World War II as Europe sought to meet its need for cheap labour. Subsequent changes in European economics decreased the demand for labour-intensive industries. As a result, the demand for cheaper labour increased; this demand could be filled only by marginal, illegal employment in the service sector.[8] Massive deindustrialisation, deskilling, and underemployment of the citizen workforce reduced the demand for higher-priced domestic labour as a whole.[9] As transnational corporations penetrate the Third World, they have taken European jobs with them.[10] Furthermore, social and economic dislocation in the Third World, due to European domination, has generated refugees and asylum-seekers eager to enter the European mother economy.

Racial differences between the European mother country and the external colonies are now used to control and exploit the majority of the population in Western Europe.[11] These differences are internal. The Western European 'common person' is now faced with a decline in the standard of living and more competition for fewer jobs. As in the days when Western Europe held external colonies, those responsible for exploitation are not held accountable. Instead, the crisis is due to the 'racialised' immigrants, refugees, and asylum-seekers.

Popular racism emerges out of and is validated by state racism. In this case, increasing class division and insecurity have led to racist stereotypes and fears. Therefore, 'in our time, the seed-bed of fascism is racism'.[12] This analysis has been supported by the findings of a number of other scholars.[13] Political and media manipulation has fostered and legitimated racialist and xenophobic ideas. The experience of those at the cutting edge, migrants and refugees, provides further validation of this crucial analysis. The Refugee Forum and Migrants Rights Action Network found that,

> it is no coincidence that countries such as Italy which did not experience racial attacks on its North African workers, began to see vicious attacks at the time when its government began imposing immigration restrictions. Unlike wealth, racism does 'trickle down' from the top, and when governments define people as unwelcome and undesirable, their populations follow.[14]

This understanding is central to the development of a strategy to challenge this racism.

The Development of Post-war State Racism

Working-class militancy after World War II created the political environment for welfare capitalism the social wage expanding the state role in providing a safety net. Working-class institutions and social democratic parties failed to build upon that militancy, and the increasing tendency of trade unionists to see themselves as an 'established' middle class led to a weakening of the working class ability to defend its gains. Imperialism and unequal international development provided populations available for recruitment to the metropolis as cheap labour. This labour was cheap not because of anything inherent, but because of the racial and national hierarchies into which it was slotted. Outsiders were brought in to do the menial work of Western society, in the hospitals, hotels, the kitchens, the foundries, on the buses, at building sites, and outside the trade unions. They arrived fully grown, fully educated, ready to work at little cost to the receiving country thus, they represented a form of foreign aid from the periphery to the metropolis.

Immigrants work for less because the historic racist view, reinforced by political parties and trade unions, excludes rather than includes them. As in the United States, European trade unionists assumed that by keeping the 'coloured' out, they were defending higher-income jobs. They were convinced that, because they were white and European, they would never have to step down to the lower-paying, dirty service jobs the class of work beneath them. This was reflected in a variety of ways, including a refusal by the post-World War II British Labour government to confront the racist culture and take measures to incorporate Afro-Caribbeans and Asians into the polity and society. The leaders of the Labour Party acted as if the white working class was naturally racist.[15] Post-war French governments, including Socialist and Communist parties, fought brutal and fundamentally racist colonial wars in Indochina and Algeria to maintain France's position in the world and to continue to validate its civilising mission. These wars reinforced racist assumptions and the presumed link between race and nationality. Other ex-colonial countries such as Belgium and the Netherlands have had similar histories and cultures, which also reinforced nationalist and racist political culture and identity.

Germany's defeat in World War II was not followed by root and branch de-Nazification primarily because of Western Europe's preoccupation with anti-Communism. The determination to leave affairs of state in 'safe' hands was accompanied by a reluctance of those safe hands to confront the ideological bases of Nazism, including its definition of what constitutes Germanness. The consequences of this failure are still playing out in Germany today. German-born children of Turkish settlers are not German citizens, yet so-called ethnic Germans from the former Soviet Union who have never lived in Germany and do not speak German are allowed entry and automatic citizenship on the basis of blood, as institutionalised in Article 116 of the German Constitution.

In the words of Oskar Lafontaine, deputy Social Democrat leader, Germany should, like France and the United Slates, adopt a 'Truly Republican understanding of nationhood', because history has shown that nationalist radicalism flourished where the 'law of blood' ruled. Cornelia Schmalz-Jacobsen, the government-appointed commissioner for foreigners, has declared, 'Nowhere has blood dripped so thickly into law. Many of the problems we have with immigrants today would not have arisen if we had allowed people who have long formed a ... part of our population to become Germans.'

Naturalisation is not granted as a rule. At the moment, only about 1,000 Turks a year manage to get through the immensely complicated process of naturalisation. If automatic citizenship were granted to children of the fourth and fifth generations, 1.5 million foreigners would be living in Germany as citizens with restricted rights. Figures show that 25 per cent of immigrants' children are under 18 years old, and that two-thirds of them were born in Germany, making up what is called 'youth without a German passport'.[16]

Migrants are at the Low End of the Totem Pole

The concentration of migrants/settlers in the worst jobs with the worst working conditions at the lowest pay and status has reinforced the view that immigrants do the jobs that host country workers no longer have to do. The 'native' race is raised in status validating the race/nation hierarchy. Racial ideological stratification is thus reinforced by material stratification. Migrants lack political rights because they are not citizens and thus their social wage is lower than the social wage of indigenous workers. They occupy the worst and most overcrowded housing, pay social security/national insurance taxes, and do not receive commensurate benefits. These workers subsidise the higher social wage of the indigenous workers. They are also more exploitable, lacking citizenship and the protection of working-class organisations. Even where migrants are skilled, or professional, a pecking order exists, with the migrant professionals occupying the lower-status sectors of the professions.

Criminalisation of Migrants

The exclusion of migrants/settlers from the political process has reinforced the processes of marginalisation and criminalisation of these communities by the media and the state. In Britain, Afro-Caribbeans, particularly young Afro-Caribbean males, are criminalised as muggers by the press.[17] An important parallel to these developments can be found in the Netherlands, where in early 1993 the chief police officer in Amsterdam, Eric Nordholt, claimed on a radio program that 'black youth from Surinam, the Antilles and Morocco committed 80 per cent of street crime' and warned of Los Angeles-style riots. However, a city police spokesman admitted that the figure referred only to suspects not those arrested and convicted and that figures for all crimes were not available as 'the police only analysed street crime on the basis of a suspect's racial origin'.[18]

Similar attempts to criminalise migrants have been made by police and politicians in France, Germany, and other EC countries and have served as the basis for legitimating increasingly repressive violations of the legal rights of migrants. In 1986, the senator for internal affairs in West Berlin called refugees 'drug containers'.[19] Linking migrants, refugees, and asylum-seekers with drugs and crime has been central to the rightward march of national politics and to EC-wide controls and restrictions. The TREVI group of interior ministers has as its mission the interdiction of terrorism, radicalism, extremism, violence and immigration.

Responding to the equation of migrants and criminality, Bashy Qureishy of Third World Voice in Denmark said at the Communities of Resistance Conference on 11 November 1989,

> In May 1980 Mrs Thatcher said, 'I did not join Europe to have free movement of terrorists, drug traffickers, animal diseases, rabies, and illegal immigrants.' I for one object to being put in the same class as a disease. At Heathrow, on my way to this conference I was treated as a suspect by racist immigration officers.[20]

The combination of criminalisation; bad housing; the worst jobs; high levels of unemployment; differential, racist education; and a racist criminal justice system has led to a black male imprisonment rate in Britain twice that of white males and a black female imprisonment rate three times that of white women. France, Germany, and other Western European countries have seen similar patterns of criminalisation and stereotyping.

The channelling of young settlers into unemployment or marginal employment has become a feature of Western European life. Although the ghettos that have been created are not so racially monolithic as those in the United States, there has been a pattern of racial concentration in areas of deprivation, poor housing, and lack of amenities. This racial concentration is then turned into a blaming-the-victim syndrome, whereby the residents of these areas, who are confined to them, are blamed for their existence and identified as the outsiders who produce such alien environments.

The European Move to the Right

In France, by the early 1990s, mainstream right-wing politicians had moved so deep into the terrain of the far-right that Jacques Chirac, mayor of Paris and now president elect, spoke of 'a family with a father, three or four wives, 20 children and 50,000 francs in welfare benefits without working'. With these neighbours 'and their noise and smell', French workers 'would go crazy' as a result of 'an overdose of immigration'.[21] In September 1991, former president Valéry Giscard d'Estaing described immigration as an 'invasion' and demanded the end of the automatic right of nationality by birth on French soil.[22] (This would bring France in line with Germany and Britain, which abolished that right in the Thatcher government's 1981 Nationality Act. One of the first acts of the right-wing French government elected in 1993 was to implement d'Estaing's recommendation.) Following these comments, Jean-Marie Le Pen declared that he now considered himself to be the leader of the centre.

This move to the right was in response to the extreme right's use of racist appeals, particularly in the area of immigration control.[23] The need for the centre to move to the right was articulated by Giscard ally and former Interior Minister Michel Poniatowski, who said that unless the right allied with Le Pen, 'France would become an African and socialist boulevard given over to anarchy'.[24] Le Pen welcomed the promise by Prime Minister Edith Cresson to fight illegal immigration with mass expulsion, including the use of charter planes — a position from which she was forced to retreat, after reviving memories of the deportation of 101 Malians on a charter plane in 1986, ordered by Charles Pasqua, right-wing Minister of the Interior.

Efforts to Force Migrants Out

There was a spectacular increase in deportation orders in France under the 1989 Joxe law, which succeeded the 1986 Pasqua laws. In 1989, 9,647 people were issued deportation orders; by 1991, the figure had jumped to 32,673 and the figures for the first quarter of 1992 maintained this increase.[25] The National Association for the Assistance of Foreigners at Frontiers (ANAFE) issued a report criticising the conditions in which refugees and immigration prisoners are kept in detention zones. In July 1992, the French government passed the Quiles law, whereby ports and airports were authorised to set up detention zones. The judicial process for detainees and the violent methods by which people are deported was described as a 'farce'.[26]

The construction of the migrant worker/settler as the outsider both limits migrants' rights during the period in which their labour is required and has laid the groundwork for attacks on them in this period of deindustrialisation, deskilling, and resurgent mass unemployment. The European governments have tried to pressure migrants to 'return' to their homelands without great success. They have even pressured migrants born in Western European countries. Attempts to buy migrants out have failed for three reasons. First, the continuing pattern of uneven economic development means that conditions for returnees in sending countries are still much worse than those in the host countries. Second, the amount of money offered was insufficient to make a fundamental change upon return to the native country. Finally, migrants have formed new social ties in their adopted countries.

All of these measures, including forced repatriation, have been insufficient to remove more than 2 million people. But state racism has been successful in labelling them as people who do not belong and reinforcing their role as lightening rods for fear and hatred, as social and economic problems have increased through no fault of the migrants'.

Ideological Justification of Repression

The ideological justifications for attempts to rid European nations of their now unwanted settlers laid the groundwork for increased racialist feeling and racist violence racism 'trickling down.' As researchers Simpson and Read conclude, there is a 'momentum which seeks to describe Europe's future in terms which are increasingly white, continental and Christian. It is, in essence, the re-creation of Christendom'.[27] In December 1982, an editorial in the *Frankfurter Allgemeine* declared:

> the interchange between Slav, Romanic, Germanic, and other Celtic peoples has become a habit. A tacit 'we-feeling' has arisen in one and the same European culture. But excluded from this are the Turk-peoples, the Palestinians, North Africans and others from totally alien cultures. They, and only they, are the 'foreigner problem' in the Federal Republic.[28]

Rathzel argues that an 'unintended "co-operation"' between left and right has constructed 'a negative image of the migrant'.[29] The liberal and highly respected newspaper *Die Zeit* published an article by the general secretary of the German Red Cross, arguing that non-Central European people should be repatriated to avoid a break in German history. About the same time, the 'Heidelberger Manifesto' was published. The work of a number of professors from different universities, it argues that the 'mixture' of different cultures would be damaging to everybody; all people should live in their own' place. And whereas the public version of their manifesto wrote of different cultures, the private version (leaked to the press) discussed people as biological and cybernetic systems with different traits passed on to subsequent generations through genes and tradition.[30]

On the European Community level, member states have constructed a range of institutions to control immigration refugee/asylum policies in a fashion that denies accountability to the European Parliament and facilitates the construction of Fortress Europe. Among these intergovernmental bodies are the TREVI group of ministers, the Ad Hoc Group on Immigration, and the Schengen Accord, in which participating nations set the agenda for a community-wide system of control. These structures are not subject to democratic controls or accountability by the European parliaments. Tony Bunyan, editor of *Statewatch* in

Britain and keen student of policing in Europe, sees lurking behind these institutions 'the beginnings of another state apparatus, made up of ad hoc and secretive bodies and separate inter-governmental arrangements, which reflects the repressive side of European political development and is largely unaccountable and undemocratic in its workings'. He makes the point that,

> Crucially, [all of these intergovernment arrangements] focus on immigration in terms of a 'law and order' issue and the development of international co-operation on policing. The equation of blacks with crime and drugs and terrorism and all of that with illegal immigration, has spread across Europe so that it now forms a basis for the new European state.[31]

Measures taken by EC countries throughout the 1980s and into the 1990s were designed to stigmatise asylum-seekers as bogus and as economic rather than political refugees. The real goal is to limit the numbers who successfully gain citizenship. In fact, there is little basis in the contemporary world for a differentiation between economic and political refugees.

The Effects of Transnational Economics

A factor that blurs the apparently clear-cut differences between political and economic refugees is also a consequence of the relationship between transnational corporations (TNCs), governments, and local elites. Local elites argue that they must offer attractive conditions for transnational capital to obtain investment, especially because they are in competition with elites from other countries of the periphery for that investment. They therefore offer cheap labour and little regulation or interference with TNC activities. This ultimately places the elites in conflict with their own populations, the majority of whom pay the price of attracting and retaining the TNC investment. Governments in such circumstances have tended to become repressive to maintain order and retain power, and often create or exacerbate ethnic, tribal, or racial differences to divide and rule. People fleeing from massacres and pogroms that have been encouraged or tolerated by governments are fleeing from the consequences of economic penetration, as are unemployed migrants displaced from rural farmland.

Refusal by governments to recognise their involvement in the situation of migrants, refugees, and asylum-seekers is purposeful and designed to limit responsibility and the rights of such people to enter their countries.[32]

Government Policies

An Amnesty International report[33] concludes that Europe's increasingly restrictive approach to asylum-seekers is threatening to undermine universal standards meant to protect people who are fleeing from serious human rights violations and that, too often, would-be asylum-seekers are treated as illegal immigrants. A 1992 study by the Organisation for Economic Co-operation and Development (OECD) concludes that,

> The relatively high refusal rate revealed by a study of claims for asylum in several OECD countries suggests that in 1990 and 1991 claims continued to be motivated by reasons that had nothing to do with the original objectives of the asylum seeking procedure. By and large, in the European OECD countries, applications are scrutinised more briefly and treated more harshly than in the past.[34]

In Germany, a controversial law aimed at speeding up asylum procedures and allowing refugees to be housed in collection camps came into force on 1 July 1992, to deal with the estimated 400,000 asylum-seekers that year. The law concentrates power over asylum-seekers and deportations in the central government and stipulates that applications that are 'obviously unfounded' must be dealt with within six weeks, after which time unsuccessful applicants will be sent back to their homeland. The head of Germany's central office for the recognition of refugees, Norbert Von Niedig, resigned in protest of the new law. He argued that existing legislation could have dealt with the backlog of 300,000 applicants if the central government had provided funding and staff. He said the new law gave the 'false impression' that all future applications would be handled in record time and would create mistaken expectations and fuel anti-foreign sentiment. Governments have committed themselves to a regime of permanent deflation, and consequently mass unemployment. The ideological remnants of the supposed triumph of free market monetarism in countries such as Britain have added to the problem because of low inflation. These economic conditions have political consequences:

> The poor, discontented and marginalised, who are in increasing numbers paying for this, will note the apparent failure of democracy. At best they will become alienated and cynical. But more and more of them are clearly turning to authoritarian and xenophobic ideologies.[35]

Gerald Holtham, then chief economist for Lehman Brothers International, discussed in similar terms the consequences of the Thatcher-Reagan agenda, which,

> cut back access to social security and unemployment benefit, reduce[d] the latter in real terms, bust the unions, [encouraged] private state enterprises to subject their workers to 'market forces,' ma[d]e the workers more insecure and the labour market more competitive. That agenda, or part of it, was followed in most OECD countries.[36]

If immigration had not been racialised and blamed for Europe's declining standard of living, the state and private sector policies responsible for the decline would be apparent. Current levels of unemployment and job flight would not be tolerated.

Trades Unions

Faced with attacks on their living standards and future opportunities, working-class Europeans have searched for support and leadership. Unfortunately, their trade unions and social democratic parties have been unable and/or unwilling to provide that leadership. A loss of militancy and awareness of interest are the outcomes of labour s participation in the welfare capitalism of the post-war period. Higher status for national labour was partly due to widespread acceptance of immigrants as non-union cheap labour. In time, European labour institutions became willing participants in their own demise. The racist compromise also led to the exclusion of the most militant and most class-conscious portions of the working class from positions of leadership within the post-war union organisations.

Migrant workers and settlers could have been valuable members of the union movement. Due to their repression and exclusion from the social benefits of compromise, they were potentially more aware of economic trends and practices that would ultimately lead to the demise of labour in Europe. Instead of being part of labour, participating in its leadership and bringing their perspective to bear, they had to fight against the racist practices of European trade unions as well as state racism.

Use of Race in Politics

Faced with the failure of their union organisations, white European working-class people had to find explanations of and solutions to their dilemma. It is not surprising that right-wing politicians and parties, whether within the mainstream or on the fringe of the political system, have used the race card to divert attention from the capitalist agenda.[37] If blacks, Turks, Algerians, and the like are 'the other', and if they 'the civilised' are being swamped by alien cultures, then it is clear that the others are the cause of problems. Hordes of aliens are trying to take over their living standards and pose a threat.

The growing appeal of far-right racist and fascist parties in Western Europe must be seen in this context. In the French regional elections of March 1992, exit polls indicated that the Front National made strong inroads into the industrial working class. The far-right continued the pattern of winning more votes than either the Socialists or the Communists in the so-called 'red belt' around Paris. The Front's 19 per cent support among workers nationally equalled that of the Socialist Party and the conservative union. The working-class vote amounted to around 28 per cent of the FN's total 13.9 per cent vote, and the FN was able to gain increased support from the people in the 18-25 age range, among whom unemployment stood at 28 per cent.[38] Although the Front National did not win any seats in the 1993 National Assembly elections, and indeed lost the only seat it had held, it gained over 12 per cent of the vote, compared to 9 per cent in 1988, emerging as the third party in many key urban areas.

In the 1992 elections in Berlin, the fascist Republikaner Partei (REP) gained its biggest support in those working-class districts of west Berlin said to be Social Democratic Party strongholds. In elections in April 1992, 13 per cent of the REP votes in Baden Wurttemberg and 7.4 per cent of the neo-Nazi Deutsche

Volksunion (DVU) vote in Schleswig-Holstein were garnered in urban areas. This support was particularly heavy among voters under 30 years of age and industrial workers in the bigger cities, where the fascists exploited resentment against foreigners with claims that 'they are taking jobs from Germans'.[39] The REP, which campaigned on law and order issues, the expulsion of 'foreign criminals', and a reduction in the number of asylum-seekers, increased its share of the vote in local elections in Hesse in March 1993. In Frankfurt, the REP won 10 seats on a 93-seat city council. An opinion poll carried out after these elections and published in *Der Spiegel* found support for the REP running nationwide at 6 per cent — up from 4 per cent before the Hesse elections and 80 per cent of Germans believing that it is 'probable', even 'certain', that the REP would gain seats in the Bundestag in the 1994 national elections.[40] However, the REP vote plummeted to less than 2 per cent.[41]

The French and German political elite have pointed to these outcomes as justifications for 'necessary' and 'pragmatic' responses to public support for increasingly restrictive immigration controls. In May 1993, the German government, with the support of the SPD opposition, pushed through the Bundestag legislation that ended the guaranteed right of all foreigners to seek asylum. The justification, accepted by the leaders of mainstream parties, was that the legislation was needed to preserve social peace in Germany. According to Wolfgang Schauble, parliamentary leader of Chancellor Helmut Kohl's Christian Democratic Union, 'Our citizens are frightened by the unchecked refugee influx .... We owe them a social order that allows Germans and foreigners to live peacefully side by side'.[42]

Restrictions against racialised foreigners were seen as another crucial step toward the construction of Fortress Europe, administered by increasingly unaccountable institutions and defined by increasing control of settlers, migrants, and blacks. The reality of the development of a common European identity an identity based on racism is that such measures leading to a new social order will not allow white Europeans and foreigners to live peacefully side by side. In Britain, the level of racist violence and harassment is much greater in the 1990s than it was in 1962, 1965, 1968, or 1971, when the state made attempts to enable whites and blacks to live peacefully side by side.

Ford[43] estimates that there was a racial attack in Britain every

26 minutes in the early 1990s. Home Office[44] figures for England
and Wales for 1992 indicate that there were nearly 9,000 reported
racial attacks that year double the number reported five years earlier.[45]

Anti-racist Strategies

Given the specific nature of contemporary European racism, it is
clear that an anti-racist policy in Europe must fight for the rights
of refugees and asylum-seekers at the same time it is fighting for
full democratic rights for settlers. Such a policy must challenge the
historical definitions of 'us versus them' rooted in the identities of
Western Europeans. European identities are integrally connected
with the history of imperialism, the slave trade, colonialism, the
ideology of bringing civilisation to other countries. The racist construction of European national identities has accompanied and
legitimated the widening class inequalities of the capitalist nations
of Western Europe. This racism has also been effective in distorting the class consciousness constructed by the European working
class.[46]

But these racist national identities have not been internalised at
all times and under all circumstances. Racism is not normal, natural, or biological. It is the product of distortion, and can be
overcome by principled struggle. The very fate of Western democracy may rest on the outcome. For just as unauthentic socialist
democracies in the East did not last, unauthentic capitalist democracies may fall under the weight of racism.

A principled anti-racist strategy is necessary to challenge the
acceptance of the new international order at home and abroad that
impoverishes people in and outside metropolitan Western Europe.
The domestic policies of corporate capitalists and their political
agents are racist, nationalist, and fascist. Settlers, migrants,
refugees, and asylum-seekers have been scapegoated by popular
racism. Meanwhile, a new and more effective system of profit seeking is being put in place that is producing high unemployment and
high insecurity for labour both in and outside Europe. Britain's
Campaign Against Racism and Fascism (CARF) argues:

> Unity needs to be worked at. And experience shows that racism can
> best be challenged by working within the working class on a long-

term basis, over issues of housing, education, employment, low pay, [and] policing football. It is around these issues that, in some areas at least, black and white unity has become a reality. But if we are to enlarge and extend that unity, we must discard old orthodoxy s and see anti-fascism not as a dogma or anti-racism as a cause, but both as being part of a creative socialist process.[47]

From a more comprehensive perspective, it is crucial to challenge the idea that racist violence can be stopped by focusing only on skinheads, neo-Nazis, and other extremists. Europe cannot rely on organising primarily against fascists, because the popular culture of racism, deriving its sustenance and sanction from state racism, provides the seed-bed of fascism. State racism is incorporated into the German Constitution in Article 116; in the increasingly restrictive and undemocratic institutions of Fortress Europe; and in the racialised educational, health, employment, housing, and criminal justice systems of European countries. These institutions shape the lives of the settlers, migrants, and refugees in Western Europe as well as the political awareness and understanding of white working people. Thus,

> the fight against fascism must begin in the fight against racism, in the community, and involve the whole community. Fighting fascism per se will not eliminate racism; but eliminating racism would cut the ground from under fascist feet.[48]

The new struggle must be organised from the bottom up rather than the top down. Organisations that have attempted top-down change, such as the Socialist Party in France, claim to lead the anti-racist struggle, but they have proved unable to organise and represent the settlers and migrants. Top-down organisations have proved unable or unwilling to challenge state racism. As a result, they are unable to stem the tide of popular racism and the rightward shift of European political institutions.

For example, although the FN lost its only seat in the French Parliament in the 1993 elections, the new right-wing government of Edouard Balladur began implementing many of the FN's proposals. On his first day as prime minister, Balladur promised to crack down on 'illegal immigrants' and to change the nationality law to oblige children of migrants to apply for French citizenship, long demanded by the extreme right.

Large and well-attended protest marches may represent for

many an expression of revulsion against neo-Nazi offences, but they are reactive. The agenda has been set by the fascists, and the presence of governmental and political leaders diverts attention from the state racism that underpins popular racism. Micha Brumlik, professor of education in Frankfurt and Heidelberg, has argued that the tens of thousands of Germans who took part in the *Lichterketten*, the recent processions of candle-carrying protesters through the streets of Germany's cities,

> overlooked ... that the heightened risk of other people being persecuted does not stem solely from torches of young arsonists, but from what took place under cold neon light the discussions and suggestions made to change Germany's asylum laws [and] in the searchlights of the border police on the River Oder.[49]

Bottom-up Organising

Examples of organising from the bottom up call be found throughout Europe. In 1991, a group of Leeds United fans decided that they could no longer allow racist and fascist recruiting activities, which had been dominant at Elland Road throughout the 1980s, to continue. They formed Leeds Fans United Against Racism and Fascism and began distributing leaflets discussing their concern about the unacceptable nature of racist behaviour. They feel they have succeeded,

> where other groups like the Anti-Nazi League failed because our campaign is based around football — for fans, by fans .... What we have succeeded in doing is to show ordinary fans of other clubs that racist behaviour can be successfully combated by fans themselves.[50]

In 1992, fans of St Pauli, a German second-division club based in a multiracial area of Hamburg, organised a strong anti-racist, anti-fascist campaign against racism in German football. The symbol of the campaign has been the St Pauli Fans Gegen Rechts (St Pauli Fans Against the Right) stickers, which have appeared all over Europe The campaign made contact with local black communities and paraded massive anti-racist banners on match days.[51]

Anti-racists have participated in campaigns against the deportation of refugees throughout Europe. In Denmark, a group of Palestinians from Lebanon sought sanctuary in a church in

Copenhagen after being served with deportation orders. They were supported by a wide range of Danish people. As a result, the Danish government was forced to allow the Palestinians to stay. Others have supported campaigns initiated by settlers and migrants, such as those in Germany calling for repeal of Article 116, so that people born in Germany can become citizens and long-term residents can have access to citizenship. Gaining citizenship would enable migrants and settlers to struggle more effectively for their democratic rights and to challenge their continuing definition as outsiders. A similar campaign is being waged in Belgium. The key to the participation of anti-racists is that they are prepared to accept the leadership of settlers and migrants rather than continuing the historic pattern of Eurocentric expectations of leadership.

A number of organisations monitor and work against racism in Europe. The Early Years Trainers Anti-Racist Network, Save the Children Fund in Scotland, and the Working Group Against Racism in Children's Resources produce anti-racist resource materials. Among the other organisations that have been monitoring and organising against both racism and fascism are the Campaign Against Racism and Fascism, with its bi-monthly publication *CARF*; the Institute of Race Relations, with its European Race Audit project and journal *Race and Class*; the Runnymede Trust, with *Runnymede Bulletin;* Statewatch, which monitors European developments in its eponymous publication; *Sage Race Relations Abstracts*; *Searchlight*; Refugee Forum and Migrants Action Network; the Anti-Racist Initiative in Berlin; the Churches Committee for Migrants in Europe in Brussels; and the Dutch Federation of Anti-Discrimination Centres.

Conclusion

The economic and political crises facing Western European societies are fundamental and interconnected. The creation and maintenance of mass unemployment and the cuts in the social wage are not only producing despair and hopelessness, they are also producing conditions suitable for the spread of authoritarianism and fascism. They enable mainstream right-wing governments to play the race card for electoral benefit and to divert systematic decisions away from the cause of social misery. The more racial stereotyping and scapegoating are used, the more historically rooted popular racism is validated.

The greater the appeal of fascists and the far-right, the greater the danger that mainstream politicians will move farther to the right to keep up with public support. Right-wing politicians will continue to play the race card, and we may very well see the re-emergence of right-wing, fascist governments in Western Europe such as those that led up to World War II. The other potential is the decreasing ability of the state to provide material benefits to enough sections of the white working class to buy their acquiescence and loyalty.

Increasing inequality and deskilling much of the white working class are necessary to advance transnational capitalism. Politics as usual is proving incapable of maintaining standards of living and has reduced the likelihood of transmitting high standards to the next generation. Conditions for Europe's black and migrant/settler communities continue to worsen. The stage is set for a repeat of Europe's worst hour.

Anti-racist and anti-fascist political education and mobilisation of both European whites and people of colour are desperately needed. A successful struggle depends upon its being inclusive. British miners and their families during the 1984-5 strike learned whose interest the state serves not theirs. A disproportionate share of the support they received came from Britain's black communities. As a result, miners were able to see common interests with blacks. Clearly, there is the potential for other white people to learn from these conditions and reject racism and fascism as part of the common best interest.

The choice facing the people of Western Europe is not one of white, indigenous democracies on one side and racism and authoritarianism for blacks, migrants, and settlers on the other. An inclusive nonracist democracy must be forged that can provide a decent standard of living for all. The alternative is an authoritarian European state. Which outcome will come to pass depends on the ability of the anti-racist movements in Europe to mobilise successfully; to organise from the bottom up; to create a vision of a humane alternative; and to unify black and white, settler, migrant, asylum-seeker, and the native-born.

9 The Political Economy of White Racism in the United States

In the fourteen years since the first edition of *Impacts of Racism on White Americans*, there has been a massive increase in racial polarisation in the United States, Britain, and the rest of Europe, both East and West. There has been an increase in racial violence in these areas and increasing scholarly recognition of the centrality of racism in the organisation of modern Western societies.[1] The successful playing of the race card in election after election has been accompanied by a rightward shift of mainstream political parties and a narrowing of the parameters of legitimate political discourse in the United States and Western Europe.[2] This rightward shift in political and governmental action led to an increase in popular racism the racism of common sense. Politicians then used this increase as a justification for further racist state actions, which in turn exacerbated popular racism .... This growth of racism has accompanied, and made politically possible, greater class inequality and a restructuring of the political economies of the advanced capitalist countries at the expense of the working classes. All these events were anticipated in the first edition chapter,[3] and developments in the decade and a half that have passed since 1981 have validated that analysis.

Another tendency that has appeared in the intervening years is an intellectual/ideological distancing of mainstream policy commentators from the analysis that sees the class implications and functions of racism in a global capitalist system. It is the argument of this chapter that the events of the 1980s and 1990s in the United States, Britain, and Europe have validated the analysis of the first edition and made it more necessary than ever for the relationship between racism and capitalism to be put on the political agenda.

The fundamental argument is not only that racism has blighted the lives of tens and hundreds of millions of people of colour all over the world. It has also functioned world-wide to maintain class-stratified societies.[4] However, this racist system has been contested terrain for its entire history. Whites and people of colour as both individuals and groups have resisted the imposition of the racist ideology and the racialised organisation of society.[5] It is important to study that resistance and to understand the conditions within which whites opted for a more inclusive definition of 'us' as opposed to the racially exclusive basis of identification that has been the dominant mode for most of the period under review.

In this chapter I will look at the development of racism during the development of capitalism, paying particular attention to the roles of slavery and imperialism. I will outline the institutionalisation of racism in the early twentieth century and its implications for different races in the metropole, and I will develop this theme in the context of the growth of working-class consciousness and organisation. Finally, I will look at the contemporary position of the working class, the crisis in the capitalist system and its impact on workers in the metropole, and the resistance to that racism and the construction of alternative visions and practices.

Slavery, Early Capitalism and the Origins of Racism

Plantation economies based on slavery in the New World provided for the development of manufacturing in the centre of the world system. The triangular trade was a stimulus for British manufacturers and for economic development in the British settler colonies in North America. It provided both the raw materials for industry and the capital for investment in new plant and equipment in the South and in New England. It was thus crucial politically and economically[6] for the United States as a whole, not merely the Southern slave states. The development of a racialised system of chattel slavery within Britain's North American colonies was a crucial development in the construction of a hegemonic racist ideology. Britain initially used both indentured white labour and black labour, either indentured or semi-enslaved. The need for a system that would meet both the demands for a controllable labour system and the continuing political domination of the large landowners was made apparent by Bacon's Rebellion in Virginia in the mid-seventeenth century. Bacon's Rebellion fundamentally threatened the status quo because it was a joint action by both racial groups. A way had to be found to maintain stability and order, to increase the supply of cheap, controllable plantation labour, and to avoid adding to the future numbers of yeoman farmers contesting for political power with the planter elite. The solution involved the enslavement of black labour and the non-enslavement of white labour. This strategy was bolstered by a series of concessions to white labour, which worked to divide the two groups further. Clearly, if no white could be a slave, and if all slaves were black, the objective conditions for racial separation were well established. This constructed a racial identity for both whites and blacks — an identity of racial superiority for the former, who could never be slaves, and of racial inferiority for the latter, who were racially suited for slavery. Furthermore, laws were passed further providing for white supremacy. For example, it was against the law for a slave not only to raise her/his hand to a master but to any Christian white. Thus, we see yet again the crucial role of state racism constructing and underpinning popular racism by providing material and psychic rewards for accepting a white identity, that is, a racialised identity in opposition to a more inclusive identity.

The political structure created by the Constitutional Convention of 1787 reflected that importance. Slavery was incorporated into the basic structure of the new political system in a number of ways: the slave trade was protected until 1807, slaves were counted as three-fifths of a human being for both taxation and representation, and a fugitive slave provision was incorporated.

The ideology of racism was incredibly effective, even given the costs to the vast majority of the Southern population. So important was this separation of whites from blacks that George Fitzhugh, the slaveholding sociologist, could declare,

> The poor (whites) constitute our militia and our police. They protect men in the possession of property, as in other countries; and they do much more, they secure men in the possession of a kind of property which they could not hold a day but for the supervision and protection of the poor.[7]

Thus, in the United States white supremacy was constructed and reinforced by race-based chattel slavery and a racialised definition of us as opposed to *them*, which was an integral part of racist ideology.[8] This white supremacy was found not only in the slave South but throughout the society. W.E.B. Du Bois argued that even when white workers received a low wage '[they were] compensated in part by a ... public and psychological wage.'[9] It is the argument of this chapter that this compensation has played a central role in the creation of a *white* identity, even among workers, farmers and the poor throughout American history. That identity has retarded the development of an inclusive class identity and has, thus, facilitated the reproduction of class inequality in the United States. David Roediger, who has written perceptively on the construction of *whiteness* has argued that:

> whiteness was a way in which white workers responded to a fear of dependency on wage labor and to the necessities of capitalist work discipline. As the US working class matured, principally in the North, within a slaveholding republic, the heritage of the Revolution made independence a powerful masculine personal ideal. But slave labor and 'hireling' wage labor proliferated in the new nation. One way to make peace with the latter was to differentiate it sharply from the former.

The effective way this was done was through

> the rallying cry of 'free labor'.... At the same time, the white working class, disciplined and made anxious by fear of dependency, began during its formation to construct an image of the black population as 'other' — as embodying the preindustrial, erotic, careless style of life the white worker hated and longed for.[10]

This was underscored by the Naturalization Act of 1790, which established the requirements for citizenship, one of which was the necessity of being white. It was not merely that one had to be white to be an American, but obviously to be white was to be superior. The construction of a white identity provided the basis for incorporation of European immigrants into the society. So the Irish driven out of their own country by the consequences of Anglo-Saxon imperialism arrive in another country largely controlled by Anglo-Saxon elites but are able to avoid permanent suppression and inferiority by virtue of being able to become white rather than remaining Irish and Celtic. Thus, angry Irish miners in Pennsylvania denounced Daniel O'Connell, the Irish Republican leader, for his call for Irish American opposition to slavery. Despite their own exploitation and the attacks on them from nativist forces, they declared that they would never accept blacks as 'brethren', for it was only as whites that they could gain acceptance and opportunity in the United States.

Furthermore, acceptance and opportunity are of crucial importance in the construction of 'whiteness'. Although the Irish suffered discrimination at the hands of the 'white, Anglo-Saxon Protestant' (WASP) elites, they had the basis of gaining acceptance in US society as whites rather than as Catholic Celts.[11] It is also conceptually important in challenging the 'ethno-racial umbrella' thesis advanced by scholars such as Nathan Glazer,[12] with the argument that ethnicity was 'an umbrella term subsuming all racial, religious and nationality groupings' to form a part of a single family of social identities.[13] Cornacchia and Nelson test the validity of this ethno-racial umbrella thesis in contrast with the 'black exceptionalism' thesis and conclude that it is the latter that has greater validity: 'The findings on the black political experience demonstrate that it would be inappropriate to treat racial minorities as merely ethnic groups competing in the interest group arena for entitlements and preferments. The political system was nearly sealed shut to blacks.'[14]

The extension of democracy in the United States, particularly during the Jacksonian era, was an extension of democracy or at least of formal incorporation into the Republic as citizens to white males. The outcome was the creation of a 'Herrenvolk democracy' or, in Roediger's terms, 'Herrenvolk Republicanism.' This incorporation of whites regardless of class played a crucial role in ensuring the triumph of racism throughout the United States, in the free states and in the slave states. Before the Civil War, poor whites and the non-slaveholding yeomanry in the South, free soil farmers in the West, and artisans and the emerging working class immigrant and native in the North were all made citizens in the great white Republic and given an identity that was oppositional to people of colour, slave or free. Not only were whites given a *psychological wage* state racism provided fundamental objective racialised rewards:

They [whites] were given public deference ... because they were white. They were admitted freely, with all classes of white people, to public functions [and] public parks .... The police were drawn from their ranks and the courts, dependent on their votes, treated them with leniency .... Their votes selected public officials and while this had small effect upon their economic situation, it had great effect upon their personal treatment .... White schoolhouses were the best in the community, and conspicuously placed, and cost anywhere from twice to ten times colored schools.[15]

To be white was to be a citizen of the Great Republic. To be white was to be a voter — unheard of for most of the immigrants. The immigrants could become American by successfully asserting their whiteness. Their whiteness and their Americanness was validated when they marched in triumphal parades to vote and then to picnics. Not only were the black slaves excluded from these public events but in most states of the ante-bellum United States, so were free blacks. Free blacks could not protect their employment, political or civil rights nor could they protect the rights of their children to a decent education and to a secure and profitable future in the American Dream. Nor could they take part in the great frontier experience, for in most territories on the frontier, free soil meant free soil for free white men. Not surprisingly, wave after wave of European immigrants opted for whiteness and free blacks were impoverished, undereducated and disproportionately imprisoned.

Because 'Herrenvolk Democracy' was not and could not be a reality in terms of 'Democracy' despite its state constructed and supported 'Herrenvolk' character, there remained a class tension within American society. This class tension became central at various points and remained more marginal at others in societal terms; for some working people it was more central to their identity than for others. The point is that it was part of an ongoing set of struggles and that the racially defined identity as whites was not always hegemonic. As Herbert Aptheker, one of the leading anti-racist scholars in the US since the 1930s, has argued, the rank and file of the anti-slavery and abolitionist movements among whites were made up largely of poor people:

> The hundreds of thousands of people who signed anti-slavery
> petitions were common people, the poor and the working class. The
> subscribers to the abolitionist newspapers had to struggle to assemble

their pennies .... It was also common white people who took risks during this period. Those who saved Garrison from lynching were plain and ordinary people.[16]

There were, therefore, white people who acted on the basis of values that were alternative to those based on an identity as whites. The triumph of the white identity, therefore, was not an inevitable consequence of natural or genetic forces but the outcome of unequal struggles. In text we find that opposition to racism could and did go hand in hand in anti-slavery movements in Britain and the United States with attitudes and politics that opposed slavery without rejecting racism. Thus, the outcomes of the struggle against slavery, including the Civil War in the United States did not lead to systems of racial justice or of class equality. For example, the ending of slavery in the British West Indies followed the rise of alternative centres of political/economic power. Fears of successful slave uprisings such as Haiti's, the increasing cost of suppressing such uprisings, and diminishing levels of profit overshadowed the moral crusade that had been waged against the evils of the slave trade and of slavery.

In the United States the Civil War was fought by the leaders of the Union less to free the slaves than to extend the sway of the emergent industrial capitalists and serve the interests of their free soil allies. Emancipation in neither the Caribbean nor the United States required the overthrow of racialist attitudes or of racist structures, despite the commitment of anti-racist whites and free people of colour and slaves struggling for freedom. Thus, slavery died so that capitalism could continue to flourish, and with it racism.

Racism in the Post-slavery Period

Prejudices, disunion, and distrust were all characteristics of the response of the major part of the working class to the triumph of capitalism. This response involved the acceptance of hierarchy itself and the situating of oneself and one's group into hierarchies based on skill, job status, ethnicity, gender, and race. One owed and was owed respect in relation to one's position along these scales. These divisions were reinforced by the distribution of material resources. State action directly and indirectly maintained this invidious social order and made possible the continued functioning of the system to control the production and distribution of the material resources. Politics based on an inclusive class consciousness had to confront and overcome these ideological and material reinforcements, including state repression, and it was not entirely surprising that such politics had an up-hill battle and were successful less frequently than they failed.

The United States

The development of class consciousness among the rapidly growing working class in the post-Civil War United States, was, as in Britain, fundamentally shaped and distorted by racism.[17] There was the presence of freed slaves and of other racially distinct colonised peoples within the metropole itself in large numbers. There was a massive immigration of European workers into the United States. Racism provided the ideological and material framework within which the millions of European immigrants who joined the labour force in the half century between 1865 and 1914 became 'American'. Then they and the indigenous white working class were given a racialised identity (or a racialised working-class identity) as an alternative to a working-class identity and this shaped their responses to being made wage-labourers.

The choice that presented itself throughout this period in US history was between a politics based on an inclusive definition of 'us' and one based on an exclusive racial definition. An inclusive definition and political strategy would have necessitated challenging the racialist ideology that had become a dominant characteristic of American identity in the ante-bellum period.[18] It would have required that workers recognise a common interest and need to cooperate to achieve common objectives. Although this was not the path chosen by most of the white working class and its organisations, there is evidence that there was consideration of such an option and evidence of attempts to develop such a politics. The Address of the National Labor Congress to the Workingmen of the United States in 1867, for example, declared that 'unpalatable as the truth may be to many', Negroes were now in a new position in the United States, and the actions of white working men could 'determine whether the freedman becomes an element of strength or an element of weakness' in the labour movement.

The solidarity option was not chosen. The exclusive racial definition of 'us' was the dominant response. This divisive definition was based both on possession of craft skills and on racial prejudice. As Du Bois put it,

> [the National Labor Union] began to fight for capital and interest and the right of the upper class of labour to share in the exploitation of common labour. The Negro as a common labourer belonged, therefore, not in but beneath the white American labour movement. Craft and race unions spread. The better-paid skilled and intelligent American labour formed itself into closed guilds and, in combination with capitalist guild-masters, extorted fair wages which could be raised by negotiation.[19]

The craft- and race-based unionisation operated to retard the development of mass unionism until the Great Depression. It culminated in the formation of the CIO (Congress of Industrial Organisations) industrial unions of the late 1930s. Exclusiveness ensured the availability of large pools of workers willing to, or having no choice but to strike-break and thus weaken the effectiveness of the craft unions. These factors were reinforced by racial and ethnic divisions in the workplace and in housing, education, and social and political activities. This situation goes a long way toward explaining the present political weakness and lack of class consciousness of the American working class.[20]

Matters were further complicated by white labour being encouraged to feel superior to non-whites and thus become 'white'. Central Pacific Superintendent Charles Crocker, for example, pointed out the benefits to white labour from Chinese immigration:

> I believe that the effect of Chinese labour upon white labour has an elevating instead of degrading tendency. I think that every white man who is intelligent and able to work, who is more than a digger in a ditch ... who has the capacity of being something else, can get to be something else by the presence of Chinese labour more than he could without it .... There is proof of that in the fact that after we got Chinamen to work, we took the more intelligent of the white labourers and made foremen of them. I know of several of them now who never expected, never had a dream that they were going to be anything but shovellers of dirt, hewers of wood and drawers of water, and they are now respectable farmers, owning farms. They got a start by controlling Chinese labour on our railroad.[21]

Not only could white male workers be elevated by the use of Chinese labour, and become 'white' men, so could white women become 'white' women. Takaki quotes an article by Abby Richardson in *Scribner's Monthly* titled 'A Plea for Chinese Labour', in which she argued: 'This is the age when much is expected of woman. She must be the ornament of society as well as the mistress of a well-ordered household.' Thus, 'Chinese labour could become a feature of both the factory and the home'. Tensions of class conflict in white society could be resolved if Chinese migrant labourers became the 'mudsills' of society, white men became 'capitalists', and their wives 'ornaments of society'.[22]

These privileges, or more correctly for many white working-class men and women, these promises of privileges were only part of the process through which racism remained a dominant characteristic of the American ideology. Repression of those who challenged that response of the working class to their designated position in society also existed. There is a long history in the United States of legal and extralegal repression, ranging from the terrorism directed against blacks and their white allies during reconstruction in the post-Civil War South, to the suppression of the Molly McGuires, a militant nineteenth-century working-class organisation, the Industrial Workers of the World (IWW) (the major class-consciousness working-class in the pre-first world war period which was suppressed by the government during the war) to the judicial murders of Sacco and Vanzetti (anarchists convicted and executed for the murder of a payroll guard in what many still regard as a political trial) then the Rosenbergs (the only Americans ever to be executed in peacetime for supposedly supplying atomic secrets to the Soviets) in the twentieth century.

Clearly, the threat posed by class-conscious interracial co-operation was perceived by the ruling class and its agents in control of the state. Repression was accompanied by propaganda campaigns against populist efforts in the last two decades of the nineteenth century. There was a massive campaign appealing to white supremacist attitudes. The spectre of black equality was used to divert the poor whites away from any incipient class consciousness, toward a renewed racial consciousness. For example, the power of racial identity was tested in Lawrence County, Alabama, which represented Alabama's 'strongest and most persistent opposition to the Democratic party' and in which 'Free labour ideology and biracial class politics survived ... because of the efforts of local black and white radical Republicans, who during congressional Reconstruction refused to be intimidated by Ku Klux Klan terror'.[23]

Horton identifies the campaign waged by the local, Democrat newspaper, the *Advertiser*:

Because the Democratic party was threatened by the possible emergence of a biracial brotherhood of working men ... the *Advertiser* resorted to a campaign of racial hatred that resembled its earlier pronouncements in support of the Klan .... To stir up racial discontent, the *Advertiser* on election day fell back on its tried and tested formula — race-baiting. The front page of the *Advertiser* was filled with reports of assaults by blacks on white women. 'The Negroes ... were getting very troublesome' in Mississippi. 'Several Negro women of Tuscumbia' were reported to 'have addressed a very insulting letter to several respectable white ladies.' Jourd White (the editor) stated that they would 'hug a barrel or look up a rope' as a just reward for the insult. The 'white men of Lawrence County' were urged by white to 'do' their 'duty' to 'protect the white race from this animalism.[24]

Horton concludes that, 'A strong tradition of free labour-oriented biracial politics coupled with worsening agricultural depression during the post-Reconstruction period could not overcome the dominance of racial politics even in a county where a legitimate space had been created for class politics'.[25]

The Southern state governments legitimated the process by establishing the Jim Crow system of *de jure* segregation, that is, of apartheid. The federal government accepted and legitimated the process through a number of Supreme Court decisions culminating in the 1896 *Plessy* v. *Ferguson* decision, which established the 'separate but equal' principle: This decision justified segregation in all aspects of life in the South. The federal government's acceptance of the disenfranchisement of the Southern black population, of the lynch terror that took hundreds of black lives a year, and of the total denial of blacks' citizenship rights were crucial developments. So was Northern capitalist support. This took the form of not recruiting Southern black labour into the growing industrial proletariat and by largely excluding the Northern black population as well. Capitalist reinforcement of racial hatred also meant recruiting blacks solely as strike-breakers. This ensured the maintenance of the controlled labour force necessary for the Southern share crop system that produced the cotton that was still so crucial to the economy of the United States. This also ensured the exclusion of black labour from the national industrial proletariat just like it had been excluded from the previous fundamental determinant of American life, the frontier. Now when blacks entered the labour force, they would be entering turf considered by whites as white.

In addition to the psychological privileges that poor whites obtained from the Jim Crow system (being told that they were superior to all African Americans regardless of their own class position), they received some material privileges. These privileges were unequally distributed within the white working class and were tenuously held. There was the ever-present threat of cheap substitute black labour if whites stepped out of line. The price white labour paid in the South for its superior position included wages significantly lower than those in other regions, lower levels of public services than in other regions, and the contempt of their ruling class 'white allies' who looked upon them in much the same way as they did the blacks. A politics characterised by the absence of issues and the absence of opportunities for poor whites to obtain benefits, even by the standards of the rest of the country, became normal. Poor whites, in effect, gave up their own suffrage through the denial of suffrage to African Americans as part of the price paid to become 'white'.

Faced with the political culture of racism, the white working class failed to create its own culture to challenge the class-based ethos or to defend and maintain the attempts to do so that were made during this period. Thus, the white working class was unable to meet the growing attacks on its interests that the rise of monopoly capital represented. The growing concentration of capital and centralisation of control brought with it increased exploitation of the population by suppressing wages and benefits. It made possible the process of 'de-skilling' and the degradation of labour associated with 'Scientific Management'.[26] The skilled/unskilled hierarchy was reinforced in ethnic and racial terms, and the craft-based unions were unable to defeat the power of the monopoly capitalists and their political allies. Rather than reconsider its basic assumptions, the American Federation of Labor (AFL) became more and more exclusionist as it faced the competition of cheaper labour. This pattern was similar to that which characterised British trade unions in the same period. In 1898 an article in the AFL's official organ, the American *Federationist*, declared that blacks were unfit for union membership because they were 'of abandoned and reckless disposition', lacking 'those peculiarities of temperament such as patriotism, sympathy, sacrifice, etc., which are peculiar to most of the Caucasian race'. The AFL therefore recommended deportation of blacks to Liberia or Cuba. Samuel Gompers, First President of the American Federation of Labor, went further in a speech in 1905 when he declared that 'the Caucasians are not going to let their standard of living be destroyed by negroes, Chinamen, Laps, or any others'.[27]

White opposition to such attitudes came from movements that posited a class, rather than a sectional or racial, analysis of society. The IWW, for example, took a principled inclusive position and was consequently the target of repressive action by state and capital. The threat that such a position would challenge the common-sense popular racism that was being pushed by capital and the state and would offer an alternative identity for the new immigrants to that of 'White American' was a serious one. This elicited a mixture of propaganda and repression, with the additional weight of science thrown in for good measure. As science and technology became more central to the economy, scientists and engineers became more important as authority figures.[28]

For example, the expanding field of psychology became an especially important ally of the capitalists, who in their role as philanthropists provided resources for scientists. Edward Thorndike received $325,000 from the Carnegie Foundation from 1918 to 1934 and was the author of one of the basic textbooks used until the 1950s in major American universities. He and his colleagues, Terman and Goddard, adapted Binet's intelligence test for American use, propagandised the theories of genetically inherited intelligence, and offered scientific 'proof' of the superiority of some races (the Nordic and Teutonic) and the inferiority of others. Coincidentally, the 'inferiors' were not only the victims of the 'white man's burden' overseas, and were the non-white superexploited races within the United States itself; they were also the recent immigrant employees of the philanthropists, such as the Italians, the Poles, the Slavs, and others. Science simply documented that the class hierarchy was as it should be. If the United States were the land of opportunity, those at the top got there because of their intelligence and hard work. Those at the bottom deserved to be there.

The scientifically objective data produced by such experts as Thorndike were used to justify the racist 1921 and 1924 Immigration Acts that kept out further immigrants from Southern and Eastern Europe. The demands for such control on immigration from the AFL and from nativist groups such as the Immigration Restriction League had all failed until after World War I. Why? Although sections of the working class supported such restriction, it was not in response to their wishes that restriction was adopted. World War I had stopped the flow of immigrant workers from Europe. There was a continuing, and indeed increasing, need for workers in the United States, first to supply the British and French war efforts and then its own. This need was met by recruiting black workers from the South. Racialist attitudes and — crucially — the construction of institutional racism by the local state, ensured that there would be antagonism between white workers and their new African-American colleagues. Racist practices ensured that the latter would be concentrated in particular low-level jobs and in particular ghetto residential areas that were then systematically denied the level of public services to which they were entitled. Thus, the labour force would continue to be divided and controllable.[29]

After the war, fear of the spread of Bolshevism made the prospect of recruiting labour from areas contaminated by its virus particularly unsatisfactory. Segregated reserves of black labour in the South made it unnecessary for capitalists and the state to take that risk. The racist culture provided the guarantee that lower levels of white immigrants and the new black industrial proletariat would be divided. The consequences for the white working class of adherence of most of its members to a system in which they were exploited as workers and were recipients of privileges, or the promise of privileges, as whites can be seen in their political weakness, low level of unionisation, high level of economic insecurity, and low level of state benefits. This situation was challenged by large sections of the working class during the Great Depression. How successful that challenge was to be and to what extent white workers would develop a class, rather than a racial, consciousness is the subject of the next section.

Racism, Welfare Capitalism, and the Authoritarian State

The development of welfare capitalism in the aftermath of the Great Depression and World War II has been one of the major developments of the contemporary period. It has been argued that capitalism has thus changed its nature. The state was now the protector of the weak and defenceless, the provider of a safety net to catch those who fell, for whatever reason, and the provider of services on the basis of need rather than the ability to pay. The corporations themselves were seen to have become 'soulful', in Harvard economist Carl Kaysen's felicitous phrase. Power was seen to have become dispersed because of widespread stock ownership, the separation of ownership and control, and the responsiveness of the new managers in the post-industrial society to interests wider than the hitherto exclusive concern for profit maximisation. There were no longer to be struggles over the distribution of scarce sources in an age of plenty and affluence. Class had become an irrelevant concept and, consequently, there was an end to ideology.

During this same period, there had been major changes in race relations. Civil rights legislation, executive action, judicial decisions, and political leadership had all been responsive to liberal ideology and political pressure from the civil rights movement. The state no longer endorsed racism, *de jure* segregation was overturned, and racial minorities could now compete and rise on the basis of their own worth. Although prejudice might still remain as a residual problem, racism was not — and could not be seen as — a structural characteristic of society in the United States.

Given the reality of capital's most recent counterattacks and revocations of most of these concessions over the past decades, it is, perhaps, hard to remember how taken-for-granted such fairy tales were in the dominant ideologies of American society from the end of the Great Depression to the present. The soulful corporation has turned out to be a transnational corporation moving production and jobs around the globe in search of ever-greater profits and using its ability to do so to force its remaining workforce in the metropole to accept an escalating series of 'take-backs' as a condition of being allowed to continue to work. The state has turned out to be more committed to capitalism than to welfare, which is being eroded as a condition of keeping and attracting jobs. The ending of *de jure* segregation did not mean the end of racial polarisation. But these challenges to the dominant ideology have not led to a reconsideration of the ideological assumptions of mainstream commentators. Far from it. It is either the genetic or cultural inferiority of the victims that accounts for continuing and increasing inequality. Indeed, it is the very welfare system itself that created a dependency culture in unemployment, homelessness, drug abuse, and so on.[30] Racism, in both its material and ideological forms, continues to be a central characteristic of American society and has played a crucial role in capital's ability, along with the state's, to overturn what were supposed to have been fundamental changes in the nature of capitalism and in the nature and operations of the liberal democratic state.

The Modern Period

The Great Depression, the New Deal, World War II, and the working-class response to these events played a major role in extracting concessions from capital and in shaping the forms of the state. The federal government came to play the central role in subsidising capital, in ensuring that a favourable investment climate existed within the United States and abroad, and in ensuring order and stability within the United States. Performing these tasks often brought the federal government into conflict with the states and with local authorities and into conflict with the belief in free enterprise, minimal government, and the inferiority of blacks. For example, in order to ensure that black struggles in the post-war period did not continue the link with the Communist Party and with issues of class, it was necessary to combine repression of those wishing to continue that link, W.E. B. Du Bois and Paul Robeson, political activist, actor and singer, for example, with sufficient concessions to ensure the triumph of Americanism, despite racism.

Such concessions required changes in the Jim Crow system of the South. *De jure* segregation was no longer necessary to maintain the Southern system of agriculture, which was being rapidly mechanised, in part supported by the policies of the New Deal. These policies served as a lightning rod for black demands and were a force of instability that the newer power centres in the South associated with industry and commerce and wished to defuse. Racial segregation was a contradiction for the United States in its efforts to shape the world order after World War II, a world in which two-thirds of the people were not white and in which US apartheid was available for the Soviets and other nationalist critics to challenge US claims to moral leadership. Plus, incorporation of African Americans into the formal democracy would channel the African American middle class into the system rather than run the danger of it becoming a counter-elite. This reasoning did not mean that the white leaders of the old order in the South would give up their power and privileges without a struggle. Also, poor whites in the South were not going to give up power either, especially after being assured by word and deed by those with power in the South and in the nation as a whole that they too were superior to blacks because they were white.

The federal government was, therefore, going to be in conflict with rural Southern elites as it attempted to overturn *de jure* segregation, with African Americans taking the lead and being beaten and killed as a necessary part of the campaign. The national administration had, at the same time, to deal with overt racial discrimination in the rest of the country where racial segregation was not legally required. Here, the federal government came into conflict with the principles of private property, which held that individuals could do whatever they wished to with their property, and could hire whom they wished, and rent to whom they wished. The level of struggle by African Americans and the imperatives of running the world required that overt racial discrimination be outlawed.[31]

The desegregation efforts of the federal government did not mean the end of institutional racism or the end of the role of the state in legitimating popular racism. Racism continued to be part of the normal operations of the state at every level. For example, one of the key engines of state intervention in support of the economy in the post-war years was support for suburbanisation, which by 1965 had led to the construction of more than $120 billion worth of owner-occupied housing — 98 per cent of which was owned and occupied by whites. This was the result of official government policies administered through the lending decisions of the Veterans Administration and the Federal Housing Agency. State and local governments made similar decisions that led to the construction of what Arnold Hirsch has called Chicago's Second

Ghetto.[32] The racialised economic consequences of encouraging and financially subsidising white flight to the suburbs included the loss of jobs, tax revenues, and affordable housing in the inner cities — which were becoming more black as African Americans were displaced from Southern sharecropping and came North looking for work. The decisions of the state at every level constructed the increasingly racialised ghettos with their underresourced education and health systems, appalling housing, and high levels of un- and underemployment. The construction of racialised criminal justice systems ensured the lack of police protection and a massively racialised disparity in imprisonment. These realities of state policy have to be set against statements in favour of tolerance and brotherhood and even against assertions of the decline of racism and the presumption that past civil rights legislation have fundamentally eliminated systematic racism in the United States.

Just as there is this contradiction between the ostensible purposes of the state in the field of race, so there is a similar contradiction in the state's relations with the white working class. An essential part of the construction of 'Pax Americana', the period of American economic, military and political hegemony following World War II, was the great or Keynesian accommodation that augmented the new era of welfare capitalism discussed above. Workers in the primary sector of the economy were allowed to enjoy high pay, job security, and a social wage. But the price they had to pay actually undermined their ability to protect these gains. The purge of the Left from the unions associated with the anti-Communist purges and the requirements of the Taft-Hartley Act (the first post-war limitation of the rights of organised labour) was accompanied by the acceptance of the ideology and practice of the Cold War, of anti-Communism, of Military Keynesianism, and by the cessation of serious attempts to unionise the non-union majority of the working class.[33]

The consequences of these concessions have proven devastating over the medium term for those workers who were to be the beneficiaries of this accommodation and devastating for those excluded. The purges of the unions had driven out those militants and activists who had wanted to challenge the structural racism within the workplace and within the unions themselves. It was these workers who wanted to create objective conditions of racial equality. The failure to continue unionising drives, particularly in the South, created a potential region where capital could locate future investment and employ labour with a lower social wage. The lack of unionisation created the basis upon which capital, the state, and the media could scapegoat organised labour as the cause of inflation and other ills of the society. The ensuing weakness of the working class made it even more difficult for members of that class to resist the transmission of the dominant racist ideology of white supremacy. The acceptance of Pax Americana helped capital and the state to define the national interest in terms most favourable to themselves.

This defining of interest included seeing any foreign government on the periphery that attempts to improve the living conditions of its people by taking control of its economy as an enemy of the United States and as part of the 'International Communist Conspiracy' of the 'Evil Empire'. The consequence of such a hegemonic definition of the national interest has been political, military, covert, and economic interventions to overthrow such governments and to put and keep in power regimes that would allow transnational capital a free run in their countries, that would sell their people more cheaply than their neighbours and thus provide opportunities for the export of jobs from the metropole to the periphery.[34] The limitation of private sector unionisation primarily to the major industrial sectors had another consequence the expanding sectors of the economy (service, sales, and clerical) were not unionised and consequently were based on cheap labour. The weakening influence of organised labour, a political system that was coming to be more and more under the control of capital, and no meaningful alternatives offered by the Democratic Party has left large parts of the white working class alienated from the system and from the Democratic Party.

The essence of the Republican strategy since 1964 has been an appeal to the white South and to whites in the rest of the country on the basis that the Democratic Party had been captured by blacks and was no longer the white Man's Party. Race has become the best single predictor of voting behaviour: For example, two thirds of all white voters voted for Reagan in 1984 and 60 per cent voted for Bush in 1988. Manning Marable, the director for the Institute of Research in African-American Studies at Columbia University, has calculated that overall white support in the South for Republican presidential candidates has been 70 per cent and among white evangelical Christians, 80 per cent. 'Since the election of Ronald Reagan in 1980, in presidential contests the Republican Party operates almost like a white united front, dominated by the most racist, reactionary sectors of corporate and finance capital, and the most backward cultural and religious movements.'[35]

Racialised politics has made it possible for capital to use the electoral system to restructure the political economy, as done in Britain under Thatcher and Major, with large portions of those who will pay, and have paid, the highest price. For example, the median family income in the United States in 1993 in real terms was lower than it was in 1973, and it takes more family members working to earn that lower income. De-skilling, deindustrialisation, decertification of trade unions, take-backs by capital from unionised workers, and cuts in the social wage have all been imposed during the decade since the first edition of this volume was published. During this period there has been an ideological assault on state and collective provision; on the supposed 'dependency culture'; and on large sections of the reserve labour force, now called the 'underclass'. The level of state attacks on African American and Latino communities has increased massively during this period, and the level of imprisonment has escalated exponentially with the United States now the most imprisoned nation in the world. The United States is racialised to the extent that an African American male is more likely to be imprisoned than to be in higher education and is five times more likely to be imprisoned than is a black African in South Africa.[36]

The racial and gender divisions of the working class have weakened its ability to resist the dominant racialised and gendered ideology. This lack of working-class consciousness and autonomous culture severely weakens its ability to respond to these attacks on its living standards and hopes for the future. The increasing level of scapegoating of African Americans and women is an indication of the determination of those in power to stay in power and to use the system to their maximum advantage. Their ability to buy acquiescence through material concessions to white working-class men is becoming more and more limited and therefore they are relying more and more on scapegoating and division.

Until the working class creates its own identity and a racially inclusive consciousness and culture, it will continue to be unable to advance its own interests. The European American working class will have to reject the white part of that identity and the illusory privileges based on racism and sexism. The damage done is not only to people of colour: European Americans are damaged as well. The dominant ideology of white racial supremacy has served, and continues to serve, the interests of capital and its political allies. Opposition has come from individuals and groups of whites, African Americans, Latinos, and others. This opposition to a racialised identity illustrates that it is possible to choose an alternative identity to that constructed and transmitted by agents of capital. Thus, it is possible for the individual effort and talent used in everyday struggles to survive and to resist class oppression, to be used to create a just and truly democratic society.

Reference Notes

Introduction

1. W.E.B. Du Bois, *Black Reconstruction in America*, London, Frank Cass, 1966, p.30.
2. J.L. Graves, Jr., 'Evolutionary Biology and Human Variation: Biological Determinism and the Mythology of Race', *Sage Race Relations Abstracts*, vol.18, no.3, 1993, pp.4-34; S. J. Gould, *The Mismeasure of Man*, New York, W.W. Norton, 1981; D. Roediger, *The Wages of Whiteness: Race and the Making of the American Working Class*, London, Verso, 1991; J.H. Stanfield, 'Racism in America and Other Race-Centered Nation-States: Synchronic Considerations', *International Journal of Comparative Sociology*, vol.32, nos3–4, 1991, pp.243–61.
3. M. Hechter, *Internal Colonialism: The Celtic Fringe in Britain's National Development*, London, Routledge & Kegan Paul, 1975.
4. B. Rolston, 'The Training Ground: Ireland, Conquest and Colonisation', *Race and Class*, vol.34, no.3, 1993, p.16.
5. Ibid., pp.16-17.
6. Ibid., p.17; See also M. Rai, 'Columbus in Ireland', *Race and Class*, vol.34, no.3, 1993, pp.25-34.
7. S.J. Smith, 'Race and Racism: Health, Welfare and the Quality of Life', *Urban Geography*, vol.11, no.6, 1990, p.607.
8. R. Bailey, 'The Slavery Trade and the Development of Capitalism in the United States: The Textile Industry in New England', *Social Science History*, vol.14, no.3, 1990, pp.373–414. See also E. Williams, *Capitalism and Slavery*, London, André Deutsch, 1967.
9. Institute of Race Relations, *Patterns of Racism*, London, Institute of Race Relations, 1982, p.26.
10. J. Pope-Hennessy, *Sins of the Fathers: The Atlantic Slave Traders, 1441-1807*, London, Sphere, 1970, p.155.
11. Leo Huberman, *Man's Worldly Goods*, New York and London, Monthly Review Press, 1968, p.167.
12. R. Bailey, 'The Other Side of Slavery: Black Labor, Cotton, and Textile Industrialization in Great Britain and the United States', *Agricultural History*, vol.68, Spring 1994, p.38.
13. J. Walvin, *The Black Presence: A Documentary History of the Negro in England*,

1555-1860, 1971, p.10.

14. P. Fryer, *Staying Power*, London, Pluto Press, 1984, p.109.
15. R. Drinnon, *Facing West*, New York, Schocken, 1980, p.138.
16. M. Marable, *Black American Politics*, London, Verso, 1985, p.141.
17. A. Briggs, 'The Language of "Class" in Early Nineteenth-Century England', in M.W. Flinn and T.C. Smout, eds, *Essays in Social History*, Oxford, Clarendon Press, 1974, p.177
18. Ibid.
19. A. Smedley, *Race in North America: Origin and Evolution of a World View*, Boulder, Westview, 1993.
20. J.H. Stanfield, op.cit., pp.246, 247.
21. M. Davis, *City of Quartz*, New York, Vintage, 1992; K.B. Hadjor, *Another America: The Politics of Race and Blame*, Boston, South End Press, 1995; A. Hirsch, *The Making of the Second Ghetto: Race and Housing in Chicago*, Cambridge and New York, Cambridge University Press, 1983; D. Massey and N. Denton, *American Apartheid: Segregation and the Making of the Underclass*, Cambridge, MA, Harvard University Press, 1993.
22. Hadjor, op.cit., p.38.
23. Ibid., p.39.
24. Ibid.
25. Massey and Denton, op.cit., p.57.
26. Hirsch, op.cit. pp.252–4.
27. Hadjor, 1995, op.cit., p.44.
28. See Lucy A. Williams, 'The Right's Attack on Aid to Families with Dependent Children', *The Public Eye*, vol.10, nos 3–4, Fall/Winter 1996, pp.1-18.
29. J. Krieger, *Reagan, Thatcher and the Politics of Decline*, Cambridge, Polity Press, 1986.
30. See *Race and Class*, "Europe: Variations on a Theme of Racism", vol.32, no.3, January-March 1991 (Special Issue).
31. P. Horton, 'Testing the Limits of Class Politics in Postbellum Alabama: Agrarian Radicalism in Lawrence County', *The Journal of Southern History*, vol.57, no.1, 1991, p.77.
32. A. Lansley, 'Accentuate the Negative to Win Again' *Observer Review*, 3 September 1995, p.4.
33. K. Eichenwald, 'Texaco Executives on Tape, Discussed Impeding a Bias Suit', *New York Times*, 4 November 1996, pp. A1, C4.
34. D. Kairys, 'Unexplainable on Grounds Other Than Race', *The American University Law Review*, vol.45, no.3, February 1996, p.737.
35. Ibid., p.748.
36. A. Sivanandan, Editorial, *Race and Class*, 'Europe: Variations on a Theme of Racism', vol.32, no.3, January-March 1991, p.v [Special Issue].
37. S. Allen and M. Macey, 'Race and Ethnicity in the European Context', *British Journal of Sociology*, vol.41, no.3, September 1990, p.378.
38. Refugee Forum and Migrant Rights Action Network, *The Walls of the Fortress: European Agreement Against Immigrants, Migrants and Refugees*, London, Refugee Forum, 1991, p.16; see also A. Simpson and M. Read, *Against a Rising Tide: Racism, Europe and 1992*, Nottingham, Spokesman for Nottingham Racial Equality Council and European Labour Forum, 1991.
39. A.D. Smith, 'Racist Party Wins Over the Workers', the *Observer*, 3 November 1996, p.21.
40. Du Bois, op.cit., p.30.
41. H. Aptheker, 'Anti-Racism in the US: An Introduction', *Sage Race Relations Abstracts*, vol.12, no.4, November 1987, pp.3*f*32.
42. James Jennings, 'Puerto Ricans and the Community Control Movement in New

York City's Lower East Side: An Interview with Luis Fuentes', *Sage Race Relations Abstracts*, vol.21, no.1, February 1996, p.28.

43. Quoted in A. Duval-Smith, 'Race Bias Back in US Schools', *Guardian*, 9 April 1997, p.7.

44. J. Kozol, *Savage Inequalities*, New York, Crown Publishers, 1991.

45. R. Herrnstein and C. Murray, *The Bell Curve: Intelligence and Class Structure in American Life*, New York, Free Press, 1994.

46. J.L. Graves, Jr. and T. Place, 'Race and IQ Revisited: Figures Never Lie, but Often Liars Figure', *Sage Race Relations Abstracts*, vol.20, no.2, May 1995, p.43.

47. See V. Polakow, 'The Shredded Net: The End of Welfare as We Knew It' *Sage Race Relations Abstracts*, vol.22, no.3, August 1997.

48. This article has been cited in the following publications: H.H. Fairchild and M.B. Tucker, 'Black Residential Mobility: Trends and Characteristics', *Journal of Social Issues*, vol.38, no.3, 1982, pp.51–74; J. Williams, 'Redefining Institutional Racism', *Ethnic and Racial Studies*, vol.8, no.3, 1985, pp.323–48; J. Gabe, 'Explaining Race: Education', *British Journal of Sociology of Education*, vol.12, no.3, 1991, pp.347–80.

49. K.B. Hadjor, 'Race, Riots and Clouds of Ideological Smoke', *Race and Class*, vol.38, no.4, April-June 1997, p.30.

50. This article has been cited by M. Ellison, 'David Duke and the Race for the Governor's Mansion', *Race and Class*, vol.33, no. 2, 1991, pp.71–9.

51. This article has been cited in the following publications: S.J. Smith, op.cit., pp.606–16; W.I.U. Ahmad, 'Reflections on the Consanguinity and Birth Outcome Debate', *Journal of Public Health Medicine*, vol.16, no.4, 1994, pp.423–8; C. Smaje, 'The Ethnic Patterning of Health: New Directions for Theory and Research', *Sociology of Health and Illness*, vol.18, no.2, 1996, pp.139–57.

52. Commission for Racial Equality, *Appointing NHS Consultants and Senior Registrars: Report of a Formal Investigation*, London, CRE, 1996, p.13.

53. S. Beishon, S. Virdee and A. Hagell, *Nursing in a Multi-Ethnic NHS*, London, Policy Studies Institute, 1995.

54. MSF, *The Ethnic Status of NHS Staff: Damning New Statistics*, London, MSF, 1997, p.1.

55. Ibid, p.2.

56. E.J. Cornacchia, D.C. Nelson, 'Historical Differences in the Political Experiences of American Blacks and White Ethnics: Revisiting an Unresolved Controversy', *Ethnic and Racial Studies*, vol.15, no.1, 1992, pp.102–24. See also P. Horton op.cit., pp.63–84; J.H. Stanfield, op.cit., pp.243–61.

57. M. Marable, 'Race and Class in the US Presidential Election', *Race and Class*, vol.34, no.3, 1993, pp.75–85.

1 Race, Class and Power
The New York Decentralisation Controversy

This chapter first appeared in the *Journal of American Studies*, 32 (2), 191–219, 1969, published by Cambridge University Press. I wish to thank the University of Manchester for the travel grant which made this research possible.

1. David Rogers, *110 Livingston Street: Politics and Bureaucracy in the New York School System*, New York, Random House, 1968, p.83.

2. Wallace Roberts quoted in 'The Battle for Urban Schools', *Saturday Review*, no.16, 1968, p.97.

3. Quoted in Mario Fantini and Richard Magat, 'Decentralizing Urban School Systems' in *The Schoolhouse in the City*, ed. Alvin Toffler, New York, Frederick A. Praeger, 1968, pp.134-5.

4. Rogers, op.cit., p.473.

5. 'For example, 39 of the 106 projects in the board's 1964-1965 building program were for local school areas where it was estimated that 90% or more of the pupils would be Negro and Puerto Rican', ibid., p.18. See also p.70.

6. Ibid., pp.63–4.

7. Ibid., p.306.

8. Ibid., p.309.

9. Cf. Kenneth Clark, *Dark Ghetto*, New York, Harper and Row, ch.6, pp.120–5.

10. *New York Times*, 13 August 1967, about release of Co-operative Research Project no.3237 of the US Office of Education's series entitled *Investigations of Fiscally Independent and Dependent School Districts*.

11. Rogers, op.cit., p.269.

12. Interview with the Rev. C.H. Oliver, 21 May 1968, in London. Cf. also Lillian S. Calhoun, 'New York: Schools and Power — Whose?', *Integrated Education*, 8, no.1, January-February 1969, p.18.

13. Ibid., p.23.

14. *Reconnection for Learning — A Community School System for New York City*, New York, Panel on Decentralization, 9 November 1967.

15. NY Civil Liberties Union, 'The Burden of Blame: A Report on the Ocean Hill-Brownsville School Controversy', New York, 9 October 1968, mimeo., p.1.

16. 'UFT Statement on Decentralization', New York, United Federation of Teachers, 10 January 1968, mimeo.

17. Edmund W. Gordon, 'Decentralization and Educational Reform', *IRCD Bulletin*, vol.4, no.5; vol.5, no.1, November 1968–January 1969, p.3.

18. Robert Rosenthal and Lenore F. Jacobson, 'Teacher Expectations for the Disadvantaged', *Scientific American*, 218, no.4, April 1968, p.19. Cf. also their book *Pygmalion in the Classroom*, New York, Holt Rinehart and Winston, 1968. Cf. also Clark, op.cit., pp.125–53, and Estelle Fuchs, 'How Teachers Learn to Help Children Fail', *Transaction*, 5, no.9, September 1968, pp.45–53.

19. Calhoun, loc.cit., p.17.

20. Private communication, November 1968.

21. 'Burden of Blame' op.cit., p.6.

22. *An Evaluative Study of the Process of School Decentralization in New York City*, New York, Bank Street College of Education, 30 July, 1968, p.95.

23. Cf. interview with John O'Neill in Fred Ferretti, 'Who's to Blame in the School Strikes', *New York Magazine*, 18 November 1968, pp.34–5.

24. New York Civil Liberties Union, Memorandum to Special Committee on Religious and Racial Prejudice, 26 November 1968, mimeo., pp.2–3.

25. *Daily Telegraph*, 11 March 1969, p.36.

26. Cf. for example, Abraham G. Duker, 'Negroes versus Jews I. Anti-Semitism is Asserted', *Patterns of Prejudice*, 3, no.2 (March-April 1969), pp.9–13. Much of the following discussion is based on the author's 'Negroes versus Jews II. Anti-Semitism is Denied', ibid., pp.13–15.

27. Gary T. Marx, *Protest and Prejudice*, New York, Harper and Row, 1967, p.131.

27. See Lucy A. Williams, 'The Right's Attack on Aid to Families with Dependent Children', *The Public Eye*, vol.10, nos 3–4, Fall/Winter 1996, pp.1–18.

28. Marx, op.cit., pp.138–9.

29. Quoted in Memorandum from Oscar Cohen on 'Negro anti-Semitism and Negro anti-Semites', 23 January 1969, mimeo., p.2.

30. Ibid.

31. Marx, op.cit., p.179.

32. Ibid., p.182.

33. Ibid., p.153 (italics in the original).

34. Ibid., pp.158–9.

35. I.F. Stone, 'The Mason-Dixon Line Moves to New York', *I.F. Stone's Weekly*,

vol.16, no.22, 4 November 1968, p.2.
36. Ibid.
37. George D. Strayer and Louis Yavner, quoted in Rogers, op.cit., p.283. Rogers also quotes Dr Mortimer Kreuter of the Center for Urban Education saying that teachers have become 'infantilised' by a system whose functionaries grade and inspect them much like children. Ibid. He also quotes a school official who said, 'It is known by everyone that headquarters doesn't know what's going on. Information does not get back from the field and people don't even know what policy actually is. They get no help from headquarters, only a mass of paper directives. It is set up like a machine, and the basic set throughout the system is not in any way toward experimenting or even pushing at a rule. A coherent plan has to aim at loosening up the central bureaucracy to begin with, and you have to build in rewards to innovate.' Ibid., pp.279–80.
38. Ferretti, op.cit. pp.34–5.
39. 'Lindsay Back to School Law Despite "Weakening"', *New York Times*, 2 May 1969.
40. Ibid.
41. Interview with the Rev. C.H. Oliver, 21 May 1969 (in London).
42. Letter from David Spencer, 3 January 1969, mimeo.

2 Race, Class and Civil Rights

This chapter was first published in *Exploitation and Exclusion* and is reproduced with permission from Hans Zell Publishers, an imprint of Bowker-Saur, a division of Reed Elsevier (UK) Ltd. I wish to thank the Nuffield Foundation's Small Grants Scheme for the Social Sciences and the University of Manchester Committee on Staff Travel Funds for Research in the Humanities and Social Sciences for their financial assistance. I thank my colleagues at the Institute of Race Relations for their years of education and encouragement and also Benjamin P. Bowser, Pat Kushnick and Jacqueline Ould and the editors of this book for their comments and suggestions.
1. L. Kushnick, 'Racism and Class Consciousness in Modern Capitalism' in B.P. Bowser and R.G. Hunt, eds, *Impacts of Racism on White Americans*, Beverley Hills and London, Sage Publications, 1981, pp.191–216.
2. N. Murray, 'Anti-Racists and Other Demons: The Press and Ideology in Thatcher's Britain', *Race and Class*, vol.27, no.3, Winter 1986, pp.1–20; N. Murray, 'Reporting the Riots', ibid. pp.86–90; C. Searle, 'Your Daily Dose: Racism and the *Sun*', *Race and Class*, vol.29, no.1, Summer 1987, pp.55–72.
3. See, for example, D. Cluster, ed., *They Should Have Served That Cup of Coffee*, Boston, South End Press, 1979; S. Evans, *Personal Politics*, New York, Alfred Knopf, 1979.
4. See A. Alkalimat, et al., *Introduction to Afro-American Studies*, Chicago, Twenty-First Century Books, 1986.
5. R.A. Hill and B. Bair, eds, *Marcus Garvey: Life and Lessons*, Berkeley, University of California Press, 1987; T. Vincent, *Black Power and the Garvey Movement*, Berkeley, Ramparts Press, 1971.
6. M. Marable, *W.E.B. DuBois, Black Radical Democrat*, Boston, Twayne Publishers, 1986, p.171; see also M. Naison, *Communists in Harlem During the Depression*, Urbana, University of Illinois Press, 1983.
7. M. Marable, *Black American Politics*, London, Verso, 1985, pp.172–3.
8. J. Bloom, *Class, Race and the Civil Rights Movement*, Bloomington, Indiana University Press, 1987, p.120.
9. Ibid., p.218.
10. Marable, *Black American Politics*, op.cit., p.193.
11. Ibid., p.140.

12. L. Finkle, 'The Conservative Aims of Militant Rhetoric', *Journal of American History*, vol.60, 1973/4, p.701.
13. Ibid., pp.707–8.
14. Ibid., p.696.
15. G. Myrdal, *An American Dilemma: The Negro Problem and Modern Democracy*, New York, Harper and Row (1944), 1962, p.1004.
16. Ibid.
17. Ibid., pp.1006–7.
18. Ibid., p.1013.
19. Ibid., p.1015.
20. Ibid., p.1016.
21. Ibid., p.1018.
22. Bloom, op.cit., 1987, p.5.
23. Quoted in H. Zinn, *A People's History of the United States*, Harlow, Longman, 1980, p.440.
24. See L.C. Gardner, *Imperial America: American Foreign Policy Since 1898*, New York, Harcourt, Brace Jovanovich, 1976; G. Kolko, *The Politics of War: The World and United States Foreign Policy (1943-1945)*, New York, Vintage Books, 1968; W.A. Williams, *Tragedy of American Diplomacy*, New York, Delta, 1972.
25. G. Horne, *Black and Red: W.E.B. DuBois and the Afro-American Response to the Cold War (1944-1973)*, Albany, SUNY Press, 1986, p.64.
26. Ibid., p.208.
27. See P. Robeson Jr, 'Paul Robeson: Black Warrior', *Freedomways*, vol.11, First Quarter, 1971, pp.24–5 for a discussion of the processes involved in books about the theatre.
28. Ibid., p.23.
29. Horne, op.cit., p.280.
30. Ibid.
31. V.H. Bernstein, 'The Anti-Labor Front', The Antioch Review, vol.3, 1943, pp.337–8.
32. Congressional Record, 66th Congress, 1st Session, vol.58, Part V, 25 August-September 1919, 4303–5. Quoted in W.A. Clark, 'An Analysis of the Relationship Between Anti-Communism and Segregationist Thought in the Deep South (1948-1964)', PhD Thesis, University of North Carolina, Chapel Hill, 1976, p.9.
33. Bernstein, op.cit., p.330
34. *Baytown Employees Federation Bulletin*, nos 72 and 9 respectively, cited in ibid.
35. Clark, op.cit., p.87.
36. D.E. Carleton, *Red Scare: Right-Wing Hysteria and Fifties Fanaticism and their Legacy in Texas*, Austin, Texas Monthly Press, 1985, p.72.
37. L.K. Adler, 'The Red Image', PhD Thesis, University of California, 1970, pp.94–5.
38. Ibid., p.97.
39. See D. Caute, *The Great Fear*, New York, Simon and Schuster, 1978; C. Pomerantz, ed., *A Quarter Century of Un-Americana*, New York, Marzani and Munsell Publishers, 1963.
40. See, for example, R.A. Freeland, *The Truman Doctrine and the Origins of McCarthyism*, New York, Schocken Books, 1971; R. Griffith and A. Theoharis, eds, *The Specter*, New York, New Viewpoints, 1974.
41. Clark, op.cit., 1974.
42. A. Dunbar, *Against the Grain: Southern Radicals and Prophets (1929-1959)*, Charlottesville, University Press of Virginia, 1981, p.256.
43. S. Rosen, 'The CIO Era (1935-55)', in J.W. Jacobson, ed., *The Negro and the American Labor Movement*, Garden City, Anchor Books, 1969, pp.199-200.
44. R.O. Boyer and H.M. Morais, *Labor's Untold Story*, New York, Marzani and Munsell Publishers, 1965, p.361.

45. C.W. Cheng, 'The Cold War: Its Impact on the Black Liberation Struggle Within the United States, Part One', *Freedomways*, vol.13, Winter 1973, p.195.
46. Adler, op.cit., pp.427–8.
47. J.F. MacDonald, *Television and the Red Menace: The Video to Vietnam*, New York, Praeger, 1985, pp.11, 12.
48. C. Carson, *In Struggle: SNCC and the Black Awakening of the 1960s*, Cambridge MA, Harvard University Press, 1981.
49. Quoted in Horne, op.cit., pp.278–9.
50. Marable 1985, op.cit., p.90.
51. Robeson Jr, op.cit., p.28.
52. Quoted in Horne, op.cit., p.184.
53. Marable, 1986, op.cit., pp.184, 188.
54. Ibid., p.198.
55. Ibid.
56. M. Marable, *Race, Reform and Rebellion: The Second Reconstruction in America, 1945-1982*, London, Macmillan, 1983, pp.28–9.
57. H. Darby and M. Rowley, 'King on Vietnam and Beyond', *Phylon*, vol.47, no.1, March 1986, p.49.
58. C.W. Cheng, 'The Cold War: Its Impact on the Black Liberation Struggle Within the United States, Part Two', *Freedomways*, vol.13, Fourth Quarter, 1973, p.288.
59. J. Forman, *The Making of a Black Revolutionary*, New York, Macmillan, 1972, p.382.
60. Ibid., pp.383–4.
61. Marable, 1983, op.cit., p.75.
62. See Carson, op.cit.
63. H.H. Haines, 'Black Radicalization and the Funding of Civil Rights: 1957-1970', *Social Problems*, vol.32, no.1, October 1984, pp.41–2.
64. Quoted in Zinn, op.cit., p.449.
65. Ibid., p.450.
66. Marable, 1985, op.cit., pp.90–1.
67. Ibid. p.92.
68. Ibid.
69. Ibid., p.95.
70. See Chapter 4.
71. Horne, op.cit., p.224.
72. Ibid., p.225.
73. Marable, 1986, op.cit., p.207.
74. D.J. Garrow, *The FBI and Martin Luther King Jr*, Harmondsworth, Penguin Books, 1981, pp.214–15.

3 British Anti-discrimination Legislation

This chapter first appeared in *The Prevention of Racial Discrimination* published by the Institute of Race Relations, 1971, and is based on research made possible by grants from the Nuffield Small Grants Scheme for the Social Sciences and from the University of Manchester. The author wishes to thank them and all those who allowed themselves to be interviewed and consulted.

1. *The Sunday Times*, 28 January 1968. Italics added.
2. *The Times*, 8 April 1969.
3. *Jewish Chronicle*, 16 April 1965.
4. See, for example, *Glasgow Herald*, 8 April 1965; *Birmingham Evening Mail*, 8 April 1965; *Daily Telegraph*, 26 May 1965.
5. House of Commons, vol.711, 3 May 1965, cols 967-8.
6. Ibid., col.1021.

7. House of Commons, vol.711, 3 May 1965, col.990.
8. Ibid., col.928.
9. Ibid., col.929.
10. Ibid., col.948.
11. Ibid., col.950.
12. House of Commons, Sixth Sitting, vol.714, 23 June 1965, col.258.
13. House of Commons, vol.716, 16 July 1965, col.1056.
14. Italics added.
15. In an address by the Home Secretary to the Institute of Race Relations, published in *Race*, vol.VIII, no.3, January 1967, pp.216–21.
16. Race Relations Board, *Report of the Race Relations Board 1966-7*, London, HMSO, 1967, p.13.
17. Italics added.
18. House of Commons, vol.738, no.119, 16 December 1966, col.938.
19. Political and Economic Planning and Research Services Ltd., *Racial Discrimination*, London, PEP, 1967.
20. *The Sunday Times*, 23 April 1967.
21. *The Times*, 10 April 1968.
22. Including *The Times*, 27 July 1967.
23. *Yorkshire Post*, 27 July 1967.
24. Harry Street, Geoffrey Howe and Geoffrey Bindman, *Report on Anti-Discrimination Legislation*, London, Political and Economic Planning, 1967.
25. House of Commons, vol.763, no.102, 23 April 1968, col.62.
26. Street et al., op.cit., p.92.
27. Ibid., p.130.

4 Parameters of British and North American Racism

This chapter first appeared in *Race and Class*, vol.23, nos 2–3, 1981–2, published by the Institute of Race Relations.

1. A. Sivanandan, *Race, Class and the State*, Race and Class pamphlet no.1, London, 1978, reprinted in A. Sivanandan, ed., *A Different Hunger*, London, Pluto Press, 1982, pp.101–252; and *From Immigration Control to Induced Repatriation*, Race and Class pamphlet no.5, London, 1978, reprinted in ibid., pp.131–40.
2. Set up by President Johnson to investigate the riots of 1967.
3. Report of the National Advisory Commission on Civil Disorders, New York, 1968, p.304, hereafter referred to as the Kerner Commission.
4. Brixton Black Women's Group, 'The Brixton Uprising', *Spare Rib*, June 1981. See also, *The Thin End of the Wedge, Manchester Law Centre* Handbook no.5, Manchester, 1980; Islington 18 Defence Committee, *Under Heavy Manners: Report of the Labour Movement Inquiry into Police Brutality and the Position of Black Youth in Islington*, London, Islington 18 Defence Committee, 1972; S. Hall, C. Critcher, T. Jefferson, J. Clarke and B. Roberts, *Policing the Crisis: Mugging, the State, Law and Order*, London, Macmillan, 1978.
5. Section 4 has now been repealed after a sustained campaign led by black organisations — but has reappeared, in another guise, in the Criminal Attempts Act.
6. Institute of Race Relations, *Police Against Black People*, Race and Class pamphlet no.6, London, 1979, p.42; see also *The Thin End of the Wedge*, op.cit.
7. Ibid.
8. See A.S. Blumber, 'Court contingencies in the Right to the Assistance of Counsel', in R. Perrucci and M. Pilisuk, *The Triple Revolution Emerging: Social Problems in Depth*, Boston, Little Brown, 1971; J. Baldwin and M. McConville, *Negotiated Justice*, London, Martin Robertson, 1977.
9. Kerner Commission. op.cit., p.337.

10. Ibid., p.340; see also Isaac D. Balbus, *The Dialectics of Legal Repression: Black Rebels before the American Criminal Courts*, New York, Russell Sage Foundation, 1973.

11. *LAG Bulletin, Legal Action* magazine, August 1981.

12. See Mike Phillips, 'Rage that Shattered Thatcher', *New Statesman*, 17 July 1981.

13. Tom Hayden, *Rebellion in Newark*, New York, Vintage Books, 1967, p.53.

14. See Gary Wills, *The Second Civil War: Arming for Armageddon*, New York, New American Library, 1968.

15. 'Toxteth's night of revenge', *The Sunday Times*, 2 August 1981.

16. Quoted in Phillips, op.cit.

17. Harold M. Baron, 'The Web of Urban Racism', in L. Knowles and K. Prewitt, eds, *Institutional Racism in America*, Englewood Cliffs, Prentice Hall, 1969.

18. Annie Stein, 'Strategies for Failure', in *Challenging the Myths: The Schools, the Blacks and the Poor*, Cambridge, Harvard Education Review, 1971, pp.133–4.

19. Malcolm X, *Autobiography of Malcolm X*, New York, Random House, 1964, p.36.

20. See L. Kushnick, 'Race, Class and Power: The New York Decentralization Controversy', *Journal of American Studies*, vol.3, no.2, 1969; chapter 1 in this volume.

21. Bernard Coard, *How the West Indian Child is Made Educationally Sub-normal in the British School System*, London, New Beacon Books, 1971.

22. Committee of Inquiry into the Education of Children from Ethnic Minority Groups, *Interim Report: West Indian Children in our Schools*, London, HMSO, 1981, p.12.

23. Center for Research on Criminal Justice, *The Iron Fist and the Velvet Glove: An Analysis of the US Police Force*, Berkeley, Center for Research on Criminal Justice, 1975, p.7.

24. Ibid., p.30.

25. Since the July uprisings in Britain, the Kerner Commission has been frequently cited politicians and the media as a source of ready-made solutions.

26. Kerner Commission, op.cit., p.336, and see also ch.12.

27. Center for Research on Criminal Justice, op.cit., p.32.

28. Kerner Commission, op.cit., p.315.

29. Ibid., p.318.

30. Pat Bryant, 'Justice vs. the movement', *Radical America*, vol.14, no.6, 1980.

31. Center for Research on Criminal Justice, op.cit., p.58.

32. Robert Allen, *Black Awakening in Capitalist America: An Analytic History*, Garden City, Anchor Books, 1969, pp.144, 147-8; Jon Frappier, 'Chase Goes to Harlem: Financing Black Capitalism', *Monthly Review*, vol.28, no.11, 1977.

33. Sivanandan, op.cit.

34. Daniel Moynihan, *The Negro Family: The Case for National Action*, 1965, in L. Rainwater and W. Yancy eds, *The Moynihan Report and the Politics of Controversy*, Cambridge, MA, and London, MIT Press, 1967.

35. E. Banfield, *The Unheavenly City*, Boston, Little Brown, 1990.

36. 'Will Whitelaw Pick a Dud?', *Daily Telegraph*, 27 July 1981.

37. See Jerry Hirsch, 'To "Unfrock the Charlatans" ', *Sage Race Relations Abstracts*, vol.6, no.2, 1981; Hilary Rose and Steven Rose, 'The IQ Myth', *Race and Class*, vol.XX, no.1, 1978.

38. Moynihan, op.cit.; Banfield, op.cit.; W. Shockley, 'A "Try Simplest Cases": Approach to the Heredity-Poverty-Crime Problem', *Proceedings of the National Academy of Sciences*, vol.57, 1967, pp.1767–74; A.R. Jensen, 'Reducing the Heredity-Environment Uncertainty', *Harvard Education Review*, vol.39, 1969, pp.449–83; R.J. Herrnstein, *I.Q. in the Meritocracy*, Boston, Atlantic/Little Brown, 1973; H.J. Eysenck, *Race, Intelligence and Education*, London, Temple Smith, 1971.

39. See City Bureau of Common Sense, 'Cities in crisis', *Radical Perspectives on the Economic Crisis of Monopoly Capitalism*, New York, Union for Radical Political Economies, 1975, p.158.
40. William Tabb, 'Civil Rights to Date: Now You Lose, Now You Lose', *Social Policy*, vol.10, no.3, 1979, p.48.
41. Ibid.
42. Frappier, op.cit., p.23.
43. Ibid., p.25.
44. See L. Kushnick, 'Racism and Class Consciousness in Modern Capitalism', in B. Bowser and R. Hunt, *The Impact of Racism on White Americans*, Beverley Hills and London, Sage Publications, 1981, pp.191–216
45. 'A Call to Action', *The Times*, 7 August 1981.
46. A. Sivanandan, 'Imperialism in the Silicon Age', London, *Race and Class*, pamphlet no.8, 1980, reprinted in A. Sivanandan, ed., *A Different Hunger*, London, Pluto Press, 1982, pp.143–200.
47. Ibid.
48. See David Edgar's 'Reagan's Hidden Agenda', *Race and Class*, vol.XXII, no.3, 1981, pp.221-38.
49. David Treadwell and Gaylord Shaw, 'Underclass: How One Family Copes', *Los Angeles Times*, 5 July 1981.
50. Ibid., and Richard E. Meyer and Mike Goodman, 'Marauders from Inner City Prey on LA's Suburbs', *Los Angeles Times*, 12 July 1981.
51. Meyer and Goodman, op.cit.
52. Ibid.

5 The United States: The Revocation of Civil Rights

This chapter first appeared in *Race and Class*, vol.32, no.1, 1990, published by the Institute of Race Relations. I would like to thank the Nuffield Foundation's Small Grants Scheme for the Social Sciences and the University of Manchester Committee on Staff Travel Funds for Research in the Humanities and Social Sciences for financial assistance.

1. One of the authors of the Fourteenth Amendment, Representative John A. Bingham, was 'later to admit that he had phrased it "word for word and syllable for syllable" to protect the rights of private property and corporations'. B.B. Ringer, *'We Are the People' and Others*, New York and London, Tavistock Publications, 1983, pp.217-18.
2. E.K. Hunt and H.J. Sherman, *Economics: An Introduction to Traditional and Radical Views*, 2nd edn, New York, Harper and Row, 1975, p.92.
3. A.P. Blaustein and R.L. Zangrando, eds, *Civil Rights and the Black American*, New York, Simon and Schuster, 1968, p.255.
4. Ringer, op.cit., p.220.
5. Ibid., p.221.
6. Ibid., p.223.
7. J.M. MacPherson, *The Negro's Civil War*, New York, Pantheon Books, 1965, p.300.
8. Where it could be shown that a set of employment practices had a differential impact on whites and blacks, the burden was on the employer to prove that these practices were justified on non-racial grounds.
9. See C. Ginsburg, *Race and the Media: The Enduring Life of the Moynihan Report*, New York, Institute for Media Analysis, 1989, pp.31–2.
10. See ibid.; *Education Week*, 30 March 1988; J. Kreiger, *Reagan, Thatcher and the Politics of Decline*, Cambridge, Polity Press, 1986, and D.H. Swinton 'Economic Status of Black Americans', National Urban League, *State of Black*

America 1, New York, 1989.
11. Interview with Frank Deale, 19 September 1989.
12. *New York Times*, 24 January 1989.
13. Ibid., 6 June 1989.
14. Ibid., 16 June and 23 June 1989.
15. D.R. Gordon, 'Last Hired ...' *The Nation*, vol.250, no.4, 29 January 1990.
16. *New York Times*, 24 June 1989.
17. Ibid., 7 August 1989.

6 Racism, the National Health Service, and the Health of Black People

This chapter first appeared in the *International Journal of Health Services*, vol.18, no.3, 1988. The author would like to thank Jackie Ould, Assistant Editor of Sage *Race Relations Abstracts*, and his colleagues at the Institute of Race Relations for their assistance, criticisms, and encouragement.
   1. B. Beverly, S. Dadzie and S. Scafe, *The Heart of the Race: Black Women's Lives in Britain*, London, Virago, 1985.
   2. P. Townsend and N. Davidson, eds, *Inequalities in Health: The Black Report*, Penguin Books, Harmondsworth, 1982, pp.58-60.
   3. J. Bourne, 'Cheerleaders and Ombudsmen: The Sociology of Race Relations', *Race and Class*, vol.21, no.4, Spring 1980, pp.331–52; Brent Community Health Council, *Black People and the Health Service*, London, Brent Community Health Council, April 1981; J. Donovan, *We Don't Buy Sickness, It Just Comes: Health, Illness and Health Care in the Lives of Black People in London*, Aldershot, Gower Publishing Co., 1986; M. Pearson, 'The Politics of Ethnic Minority Health Studies', *Radical Community Medicine*, 16, 1983, pp.34–44.
   4. S. Castles and G. Kosack, *Immigrant Workers and Class Structure in Western Europe*, 2nd Edition, Oxford University Press, Oxford, 1985; A. Sivanandan, *Race, Class and the State: The Black Experience in Britain*, reprinted in A. Sivanandan, ed., *A Different Hunger: Writings on Black Resistance*, London, Pluto Press, 1982, pp.106–26.
   5. Commission for Racial Equality, *Ethnic Minority Hospital Staff*, London, 1983.
   6. M. Anwar and A. Ali, *Overseas Doctors: Experience and Expectations. A Research Study*, Commission for Racial Equality, London, January 1987, p.73.
   7. Ibid., p.74.
   8. Ibid., p.75.
   9. Sir Raymond Hoffenberg, *The Health Service and Race*, London, Centre for Contemporary Studies, London, 1985.
  10. Ibid.
  11. S. Watkins, 'Racialism in the National Health Service', *Radical Community Medicine*, vol.16, 1983, pp.55–60.
  12. Ibid., pp.58–9.
  13. Hoffenberg, op.cit., p.5.
  14. Black Health Workers and Patients Group, *Bulletin no.1*, London, November 1981, pp.7–8.
  15. L. Doyal et al., with the support of N. Parry, *Migrant Workers in the National Health Service: Report of a Preliminary Survey*, Polytechnic of North London, Department of Sociology, London, June 1980.
  16. A. McNaught, *Race and Health Care in the United Kingdom*, Occasional Papers in Health Service Administration, Centre for Health Service Management Studies, Polytechnic of the South Bank, London, 1984.
  17. Ibid.
  18. Greater London Council Health Panel, *Ethnic Minorities and the National Health Service in London*, London, 1985.

19. P. Townsend and N. Davidson, eds, *Inequalities in Health: The Black Report*, Harmondsworth, Penguin Books, 1982, pp.58–60.
20. M. Whitehead, *The Health Divide: Inequalities in Health in the 1980s*, London, Health Education Council, March 1987, p.1.
21. A. McNaught, *Race and Health Care in the United Kingdom*, Occasional Papers in Health Service Administration, London, Centre for Health Service Management Studies, Polytechnic of the South Bank, 1984, p.26; see also M. Whitehead, *The Health Divide: Inequalities in Health in the 1980s*, London, Health Education Council, March 1987, pp.30–4.
22. *Guardian*, London, 8 November 1985.
23. M. Whitehead, op.cit., p.34.
24. Greater London Council Health Panel, op.cit., p.5.
25. Ibid., p.11.
26. N.P. Torkington, *The Racial Politics of Health — A Liverpool Profile*, Merseyside Area Profile Group, Liverpool, Department of Sociology, University of Liverpool, May 1983.
27. Ibid., pp.26–8.
28. C. Brown, *Black and White Britain: The Third PSI Survey*, London, Heinemann, 1984, p.256.
29. Greater London Council Health Panel, *Mental Health Services in London*, London, 1985, pp.18–19.
30. Hoffenberg, op.cit., p.8.
31. Brent Community Health Council, op.cit., p.13.
32. A. Henley, *Asian Patients in Hospital and at Home*, Oxford, Oxford University Press, 1982.
33. Brent Community Health Council, op.cit., p.14.
34. Torkington, op.cit., p.64.
35. A. Oakley and A. MacFarlane, 'A Poor Birth Right', *New Society*, vol.53, no.923, 24 July 1980, pp.172–3.
36. Ibid., p.173.
37. Greater London Council Health Panel, *Ethnic Minorities*, op.cit., p.13.
38. Ibid.
39. SUS refers to that part of a law dating from 1834 that makes it a criminal offence to be a suspicious person loitering with intent to commit a crime. This had been widely used against Afro-Caribbean youths; a major community campaign was conducted against it.
40. Brent Community Health Council, op.cit., p.18.
41. Greater London Council Health Panel, *Ethnic Minorities and the National Health Service in London*, London, 1985, p.6.
42. U. Prashar, E. Anionwu and M. Brozzovic, *Sickle Cell Anaemia-Who Cares? A Survey of Screening and Counselling Facilities in England*, The Runnymede Trust, London, 1985, p.38.
43. P. Foot, *Immigration and Race in British Politics*, Harmondsworth, Penguin Books, 1965, p.168.
44. Ibid., p.169.
45. *Pulse*, vol.41, no.6, 7 February 1981.
46. *Guardian*, London, 17 March 1980.
47. P. Gordon and A. Newnham, *Passport to Benefits? Racism in Social Security*, London, Child Poverty Action Group and The Runnymede Trust, 1985, pp.68–9; P. Gordon, *Policing Immigration: Britain's Internal Controls*, London, Pluto Press, 1985, pp.77–83.
48. Manchester Law Centre, *From Ill Treatment to No Treatment*, Law Centre Immigration Handbook no.6, Manchester, Manchester Law Centre, 1982, p.20.
49. Beverly, Dadzie and Scafe, op.cit., 1985, p.46.

7 The Political Economy of White Racism in Great Britain

This chapter was first published as Occasional Paper no.34, 1996 for the William Monroe Trotter Institute, University of Massachusetts. It was made possible by generous financial support from The Faculty of Arts, The University of Manchester; from the University of Manchester fund for Staff Travel for Research in the Humanities and Social Sciences; and from the Small Grants Scheme in the Social Sciences of the Nuffield Foundation. I would like to thank James Jennings and Gemima Remy and their colleagues at the William Monroe Trotter Institute; A. Sivanandan and my colleagues at the Institute of Race Relations for their years of dedicated and principled anti-racist practice; and Huw Beynon, Simon Katznellenbogen and Patricia Kushnick for their contributions and support.

1. W.E.B. Du Bois, *Black Reconstruction in America*, London, Frank Cass, 1966, p.30.
2. E. Williams, *Capitalism and Slavery*, London, André Deutsch, 1967. For a discussion on the role slavery and the economic system based on slavery had in funding the development of the New England economic system, see R. Bailey, 'The Slavery Trade and the development of Capitalism in the United States: The Textile Industry in New England', *Social Science History*, vol.14, no.3, 1990, pp.373–414.
3. J. Pope-Hennessy, *Sins of the Fathers: The Atlantic Slave Traders, 1441-1807*, London, Sphere, 1970, p.155.
4. Leo Huberman, *Man's Worldly Goods*, Monthly Review Press, New York and London, 1968, p.167.
5. P.Fryer, *Staying Power*, London, Pluto Press, 1984.
6. R. Drinnon, *Facing West*, New York, Schocken, 1980.
7. For a discussion on anti-Irish racism, see M. Hechter, *Internal Colonialism: The Celtic Fringe in British National Development, 1536-1966*, London, Routledge and Kegan Paul, 1975. Also see, M. Rai, 'Columbus in Ireland', *Race and Class*, vol.34, no.4, 1993, pp.25–34; and B. Rolston, 'The Training Ground: Ireland, Conquest and Colonization', *Race and Class*, vol.34, no.4, 1993, pp.13–24. For a discussion on anti-African racism, see P. Fryer, *Staying Power*, op.cit.
8. J. Foster, 'Nineteenth-Century Towns: A Class Dimension', in M.W. Flinn and T.C. Smout, eds, *Essays in Social History*, Oxford, Clarendon Press, 1974.
9. Ibid.
10. Richard Cobden, quoted in A. Briggs, 'The Language of "Class" in Early Nineteenth-Century England', in M.W. Flinn and T.C. Smout, eds, *Essays in Social History*, Oxford, Clarendon Press, 1974.
11. The London Working Men's Association, quoted in A. Briggs, op.cit.
12. W. Woodruff, 'The Emergence of an International Economy, 1700-1914', in C.M. Cipolla, ed., *The Fontana Economic History of Europe: The Emergence of Industrial Societies*, Part 2, London, Collins Fontana, 1973.
13. L.E. Davis, and R.A. Huttenback, *Mammon and the Pursuit of Empire: The Political Economy of British Imperialism, 1860-1912*, Cambridge, Cambridge University Press, 1986.
14. E. Hobsbawm, *Industry and Empire*, Harmondsworth, Penguin Books, 1968.
15. Ibid., pp.154-71.
16. M. Ellison, *Support for Secession: Lancashire and the American Civil War*, Chicago: University of Chicago Press, 1972.
17. V.G. Kiernan, *The Lords of Human Kind: European Attitudes Towards the Outside World in the Imperial Age*, London, Weidenfeld and Nicolson, 1969, pp.28-9.
18. P. Horn, 'Print Imperials', *Times Educational Supplement*, 1987, vol.3707, no.19, p.19.

19. Ibid.
20. J.A. Mangan, 'Images for Confident Control: Stereotypes in Imperial Discourse', in J.A. Mangan, ed., *The Imperial Curriculum*, London, Routledge, 1993, pp.6-22.
21. The Empire Day Movement was formed by Meath in 1903. Its first public celebrations were on 24 May 1904, which was also Queen Victoria's birthday. Government support came during World War I when there was general public enthusiasm. Support waned in the interior years but was revived by World War II. Interest waned in the post-war period and began to decline by 1959 when it became Commonwealth Day. J.M. MacKenzie, '"In Touch with the Infinite": The BBC and the Empire, 1923-53', in J.M. MacKenzie, ed, *Imperialism and Popular Culture*, Manchester, Manchester University Press, 1986, pp.168–81.
22. P. Horn, "Children of the Empire", *Times Educational Supplement*, vol.3648, no.19, 1986, p.19.
23. Roberts, quoted in Horn, ibid.
24. J.M. MacKenzie, *Propaganda and Empire*, Manchester, Manchester University Press, 1984, p.45.
25. K. Marx and F. Engels, *On Britain*, 2nd edn, Moscow, Foreign Languages Publishing House, 1962, pp.551, 552.
26. D. Nandy, 'Foreword', in J. McNeal and M. Rogers, eds, *The Multi-Racial School*, New York, Viking, 1971.
27. R. May and R. Cohen, 'The Interaction Between Race and Colonialism: A Case Study of the Liverpool Race Riots of 1919', *Race and Class*, vol.16, no.2, 1974, pp.111–26. Also see, Fryer, op.cit.; and N. Evans, 'Across the Universe: Racial Violence and the Post-War Crisis in Imperial Britain, 1919-25', *Immigrants and Minorities*, vol.13, nos 2 and 3, 1994, pp.59-88.
28. D. Byrne, 'The 1930 Arab Riot in South Shields', *Race and Class*, 1977, vol.18, no.3, pp.261–77. Also see, D. Byrne, 'Class, Race and Nation: The Politics of the "Arab Issue" in South Shields, 1919-39', *Immigrants and Minorities*, vol.13, nos 2 and 3, 1994, pp.89–104.
29. House of Commons, 4 December 1934, 1458.
30. N. Evans, op.cit.
31. See A. Sivanandan, 'Race, Class and the State', in A. Sivanandan, ed, *A Different Hunger*, London, Pluto Press, 1990, pp.101–25. Also see, L. Kushnick, 'Racism, the National Health Service and the Health of Black People', *International Journal of Health Services*, vol.18, no.3, 1988, pp.457–70; and C. Brown, *Black and White Britain: The Third PSI Survey*, London, Heinemann, 1984.
32. G. Smith, *When Jim Crow Met John Bull*, London, I.B. Tauris, 1987.
33. S. Joshi and B. Carter, 'The Role of Labour in the Creation of a Racist Britain', *Race and Class*, vol.25, no.3, 1984, pp.53–70. Also see, C. Harris, 'Configurations of Racism: The Civil Service, 1945-60', *Race and Class*, vol.33, no.1, 1991, pp.1–30.
34. Louis Kushnick, 'British Anti-Discrimination Legislation', in S. Abbott, ed, *The Prevention of Racial Discrimination in Britain*, Oxford, Oxford University Press for the United Nations Institute of Training and Research and the Institute of Race Relations, 1971, pp.223–68.
35. Fryer, op.cit., p.390.
36. J. Westegaard and H. Resler, *Class in a Capitalist Society: A Study of Contemporary Britain*, London, Heinemann Educational Books, 1975. Also see, P. Townsend and N. Davidson, eds, *Inequalities in Health: The Black Report*, Harmondsworth, Penguin Books, 1982; and C. Oppenheim, *Poverty: The Facts, Revised and Updated Edition*, London, Child Poverty Action Group, 1993.
37. Paul Foot, Immigration and Race in British Politics, Harmondsworth, Penguin Books, 1965.

38. See Louis Kushnick, 'Racism, the National Health Service and the Health of Black People', op.cit.
39. N. Murray, 'Anti-Racists and Other Demons: The Press and Ideology in Thatcher's Britain', *Race and Class*, vol.27, no.3, 1986, pp.1–20. Also see Searle, 'Your Daily Dose: Racism and the Sun', op.cit.
40. A. Sivanandan, 'A Different Hunger', op.cit., p.132.
41. See Murray, 'Anti-Racists and Other Demons', op.cit., and Searle, 'Your Daily Dose', op.cit.
42. *Daily Mail*, 7, 8, and 9 October, 1991.
43. Ibid.
44. *Daily Star*, 15 June 1991.
45. *Daily Star*, 25, 27 and 29 May 1991.
46. Searle, 'Your Daily Dose', op.cit.
47. *Daily Express*, 2, 7, 8 and 9 April 1992.
48. 'Paddy Puts Out the Welcome Mat for 4m from Hong Kong', *Daily Mail*, 7 April 1992.
49. 'Race and the Rapist: Cultural Differences are Behind Some Sex Attacks, says Expert', *Daily Mail*, 27 March 1992.
50. *Daily Mail* 7 April 1992.
51. Winston Churchill, MP, 28 May 1993, quoted in the *Daily Express*, 29 May 1993.
52. Paul Johnson, 'The Lying Game', *Daily Mail*, 13 February 1995.
53. See L. Fekete, 'Racist Violence: Meeting the New Challenges', *Race and Class*, vol.30, no.2, 1988, pp.71-6. Also see, N. Ginsburg, 'Racial Harassment Policy and Practice: The Denial of Citizenship', *Critical Social Policy*, vol.26, no.26, 1989, pp.66-81; Institute of Race Relations, *Policing Against Black People*, London, Institute of Race Relations (IRR), 1987; and K. Tompson, *Under Siege: Racism and Violence in Britain Today*, Harmondsworth, Penguin Books, 1988.
54. Home Office, *Racial Attacks: Report of Home Office Study*, London, HMSO, 1981.
55. Brown, op.cit.
56. Greater London Council, *Racial Harassment in London*, London, 1984.
57. Commission for Racial Equality, *Racial Attacks Survey of Eight Areas of Britain*, London, Commission for Racial Equality, 1987.
58. Sheffield Racial Harassment Project, *Because their Skin is Black*, Sheffield, Sheffield City Council, 1988.
59. Independent Committee of Inquiry into Racial Harassment, *Racial Harassment in Leeds 1985-6*, Leeds, Leeds Community Relations Council, 1987.
60. D. Walsh, *Racial Harassment in Glasgow*, Glasgow, Scottish Ethnic Minorities Research Unit, 1987.
61. G. Ford, *Fascist Europe: The Rise of Racism and Xenophobia*, London, Pluto Press, 1992.
62. R. Klein, 'Where Prejudice Still Flares in Violence', *Times Educational Supplement*, 6 January 1995, no.4097, p.9.
63. Home Affairs Committee, House of Commons, Session 1993-4, Third Report, *Racial Attacks*, vol.II, London, HMSO, 1994, 1.
64. Klein, op.cit.
65. *Guardian*, 14 March 1995.
66. See Louis Kushnick, 'Immigration and Asylum in the European Union', *Outsider*, no.42, April 1995, 3.
67. *Guardian*, 14 March 1995.
68. *Financial Times*, 8 March 1995.
69. *Financial Times*, 26 October 1995.
70. A similar process is in operation throughout Europe — see Kushnick 1995, op.cit.

71. *Guardian*, 20 March 1995.
72. J. Krieger, *Reagan, Thatcher and the Politics of Decline*, Cambridge, Polity Press, 1986.

8 Racism and Anti-Racism in Western Europe

This chapter first appeared in *Racism and Anti-racism in World Perspective*, Sage Publications, pp.181–202.

1. S.J. Gould, *The Mismeasure of Man*, New York, Norton, 1981. See also J.H. Stanfield, 'Racism in America and Other Race-centred Nation-states: Synchronic Considerations', *International Journal of Comparative Sociology*, vol.32, no.3-4, 1991, pp.243–61. H. Winant, and M. Omi, *Racial Formation in the United States: From the 1960s to the 1980s*, London, Routledge, 1986.
2. M. Hechter, *Internal Colonialism: The Celtic Fringe in British National Development, 1536-1966*, London, Routledge and Kegan Paul, 1975.
3. M. MacEwan and A. Prior, *Planning and Ethnic Minority Settlement in Europe: The Myth of Thresholds of Tolerance*, research Paper no.40, Edinburgh, Edinburgh College of Art/Heriot-Watt University School of Planning and Housing, 1992.
4. J.N. Pieterse, 'Myths and realities', *Race and Class*, vol.32 no.3, January-March 1991, pp.3–10.
5. A. Sivanandan, 'Editorial', *Race and Class*, vol.32, no.3, January-March 1991, pp.v-vi.
6. *Daily Mail*, 26 March 1992.
7. S. Castles and M.J. Miller, *The Age of Migration*, London, Macmillan, 1993. See also L.P. Moch, *Moving Europeans: Migration in Western Europe since 1650*, Bloomington, Indiana University Press, 1992; L. Potts *The World Labour Market: A History of Migration*, London, Zed Books, 1990.
8. G. Wallraff, *The Lowest of the Low*, London, Methuen, 1988.
9. J.P. Hollifield, *Immigrants, Markets and States: The Political Economy of Post-war Europe*, Cambridge, Harvard University Press, 1992.
10. E. Gaffiken and M. Morrisey, *The New Unemployed: Joblessness and Poverty in the Market Economy*, London, Zed Press, 1992. See also J. Michie and J.G. Smith, eds, *Unemployment in Europe*, London, Academic Press, 1994. See also J. Mitter, *Common Fate, Common Bond, Women in the Global Economy*, London, Pluto Press, 1986. See also S. Sassen, *The Mobility of Labour and Capital*, Cambridge, Cambridge University Press, 1988.
11. L. Fekete and F. Webber, *Inside Racist Europe*, London, Institute of Race Relations, 1994.
12. A. Sivanandan, 'Racism: The Road from Germany', *Race and Class*, vol.34, no.3, January-March 1993, pp.67–73.
13. A. Dummett, A. Nicol, *Subjects, Citizens, Aliens and Others: Nationality and Immigration Law*, London, Weidenfeld & Nicolson, 1990. See also P. Hainsworth, 'Introduction: The Cutting Edge: The Extreme Right in Post-war Western Europe and the USA' in P. Hainsworth, ed., *The Extreme Right in Europe and the USA*, London, Pinter, 1992. See also MacEwan and Prior, op.cit., 1992.
14. Refugee Forum and Migrant Rights Action Network, *The Walls of the Fortress: European Agreement against Immigrants, Migrants and Refugees*, London, Refugee Forum and Migrant Rights Action Network, 1991, p.16.
15. B. Carter, C. Harris and S. Joshi, *The 1951-55 Conservative Government and the Racialisation of Black Immigrants*, Policy Paper in Ethnic Relations, no.11, Coventry, University of Warwick, Centre for Research in Ethnic Relations, 1987. See also C. Harris, 'Configurations of Racism in the Civil Service', *Race and Class*, vol.33, no.1, July-September 1991, pp.1–30. See also S. Joshi and B. Carter, 'The

Role of Labour in the Creation of a Racist Britain, *Race and Class*, vol.25, no.3, winter 1984, pp.53–70.

16. *Guardian*, 2 March 1993.
17. S. Hall, C. Critcher, T. Jefferson, J. Clarke and B. Roberts, *Policing the Crisis: Mugging, the State, and Law and Order*, London, Macmillan, 1978. See also Institute of Race Relations. *Policing against Black People*, London, Institute of Race Relations, 1987. See also D.J. Smith, *Police and People in London*, 4 vols, London, Policy Studies Institute, 1983.
18. *Statewatch*, vol.3, no.2, March-April, 1993, p.3.
19. N. Rathzel, 'Germany: One Race, One Nation?', *Race and Class*, vol.32, no.3, pp.31–48.
20. Communities of Resistance Network, *Communities of Resistance*, first launch report, London, Communities of Resistance Network, 1992, p.11.
21. *Guardian*, 21 June 1991.
22. *Guardian*, 24 September 1991.
23. Hainsworth, op.cit., 1992.
24. *L'Humanité*, 17 February 1993. *Le Monde*, 18 February 1993.
25. *Le Monde*, 14 January 1993.
26. *L'Humanité*, 17 February 1993. Le Monde, 18 February 1993.
27. A. Simpson and M. Read, *Against a Rising Tide: Racism, Europe and 1992*, Nottingham, Spokesman Books, 1991, p.33.
28. F. Webber, 'From Ethnocentrism to Euro-racism', *Race and Class*, vol.32, no.3, January 1991, pp.11–18.
29. Rathzel, op.cit., p.38.
30. Ibid.
31. T. Bunyan, 'Toward an Authoritarian European State', *Race and Class*, vol.32, no.3, January-March 1991, pp.19–30. See also M. Baldwin-Edwards, 'Immigration after 1992', *Policy and Politics*, vol.19, no.3, 1991, pp.199–211. See also A. Cruz, *An Insight into Schengen, TREVI and other European Intergovernmental Bodies*, Briefing Paper no.1, 2nd edn, Brussels, Churches Committee for Migrants in Europe, 1991. See also Refugee Forum and the Migrants Rights Action Network, op.cit., 1991. See also M. Spencer, *1992 and All That: Civil Liberties in the Balance*, London, Civil Liberties Trust, 1990.
32. A. Sivanandan, *A Different Hunger*, London, Pluto Press, 1982. See also A. Sivanandan, *Communities of Resistance*, London, Verso, 1990.
33. Amnesty International, *Europe: Human Rights and the Need for a Fair Asylum Policy*, Geneva, Amnesty International, 1991.
34. Organisation for Economic Co-operation and Development, *SOPEMI: Trends in International Migration*, Paris, Organisation for Economic Co-operation and Development, 1992, p.13.
35. J. Toporowski, 'Fascist Spectre Looms over Stagnant Europe', *Observer*, 27 September 1992, p.24.
36. *Independent on Sunday*, Business Section, 10 January 1993.
37. J. Krieger, *Reagan, Thatcher and the Politics of Decline*, Cambridge, Polity Press, 1986.
38. *Searchlight*, May 1992, p.18.
39. Ibid., p.15.
40. *Independent*, 21 March 1993.
41. *Searchlight*, November 1994, p.21.
42. *Guardian*, 27 May 1993.
43. G. Ford, *Fascist Europe: The Rise of Racism and Xenophobia*, London, Pluto Press, 1992.
44. House of Commons, Home Affairs Committee, *Third Report: Racial Attacks and Harassment*, vol.III, London, House of Commons, 1994.

45. R. Klein, 'Where Prejudice Still Flares into Violence', *Times Educational Supplement*, no.4097, 6 January 1995, p.9. For a general discussion of racial violence, see C. Brown, *Black and White Britain: The Third PSI Survey*, London, Heinemann, 1984. Commission for Racial Equality, *Racial Attacks - Survey of Eight Areas of Britain*, London, Commission for Racial Equality, 1987. J. Cooper and T. Qureshi, *Through Patterns not our Own*, London, New Ethnicities Research and Education Group, 1993. L. Fekete, 'Racist Violence: Meeting the New Challenges', *Race and Class*, vol.30 no.2, 1988, pp.71-6, N. Ginsburg, 'Racial Harassment Policy and Practice: The Denial of Citizenship', *Critical Social Policy*, 26(26), 1989, pp.66–81. Greater London Council, *Racial Harassment in London*, London, London Commission for Racial Equality, 1984. Independent Committee of Inquiry into Racial Harassment, *Racial Harassment in Leeds, 1985-6*, Leeds, Leeds Community Relations Council/Institute of Race Relations, 1987. London Borough of Waltham Forest, *Beneath the Surface: An Inquiry into Racial Harassment in the London Borough of Waltham Forest*, London, London Borough of Waltham Forest, 1990. Sheffield Racial Harassment Project, *Because their Skin is Black*, Sheffield, Sheffield City Council, 1988. K. Tompson, *Under Siege: Racism and Violence in Britain Today*, Harmondsworth, Penguin, 1988. D. Walsh, *Racial Harassment in Glasgow*, Glasgow, Scottish Ethnic Minorities Research Unit, 1987.

46. L. Kushnick, 'Racism and Class Consciousness in Modern Capitalism', in B.P. Bowser and R.G. Hunt, eds, *Impacts of Racism on White Americans*, Beverly Hills, Sage, 1981, pp.191-216. See also L. Kushnick, 'Political Economy of White Racism in the United States and Great Britain' in B.P. Bowser ed., *Impacts of Racism on White Americans*, 2nd edn, Thousand Oaks, Sage, 1996.

47. *Campaign Against Racism and Fascism* (CARF), no.6, Jan./Feb. 1992, p.4.

48. Sivanandan, op.cit, 1993, p.69.

49. Reprinted in the *Guardian*, 5 February 1993.

50. CARF, no.2, April/May 1991, p.12.

51. CARF, no.8, May/June 1992, p.15.

9 The Political Economy of White Racism in the United States

This chapter first appeared in *Impacts of Racism on White Americans*, 2nd edition, ed. B.P. Bowser, Sage Publications, pp.48–67, 1996. Reprinted by permission of Sage Publications Inc.

1. E.J. Cornacchia and D.C. Nelson, 'Historical Differences in the Political Experiences of American Blacks and White Ethnics: Revisiting an Unresolved Controversy', *Ethnic and Racial Studies*, vol.15, no.1, 1992, pp.102–24. See also P. Horton, 'Testing the Limits of Class Politics in Postbellum Alabama: Agrarian Radicalism in Lawrence County', *Journal of Southern History*, vol.57, no.1, 1991, pp.63–84. J.H. Stanfield, 'Racism in America and Other Race-Centered Nation-States: Synchronic Considerations', *International Journal of Comparative Sociology*, vol.32, nos 3–4, 1991, pp.243–61.

2. L. Kushnick, 'Racism and Anti-Racism in Western Europe', in B.P. Bowser, ed., *Racism and Anti-Racism in World Perspectives*, Thousand Oaks and London, Sage Publications, 1995; chapter 8 in this volume. See also M. Marable 'Race and Class in the US Presidential Election', *Race and Class*, vol.34 no.3, January-March 1993, pp.75–85.

3. L. Kushnick 'Parameters of British and North American Racism', *Race and Class*, vol.23, nos 2–3, 1981–2, pp.187–206; chapter 4 in this volume.

4. W.E.B. DuBois, *Black Reconstruction in America*, London, Frank Cass, 1966, p.30.

5. H. Aptheker, 'Anti-Racism in the US: An Introduction', *Sage Race Relations Abstracts*, vol.12, no.4, November 1987, pp.3–32.

6. R. Bailey, 'The Slavery Trade and the Development of Capitalism in the United States: The Textile Industry in New England', *Social Science History*, vol.14, no.3, 1990, pp.373–414. See also E. Williams, *Capitalism and Slavery*, London, André Deutsch, 1967.

7. T. Allen, 'They Would Have Destroyed Me: Slavery and the Origins of Racism', *Radical America*, vol.9, no.3, 1975, p.42.

8. R. Drinnon, *Facing West*, New York, Schocken, 1980; see also B.B. Ringer, *We the People and Others*, New York, Norton, 1983; D.R. Roediger, *The Wages of Whiteness: Race and the Making of the American Working Class*, London, Verso, 1991; A. Saxton, *The Rise and Fall of the White Republic: Class Politics and Mass Culture in Nineteenth-Century America*, London, Verso, 1991; R.T. Takaki, *Iron Cages: Race and Culture in Nineteenth-Century America*, London, Athlone, 1980.

9. Du Bois, op.cit., pp.633–4.

10. Roediger, op.cit., 1991 pp.13, 14.

11. Ibid.

12. N. Glazer, 'Blacks and White Ethnics: The Difference and the Political Difference It Makes', *Social Problems*, vol.18, 1971. pp.444–61.

13. Cornacchia and Nelson, op.cit., p.103.

14. Ibid., p.120.

15. Du Bois, op.cit., pp.700-01; See also I. Katznelson and M. Weir, *Schooling for All: Class, Race and the Decline of the Democratic Ideal*, New York, Basic Books, 1985.

16. Aptheker, op.cit.

17. Saxton, op.cit.

18. Roediger, op.cit.

19. Du Bois, op.cit.

20. M. Davis, *Prisoners of the American Dream*, London, Verso, 1980.

21. Takaki, op.cit., p.238.

22. Ibid., p.239.

23. Horton, op.cit., p.65.

24. Ibid, pp.76, 77.

25. Ibid, p.83.

26. H. Braverman, *Labor and Monopoly Capital*, New York, Monthly Review Press, 1974.

27. A. Saxton, 'Race and the House of Labor', in G. Nash and R. Weiss, eds, *The Great Fear: Race in the Mind of Americans*, New York, Holt, Rinehart and Winston, 1970, p.115.

28. D. Noble, *America by Design*, Oxford, Oxford University Press, 1977.

29. W. Tuttle, *Race Riot, Chicago in the Red Summer of 1977*, Urbana, University of Illinois Press. See also S. Vittoz, 'World War I and the Political Accommodation of Transitional Market Forces: The Case of Immigration Restrictions', *Politics and Society*, vol.8, 1978, pp.49–78.

30. G. Gilder, *Wealth and Poverty*, New York, Bantam Books, 1982. See also C. Murray, *Losing Ground: American Social Policy 1950–1980*, New York, Basic Books, 1986. For a critique of these see T. Boston, *Race, Class and Conservatism*, Boston and London, Unwin Hyman, 1988. See also A. Reed, 'The Underclass as Myth and Symbol: The Poverty of Discourse about Poverty', *Radical America*, vol.24, no.1, 1992, pp.21–40.

31. L. Kushnick, 'Race, Class and Civil Rights', in A. Zegeye, L. Harris, J. Maxted, eds, *Exploitation and Exclusion: Race and Class in Contemporary US Society*, 1991, pp.158-9. Oxford, Hans Zell. Chapter 2 in this volume. See also M. Marable, *Race, Reform and Rebellion*, 2nd edition, London, Macmillan, 1991.

32. A. Hirsch, *Making the Second Ghetto: Race and Housing in Chicago*, Cambridge and New York, Cambridge University Press, 1983.

33. S. Bowles, D. Gordon and H. Gintis, *Beyond the Waste Land*, Garden City, Anchor Books, 1984.
34. A. Sivanandan, *A Different Hunger*, London, Pluto Press, 1990.
35. M. Marable, op.cit, 1993, p.76.
36. M. Mauer, *Young Black Men and the Criminal Justice System: A Growing National Problem*, Washington, DC, The Sentencing Project, 1990. See also C. Shine and M. Mauer, *Does the Punishment Fit the Crime? Drug Users and Drunk Drivers, Questions of Race and Class*, Washington, DC, The Sentencing Project, 1993.

Index

Ad Hoc Group on Immigration (European Union) 192
Adler, Leslie 62, 64, 229, 230
Advertiser (US) 13, 213
AFDC, Aid for Families with Dependent Children 10
Affirmative action 14, 20, 108, 113, 141–2, 144
Africa 3, 4, 5, 6, 67, 68, 69, 160, 166, 167, 176, 181
African National Congress (ANC) 69
African-Americans 9, 14–15, 19–20, 23, 46, 48, 50, 52, 138–9, 214, 219–20, 223
Afro-Caribbeans 10, 79–82, 104, 117–18, 121, 128, 131, 158-9, 174, 183, 187, 189, 235
Agricultural Adjustment Act (AAA) 49
Ahmad, W.I.U. 226
Alabama 66, 67, 75, 144, 212, 225, 241
Ali, A. 234
Alien's Restriction Order (Coloured Seamen), 1925 (UK) 173
Alkalimat, A. 228
Allen, R. 232
Allen, S. 16, 225
Allen, T. 241
Ambulance service (UK) 151
American Creed 53
American Federation of Labor 64, 214, 215, 216
American Federationist 215

American National School Board Association 27
Amnesty International 12, 194, 240
Ancillary Workers' Strikes (UK) 164
Anionwu, E. 235
Ante-natal provisions (UK) 156, 157
Anti-Communism 58, 59, 68, 69, 70, 71, 72, 77; and NAACP 58, 59, 68, 69, 70; and SNCC refusal to co-operate with 71, 72
Anti-discrimination legislation: assumptions underlying 81–2, 87, 92, 96–7, 102, 111; attitudes of trades unions 85, 99–100, 102, 105; declaratory nature 81, 102, 111; enforcement provisions 83, 87-97, 99–103, 106-10, 112-13; and Labour Party 79, 85, 86, 88; opposition to 88-9, 99–101, 103; relationship to immigration restriction 86; support for 87, 98-9, 104; in UK 21, 79–113, 175; in US 60, 110, 138, 144–5, 219
Anti-slavery movement 5, 167, 171, 208–09
Anti-war movement 48, 125, 127
Anwar, M. 234
Apartheid: American and housing 8, 15, 57, 225; Southern system of Jim Crow 49, 58, 138, 140, 213, 219; in UK labour market 151; used as argument against anti-discrimination legislation 89
Aptheker, Herbert 208, 225, 241, 242

Arab workers (UK) 173
Article 116 of the German
  Constitution 188, 199, 201
Asians in UK 10, 98, 153, 155, 159,
  161, 175, 178, 183, 187
Association of Jewish Ex-Servicemen
  and Women (UK) 88
Asylum Bill 1991 12
Asylum-seekers 11, 13, 15, 176, 179,
  180, 184, 185, 186, 189, 193, 194,
  197, 198
Attorney General's List of Subversive
  Organizations (US) 63
Attorney General (UK) 91, 92, 95, 99,
  110
Australia 183

Babcock's Valuation of Real Estate 8
Bacon's Rebellion 205
Baden Wurttemberg (Germany) 196
Bailey, R. 4, 224, 236, 241
Bair, B. 228
Baker, Alfred 60
Baker, Kenneth 11, 13, 177
Balbus, I. D. 231
Baldwin, J. 231
Baldwin-Edwards, M. 240
Balladur, Edouard (Prime Minister,
  France) 199
Banfield, Edward 129, 232
Bangladeshis in UK 153-4
Bank Street College of Education 39,
  227
Beale, Dr Norman 152
Beaumont, Texas 61
Beishon, S. 226
Belgium 12, 183, 187, 201
'Benign Neglect' 141
Bernstein, Victor 60, 61, 229
Beverly, B. 234, 235
Bindman, G. 231
Bingham, Representative J.A. 233
Birmingham (Alabama) 26, 67, 75,
  144
Birmingham (UK) 81, 230
Birmingham *Evening Mail* (UK) 230
Black capitalism 129–31, 232
Black children: in UK 123, 164; in US
  28-32, 36, 38, 66, 122-3
Black Health Workers and Patients
  Group (UK) 234
Black militancy 53, 73, 143
Black Nationalism 32, 50, 228

Black Panther Party (US) 119, 127
Black parents: in UK 123; in US 30,
  32, 37, 45, 66
Black People and the Health Service,
  Brent Council Report 155, 234, 235
Black Power 26, 40, 228
Black Report, The 148, 151, 234, 235,
  237
Blackmun, Justice Harry 144
Blaming the Victim 19, 48, 122, 134,
  155, 190
Blom-Cooper, Louis 89
Bloom, Jack 51, 55, 228, 229
Blumber, A.S. 231
Board of Deputies of British Jews 88
Board of Education (New York) 29,
  33, 34, 35, 43, 44, 45
Board of Examiners (New York) 44
Boer War 170
Bonham-Carter, Mark (Chair of Race
  Relations Board) UK 95
Boston, T. 242
Bourne, J. 234
Bowles, S. 242
Bowser, B. P. 228, 241
Boyer, R.O. 63, 229
Boyle, Sir Edward, MP 104
Bradley, Tom 135
Brauer, Carl 67
Braverman, H. 242
Brennan, Justice 145
Brent Community Health Council 155,
  234, 235
Briggs, A. 225, 236
British Refugee Council 12
Brixton 21, 22, 117, 120, 121, 132,
  231
Brockway, Fenner, MP 85, 86, 175
Bronx (New York) 30, 37
Brooke, Henry, MP (Home Secretary)
  88, 89
Brooke, Senator Edward 70
Brooklyn (New York) 27, 29, 33, 34
*Brown v. Board of Education of
  Topeka*: 18, 55, 58, 65, 66, 146; and
  Brown II 66
Brown, C. 235, 237, 238, 240
Brozzovic, M. 235
Bruges 6
Bryant, P. 232
Bunche, Ralph 70
Bundy, McGeorge 33, 36, 38
Bunyan, Tony 192, 240

Burger, Chief Justice Warren 140
Burrell, Berkely G. 131
Bush, George 11, 14, 22, 142, 221
Byrne, D. 237
Byrnes, James F. 60

Calhoun, L. 227
Callaghan, James, MP (Home
    Secretary, later Prime Minister) 81,
    97, 108
Campaign Against Racial
    Discrimination (CARD) 87, 98
Campaign Against Racism and
    Fascism 198, 201
Canny, Nicholas 2
Capitalism 1, 4, 22, 69, 78, 115,
    129–31, 165, 167, 170, 175, 186,
    195, 202, 204, 209, 217–18, 224,
    228, 232-3, 236-7, 241
Cardiff, Wales (UK) 173
Carey, George 12
CARF 198, 201, 257
Carleton, D.E. 62, 229
Carmichael, Stokely 72, 75
Carnegie Foundation 215
Carson, C. 230
Carter, B. 237, 239
Castles, S. 234, 239
Caute, D. 229
Center for Constitutional Rights 143
Center for Research on Criminal
    Justice (US) 125, 232
Chamber of Commerce 62
Chapman, Donald, MP 92, 93
Chartists 169
Cheng, Charles W, 64, 70, 229, 230
Chicago: and 1919 race riot 46, 242;
    and Great Migration 50; and
    institutional racism 50, 219, 220;
    and Second Ghetto 219, 220, 225;
    and post-Civil Rights Movement
    mobilisation 76; and Black Panther
    Party 127; and political repression
    127; and images of welfare mothers
    134
Chirac, Jacques (President, France)
    190
Christian Democratic Party (Germany)
    16, 197
Churches Committee for Migrants in
    Europe (Belgium) 201, 240
Churchill, Winston MP (Prime
    Minister) 3

Churchill, Winston MP (grandson)
    177, 251
Cipolla, C.M. 236
City Bureau of Common Sense 232
Civil Rights: Act 1866 45; 1875 138;
    1964 75; Cases 1875 138;
    Legislation and attacks upon gains
    143, 146
Civil Rights Movement: and anti-
    Communism 19, 47, 63, 65, 70, 72;
    as a catalyst for other change-
    oriented groups 48, 125, 140;
    corporate sector and 49, 55, 219; *de
    jure* segregation and 46, 217, 220;
    economic status of blacks and 75,
    77, 127, 140, 233; funding of 72,
    230; liberals and 26, 28, 55, 74–5,
    217; non-violent direct action and
    67, 75, 77; and opposition to the
    Vietnam War 70, 125; relations with
    whites 26, 29, 42-3, 72;
    shortcomings of 75–6, 130, 136,
    140, 233; successes of 75, 130, 136,
    140, 217, 220, 233; US Government
    and 29, 57, 67, 74–5, 125–6, 136,
    140, 143–6, 208, 219
Civil War (US): 136, 139, 207, 209;
    post-Civil War period and class
    consciousness 210, 212
Clark, Jim 56
Clark, Kenneth 227
Clark, Mark (Black Panther Party)
    127
Clark, Wayne 61, 229
Clarke, J. 231, 239
Cluster, D. 228
Coard, B. 232
Cobden, R. 6, 236
Cohen, O. 227
Cohen, R. 237
COINTELPRO (FBI's counter-
    insurgency programme) (US) 127
Cold War: and corporate power 10;
    and anti-Communist purges 47, 57,
    59, 60, 63, 65, 70, 71, 77, 229, 230;
    and Civil Rights Movement 47, 63,
    65, 70, 71, 77, 229, 230; liberalism
    70, 71; and national security state
    65; and permanent war-time
    economy 57, 142, 220; and racism
    60, 63
Commission for Racial Equality (UK)
    12, 23, 128, 149, 161, 178, 226,

234, 238, 240–1
Committee of Inquiry into the
  Education of Children from Ethnic
  Minority Groups 232
Committee on Civil Rights (Truman
  Administration) 57
Commonwealth Immigrants Act 1962
  79, 86
Communist Party (USA) 16, 50, 53,
  218
Communist Party (France) 187
Community Control of Education 28,
  34, 36, 38, 123
Community Relations Service
  (Department of Justice, US) 126,
  134
Community Relations Commission
  (UK) 128; local community relations
  committees, 128
Comsymps 58
Confederation of British Industry
  (CBI) (UK) 99, 100, 102, 107
Confederation of Health Service
  Unions 161
Congress of Racial Equality (CORE)
  70, 74, 127
Connor, Bull 56
Conservative Party (UK) 11, 13, 77,
  79, 105, 177; *see also* Anti-
  discrimination legislation;
  Conservative Government
Constantine, Sir Learie 95
Constitutional Convention, 178, 205
Cooper, Dr Peter 161, 235
Cooper, J. 240
Cornacchia, E. J. 207, 226, 241
Council of Supervisory Associations
  (New York) 33
Council on African Affairs 69
Cresson, Edith (Prime Minister,
  France) 190
Critcher, C. 231, 239
Crocker, Charles 211
Crow, Jim 19, 48–50, 56, 58, 60,
  76–7, 140, 213–14, 218, 237
Cruz, A. 240
Cuba 215
'Cultural deprivation' 123

Dadzie, S. 234, 235
Daily Express (UK) 12, 177, 238
Daily Mail (UK) 12, 176–8, 238–9
Daily Star (UK) 12, 176, 238

Daily Telegraph (UK) 129, 227, 230,
  232
Darby, Henry 70, 230
Davidson, N. 234, 235, 237
Davis, L.E. 236
Davis, M. 225, 242
De jure segregation 9, 18–19, 46,
  48–50, 54–6, 60, 75, 122, 140, 213,
  217–19
Deakin, Nicholas 98
Deale, Frank 143
Debs, Eugene 61
Decentralisation: of police control
  127; of schools (New York) 17, 26,
  28, 30, 33, 34, 35, 36, 37, 38, 39,
  40, 41, 42, 43, 44; *see also*
  Community control; United
  Federation of Teachers; Whites
Democratic National Convention,
  1964 72
Democratic Party (US): and Civil
  Rights Movement 55; and
  Mississippi Freedom Democratic
  Party 72; and Solid South 212, 213,
  221
Denmark 200
Denton, N.A. 8, 9, 225
Department of Employment and
  Productivity (UK) 100
Department of Health and Social
  Security (DHSS) (UK) 155, 161, 163
Dependency 10, 141–2, 206, 218, 222
Depo-Provera 158
Der Spiegel (Germany) 197
D'Estaing, Valéry Giscard (President,
  France) 190
Detroit and Great Migration 50; and
  institutional racism 50; and urban
  uprisings 120
Deutsche Volksunion (DVU)
  (Germany) 196, 197
Die Zeit (Germany) 192
Discrimination: in US 7, 9, 14, 41, 52,
  55–7, 138, 140, 144, 207, 219; in
  UK 20, 23–4, 80–1, 83–4, 88–90,
  93, 96, 98, 101–03, 149–50, 163
Dodd, Edward H., Jr 59
Donovan, J. 234
Douglass, Frederick 139
Doyal, L. 234
Driberg, Tom, MP 175
Drinnon, R. 225, 236, 241
DuBois, Dr W.E.B.: 1, 52, 58–9,

68–70, 76–8, 218, 228–9, 241; and class divisions within black community 76–7; and CNNCP 52, 58; and March on Washington 76; and support for African independence 69–70; and need for fundamental economic restructuring 77–8, 218; and critique of petit bourgeois leaders of black community 69; and anti-Communist purges 68–70
Duker, Abraham G. 227
Dummett, A. 239
Dunbar, A. 63, 229
Dutch Federation of Anti-Discrimination Centres (the Netherlands) 201
Duval-Smith, A. 226

Early Years Trainers Anti-Racist Network (UK) 201
East Harlem (New York) 33, 34, 44
Edgar, D. 233
Education and the European Union 199
Education in UK: and anti-discrimination legislation 83, 95; and black demands 123, 162; and class inequalities 160, 175, 182, 199; and inner cities 83, 189; racially differential outcomes 123–4, 189; and racism in 23–4, 123–4, 128, 160, 182, 184, 189, 232; and racist curricula 6, 123, 169–72, 237
Education in US: and black demands 18, 26, 28, 30, 32, 34–7, 42–3, 45, 66, 123, 141, 208; and *de jure* segregation 18, 55, 62, 75, 146; and discrimination in employment 31, 33, 35; and racial segregation 18, 28-9, 31-2, 208, 211; and racially determined resource allocation 10, 17–19, 32, 37, 46, 75, 122, 220; and racially differential outcomes 28, 30, 36, 38, 75, 122-3; and racist ideology 4, 17, 37–8; and teachers and administrators 17, 27, 29, 31–4, 37–8, 43–4, 228; and teachers' union 17, 27, 33, 36, 38, 43–4
Education Week (US) 233
Eichenwalk, K. 225
Eisenhower, President Dwight D.: and Civil Rights Movement 58, 66; and

failure to support the moral imperative of *Brown v. Board of Education* decision 66; and Military Industrial Complex 10
Elections in France: 1992 regional elections 196; 1993 National Assembly elections 196, 199
Elections in Germany: 1992 local elections in Berlin, Baden Wurttenburg 196; 1993 elections in Hesse 197; 1994 Bundestag elections 197
Elections in UK: 1964 81; 1979 11; 1992 13, 177; 1994 13; see also Race card
Elections in US: 1876 137; 1968 131; 1980 222; 1984 221; 1988 221; 1992 226, 241; 1996 22
Ellison, M. 226, 236
Empire Day Movement 171, 236, 237
Employment in Europe: and marginal labour forces 185, 190-1; and structural unemployment 194–5; and unemployment levels 7, 191; and teenage unemployment 190; and unemployment and support for Far Right 196, 201
Employment in UK: and anti-discrimination legislation 83, 85, 87, 90, 93, 96–7, 99–100, 106, 109; and economic restructuring 133; and enforcement of anti-discrimination legislation 99–100, 112–13; and equal opportunities policies 24; and National Health Service 148; and New Right rejection of unemployment as cause of uprisings 129; and racially stratified labour markets 120-2, 148, 151-3; and racism 23–4, 97, 120–2, 148, 151, 160, 189; and racism in education system 123; and scapegoating black/Chinese as cause of white unemployment 162, 173; and teenage unemployment 121–3; and unemployment 121, 132–3, 152, 189
Employment in US: and anti-discrimination legislation 74, 144; and anti-discrimination programs 59; and limitations of Civil Rights Movement 195; and New Right rejection of unemployment as cause

of uprisings 129; and racism 7, 14, 42, 46, 120, 123, 130, 208, 218, 220; and racism in educational system 123; and Supreme Court decisions affecting anti-discrimination legislation 144, 233; and teenage unemployment 120–1, 123; and underemployment 14, 130; and unemployment 14, 28, 120–1, 130–1, 218, 220
Engels, F. 172, 237
Ennals, David, MP 89, 92, 106
Equal Rights (lobby group, UK) 101, 104
Equiano, O. 5, 167
European Community 12, 179, 184, 192
European Parliament's Committee of Enquiry into Racism and Xenophobia 179, 238, 241
Evans, Neil, 173, 237
Evans, Roger Warren 98
Evans, Sara 228
Eysenck, Hans 129, 232

Fabian Society 98
Fairchild, H. H. 226
Family in Europe: and stereotype of immigrant family 190; white and suburbanisation 9
Family in UK: Afro-Caribbean, and stereotypes of pathological family 159, 164; Asian, and child birth 156; and family planning 158; and immigration rules keeping families divided 195; and refugees and asylum-seekers and immigration laws 12; and social workers 164; and stereotypes of Asian illegal immigrants 177; white, and example of landlord and family in anti-discrimination legislation 109
Family in US: black, and stereotype of pathological family 48, 134, 141, 232–3; and decline in family income since 1973 143, 222; and family income 130; and decline in family-owned businesses 131; and New Right and patriarchal family 141; and women's challenge to patriarchal family 140
Fantini, M. 226
Farmer, James 70

Fascism 19, 88, 173, 186, 199, 200, 201, 202
FDR/Woodrow Wilson Club 26
Federal Bureau of Investigations 58, 63, 66, 72, 230
Federal Government: and anti-Communist purges 60, 62, 218; and Civil Rights Movement 58, 60, 62, 66, 72, 218, 219; and Kerner Commission 125, 126
Federal Housing Agency 9, 219; and repeal of the First Reconstruction 136, 137, 213; and suburbanisation 50
Fekete, L. 238, 239, 240
Fellow Travellers 58
Feminism (second wave) 48
Ferretti, F. 227, 228
Financial Times (UK) 180, 238
Finkle, L. 52, 228
First Reconstruction 22, 51, 136, 139
First World War 49-50, 137, 212
First World War: and Black Migration, 49, 137; post-First World War period and UNIA 50; pre-First World War period and Industrial Workers of the World 212
Fitzhugh, George 205
Flinn, M.W. 225, 236
Foley, Maurice, MP 98
Foot, P. 235, 237
Ford Foundation, 33, 34, 127
Ford, Glyn 197, 238, 241
Forman, James 71, 72, 74, 75, 230
'Fortress Europe' 15, 183, 184, 192, 197, 199
'Forty Acres and a Mule' 137
Foster, John 169, 236
France 12, 16, 183–5, 187–91, 199
Frankfurt (Germany) 197
Frankfurter Allgemeine (Germany) 192
Frappier, J. 232
Freeland, R.A. 229
Freeson, Reginald, MP 92
Front National (France) 16, 183, 196, 199
Fryer, P. 225, 236, 237
Fuentes, L. 226
Fullilove v. Klutznick 143

Gabe, J. 226
Gaffiken, E. 239

Gardner, L.C. 229
Garrison, William Lloyd 209
Garrow, David 77, 230
Garvey, Marcus 50, 228
Genocide 2
Georgia 75
Germany 12, 16, 176, 179, 183–85, 187–90, 194, 197, 200-01, 239–40
Gideon v. Wainwright 140
Gilder, G. 242
Ginsburg, C. 233
Ginsburg, N. 238, 240, 241
Gintis, H. 242
Glasgow Herald 230
Glasgow, Scotland (UK) 179, 241
Glazer, Nathan 207, 242
globalisation 15–16
Gompers, Samuel 215
Goodman, M. 233
Gordon, D.R. 234, 242
Gordon, E.W. 36, 227
Gordon, P. 235
Gordon-Walker, Patrick, MP 81
Gould, S.J. 224, 238
Graves, J.L., Jr. 224, 226
Greater London Council: Health Panel 151, 234, 235; and racial harassment 178, 237, 241; Women's Committee 158
Griffith, R. 229
Griffiths, E., MP 107
Guardian (London) 161, 179-81, 226, 234-5, 238-41
'Guinea Cargo' 4, 166
Gunter, Ray, MP 100

Hadjor, K.B. 8–9, 225–6
Hagell, A. 226
Haines, Herbert 72, 230
Hainsworth, P. 239
Haiti 209
Hall, S. 231, 239
Hampton, Fred (Black Panther Party) 127
Haringey, London 123
Harlan, Justice John Marshall 139
Harlem: and attitudes towards Second World War 52; and black capitalism 232; and East Harlem and community control conflict 33, 34, 44; and New Negro 55; and US Communist Party 228; and urban uprisings 76, 127

Harris, C. 237, 239
Harris, L. 242
Hayden, Tom 119, 232
Health in Europe: 184, 199
Health in UK: 23–4, 147–64, 175, 182, 184, 199, 224, 226, 234–6; and concentration of health education material for Asians and Afro-Caribbeans on birth control 156, 158; and consequences of living in inner-cities 153; and consequences of working conditions 153; and demands for immigration control 160-1; and employment in health care delivery service 23–4, 148–51, 234–6; and health consequences of racism 23, 147–54, 156, 158, 160, 224, 226, 234–5; and health workers' militancy 164; and lack of concern with racial inequality in health care 148; and link with unemployment 152; and links between racism and social and economic factors determining health 151–3, 234–5; and Liverpool 153, 235; and meaning of good health 147; and mental health 152, 154, 158, 235; and National Health Service 23–4, 147–51, 159, 234–5; and quality of primary health care 153; and racial harassment 23; and racialised access to services 161-2; and specific health problems such as Sickle Cell Anaemia 147, 159; and racial violence 153; and stereotypes about Asian and Afro-Caribbean cultures 156, 158–9
Health in US: 46, 75, 142, 220; and health and safety protection in workplace 142; and racialised access to health care 46, 75, 220; and unionised workers access to health care 142
Health Divide, The: Inequalities in Health in the 1980s 151
Health Education Council (UK) 151
Heath, Edward 11
Hechter, Michael 1, 224, 236, 239
'Heidelberger Manifesto' 192
Henley, Alix 156
Herrenvolk: Democracy, 46, 207-08; Republicanism 207
Herrnstein, Richard 19, 129, 226, 232

Heseltine, Michael, MP (Cabinet
Minister) 131, 132
Hesse (Germany) 197
Hill, R. A. 228
Hirsch, A. 9, 219, 225, 241
Hirsch, J. 232
Hobsbawm, E. 236
Hoffenberg, Sir Raymond 149, 150,
155, 234
Hogg, Quintin, MP 103
Hollifield, J. P. 239
Hollywood 59, 64
Holmes, Edmund 171
Holtham, Gerald 195
Home Office 12, 100, 153, 162–3,
178–9, 198, 238
Home Owners Loan Corporation 8
Horn, Patricia 171, 236, 237
Horne, Gerald 58, 59, 60, 69, 229,
230
Horton, P. 213, 225, 226, 241, 242
Houghton, Douglas, MP 86
House of Commons: Hansard 230,
231; Select Committee on Home
Affairs (UK) 179, 238; Social
Services Committee (UK) 150
House Unamerican Activities
Committee (HUAC) (US) 59, 63, 64,
65
Houston, Texas 62, 229
Howard, Michael, MP (Home
Secretary) 13, 179, 180
Howe, G. 231
Huberman, L. 224, 236
Hughes, Langston 59
L'Humanité (France) 240
Hume, Basil 12
Hunt, E. K. 233
Hunt, John, MP 92
Hunt, R. G. 228, 241
Hurd, Douglas, MP (Foreign
Secretary) 11, 13, 184, 185
Huttenback, R. A. 236
Hynd, Harry, MP 160

Ideology: and class 203, 222; and
hegemony of corporate America
64–5, 129; and ideological
opposition to discrimination in UK
85; to slavery 167
Ideological racism in European Union,
184, 187–8, 192; in UK 23, 169–70,
172, 174, 184; US 2, 7–8, 17,

19–20, 128, 131, 134, 143, 210,
218, 226
Immigration and legislation in
European Union 12, 192–3; in
France 16, 190–1; in Germany 190,
197
Immigration and legislation in UK: 11-
13, 24–5, 79, 81, 86, 117-18,
147–8, 158-63, 175, 177, 182,
184–5, 231, 235, 238–40, 242;
Immigration and Asylum Bill 1996
13; and Conservative Party 79; and
Labour Party 79, 86, 175, 185;
White Paper of 1965 11, 25, 86,
175 see also Race card; Whites;
Working class
Immigration and legislation in US:
210–11, 216, 242; Immigration
Restriction League 216
Independent (UK) 240
Independent Committee of Inquiry
into Racial Harassment (UK) 178,
238, 241
Independent on Sunday (UK) 240
India 3, 20, 115, 149, 174
Indians in UK 153, 171, 174, 177
Indonesians (The Netherlands) 183
Industrial Workers of the World
(IWW) 61, 212, 215
Institute of Race Relations (UK) 20,
78, 96–7, 117, 201, 224, 231,
236–9, 241
Institutional racism 6, 19, 21, 46, 48,
50, 140, 148, 176, 216, 219, 226,
232
Institutional racism in UK: 21, 148,
176; and health 148; and link with
popular racism 176; and Lord
Scarman's denial of its existence 21
Institutional racism in US: 6, 19, 46,
48, 50, 216, 219, 226, 232; and
differences with *de jure* segregation
48, 219; implications for
employment/unemployment 220;
links with popular racism 216; and
role of government in housing
segregation 50, 216, 219; resistance
to 48; see also Structural racism
Integration 6, 14, 63, 66-8, 72, 88
95–6, 99, 101–02, 123
Internal colonialism 1–2, 224, 236, 239
International Working Man's
Association 170

Ireland 2, 169, 183, 224, 236
Irish: and England 1, 2-3, 5–6, 115, 168-9, 171–2, 183, 236; and US 206–7
IRR European Race Audit Project 201
IS201 (demonstration district, New York) 33, 34, 44, 45
Islington 18 Defence Committee (UK) 231
Israel 68, 135
Italy 12, 16, 186

Jackson, George 119
Jacobson, L. F. 227
Jefferson, T. 231, 239; Jeffersonian economic democracy 137
Jenkins, Roy, MP (Home Secretary) 95, 96, 97, 105
Jennings, J. 17, 225
Jensen, Arthur 129, 232
Jett v. Dallas Independent School District 145
Jewish Chronicle (UK) 230
Jewish Defence Committees (UK) 88
Jewish Vanguard (US) 40
Johnson, Charles S. 6
Johnson, Paul, 178, 238
Johnson, President Lyndon B. 128, 130, 231
Joint Council for the Welfare of Immigrants (UK) 161, 162
Jones, Clarence 74
Jones, Dorothy B. 64
Jordan, Colin 88
Joshi, S. 237, 239
Joxe Law of 1989 (France) 191
Justice Department of (US) 71, 74

Kairys, D 14, 225
Kalodner, H. 38
Katznelson, I. 242
Kaysen, Carl 217
Kennedy, John F.: 58, 67, 72-4; and anti-Communism 72; on Civil Rights Legislation 67, 74–5; and impact of world opinion on support for civil rights 58, 67; and electoral interests 67; and March on Washington 73–4
Kenya Asians Act, 1968 (UK) 175
Kerner Commission 21, 116, 118, 119, 124, 126, 231, 232; *see also* National Advisory Commission on Civil Disorders

Keynesian Accommodation 128, 142, 220
Khan, Ibrahim 162
Kiernan, V. G. 236
King, Dr Martin Luther, Jr: 66, 70, 72, 77–8, 114, 235-6; and anti-Communist purges 72; and need for fundamental economic restructuring 77–8; and non-violent direct action 66; and opposition to Vietnam War 70, 77, 235–6
Klein, R. 238, 240
Kohl, H 16, 197
Kolko, G. 229
Kosack, G. 234
Kozol, J. 18, 226
Krenz, F. 12
Krieger, J. 225, 238, 240
Ku Klux Klan 213

Labour Party 11, 77, 79, 85, 86, 88, 133, 174, 175, 180, 1881, 185, 187; *see also* Anti-discrimination legislation; Whites; Working class
Lafontaine, Oskar (German Social Democratic Party) 188
Lambeth 117
Lancashire textile industry (UK): 174; and workers 171
Langton, Alderman Bernard 95
Lansley, A 13, 225
Latency, Reverend George 74
Latinos 10, 17-18, 57, 145, 222-3
'Law and Order' 141
Law Enforcement Assistance Administration (LEAA) (US) 125
Lawrence County 13, 212-13, 225, 241
Le Pen, Jean-Marie (leader, Front National, France) 190
Leeds (UK): 178, 238, 241; Community Relations Council 178, 238, 241; Fans United Against Racism and Fascism 200
Legal Action Group (UK) 119, 231
Lester, Anthony 87, 98
Lewis, John 74, 75
Leyton 86
Liberal democracy 19, 168, 181, 218
Liberalism: UK 82, 104, 107, 132; US 22, 26, 53, 57, 70–2, 130, 140, 217; and limitations of 26
Liberia 215

Lichterketten (processions of candle-carrying protestors, Germany) 200
Lilley, Peter MP (Cabinet Minister) 13, 180
Lindsay, Mayor John 27, 32, 33, 40
Liverpool 4, 120, 153, 159, 166, 173, 234, 237
Lloyd, Peter, MP (Home Office Minister) 179, 238
Local Government Act of 1966 (UK) 83
Logan, David, MP 173
London Programme (UK) 178
London Working Men's Association (UK) 7, 236
Los Angeles Times (US) 134, 233
Los Angeles Urban League (US) 135
Lower East Side (New York) 33, 34, 35, 225
Loyalty Security Program 63
Luxembourg 12, 38, 39, 40, 44

McCarthyism 71, 229
McConville, M. 231
McCoy, Rhody (Ocean Hill-Brownsville Administrator) 27, 30, 331,
MacDonald, J. Fred 64, 230
MacDonald, Kenneth (Chair, Washington State Board Against Discrimination) 110, 111
MacEwan, M. 239
MacFarlane, A. 157, 235
MacKenzie, J.M. 172, 237
McMichael's Appraising Manual 8
McNaught, A. 151, 152, 234, 235
McNeal, J. 237
MacPherson, J.M. 233
Mack, John 135
Macey, M. 16, 225
Magat, R. 226
Major, John (Prime Minister) 10, 11, 222
Malcolm X: 73–4, 77, 122, 239; and March on Washington, 73–4; and racist teacher 122
Manchester (UK): 4, 149, 159, 166, 170, 231, 235; Law Centre (UK) 231, 235
Mangan, J.A. 171, 236
Mapp v. Ohio 140
Marable, Manning 51, 69, 74, 221, 228, 230, 241, 242

March on Washington, 1963 72, 73, 74, 75, 76; see also DuBois; Kennedy; King, Jr; Malcolm X
Marshall, Burke 71
Marshall, Thurgood 144, 146
Martin v. Wilkes 144
Martin, Andrew 86
Martin Committee, The 86
Marx, Gary 41, 42, 227
Marx, K. 172, 237
Massey, D.S. 8-9, 225
Mauer, M. 242
Maxted, J. 242
May, R. 237
Media 8, 15, 40, 46–7, 66–7, 69, 118, 121, 132-3, 140, 158, 162, 172, 176-80, 184, 186, 189, 230, 240-1
Media in UK: 12-13, 88, 99–100, 118, 132-3, 158, 176, 179, 184, 189, 227, 230, 232-3, 237-8; and anti-discrimination legislation 88, 99-100, 132-3; and black youth 221, 228; and Conservative Government 12-13, 176-8, 184, 228, 237–9; and criminalising Afro-Caribbean youth 118, 189; and elections 12, 177–8, 180, 184, 228, 237–9; and explanation of rise of neo-Nazis in Germany 184; and labelling asylum-seekers as bogus 13; and mugging 118; and the Race Card 10, 13, 176–8, 180–1, 196, 201–3, 225; and racial violence 179; and racism 13, 158, 162, 177–9, 184, 228; and response to black uprisings 132, 228, 232; and support for racist immigration laws 184
Media in US: 19, 40–1, 47, 66, 69, 140, 221, 232–3; and attacks on organised labour 221; and Civil Rights Movement 66–7; and Dr W.E.B. DuBois 69; and 1960s critique of press 140; and racism 46; and support for the Moynihan Report 141–2, 233; and support for charges of black anti-Semitism 40; and uncritical support for *The Bell Curve* 19
Media in Europe 15, 186, 196, 201, 240
Medical Foundation for the Care of Victims of Torture 12

Medical Practitioners' Union (UK) 149
Menjou, Adolph 59
Mental Health Services (UK) 154, 235
Merrivale, H. 4, 166
Merseyside Regional Health Authority
  (UK) 149
Messenger (US) 61
Meyer, R. E. 233
Michie, J. 239
Middle class: black 50, 55–6, 75–6,
  130–1, 140, 219; white and Civil
  Rights Movement 55
Militancy: black, 53, 73, 143;
  working-class 7, 186; loss of
  working-class 195
Military Industrial Complex 10, 60
Military Keynesianism 10, 114, 220
Miller, Dr Maurice, MP 92
Miller, M. J. 239
Ministry of Labour (UK) 100
Miranda v. Arizona 140
Mississippi: 13, 70–2, 75, 213;
  Freedom Democratic Party 72;
  Freedom Summer 70, 71
Mitchison, Gilbert, MP 86
Mitter, J. 239
Mitterrand, François (President,
  France) 16
Moch, L. P. 239
Molly McGuires 212
Le Monde (France) 240
Montesquieu, comte de 5, 167
Montgomery (Alabama) 55, 66
Moore, David 120
Morais, H. M. 63, 229
Morrisey, M. 239
Moynihan, Daniel Patrick (US
  Senator) 128, 129, 131, 141, 232,
  233; and 'benign neglect' 141; and
  Moynihan Report 128, 129, 232,
  233
MSF Union (UK) 24, 226
Mugging 118, 231, 239
Murray v. Giarrantano 145
Murray, Charles 19, 242
Murray, Nancy 237
Muste, Vance 60
Myrdal, Gunnar and *An American
  Dilemma* 53, 54, 57, 229

NAACP Legal and Defence Fund 145
Nancy, D. 237
National Advisory Commission on

Civil Disorders *see* Kerner
  Commission
National Association for the
  Advancement of Colored People
  (NAACP) (US): 52, 58–60, 66,
  68–72, 74, 146; 58, 69–71; and
  Council on African Affairs 69; and
  Dr W.E.B. DuBois 52, 58; and
  March on Washington 72-3; and
  successful strategy of lobbying and
  litigation, 66; and support for anti-
  Communist purges 58, 69–71; and
  support for US foreign policy 60,
  68–70
National Association for the
  Assistance of Foreigners at Frontiers
  (ANAFE) (France) 191
National Business League (US) 131
National Committee for
  Commonwealth Immigrants (UK)
  83, 97, 98, 99
National Co-ordinating Conference of
  Voluntary Liaison Committees (UK)
  95
National Council for Civil Liberties
  (UK) 88
National Health Service (NHS) (UK)
  23, 24, 147, 148, 149, 150, 151,
  159, 160, 161, 226, 235, 237; *see
  also* Employment, UK; Health, UK;
  Racial discrimination, UK; Women,
  UK; Working class, UK
National Labor Congress (US) 210
National Labor Union (US) 211
National Lawyers Guild (NLG) (US)
  70, 71
National security state 65
National Socialist Movement (UK) 88
National Union Seamen (UK) 173
National Urban League (US) 72, 74,
  233
Native Americans 2, 57
Naturalization Act of 1790 (US) 206
Nazism 56, 186
Nehercott, Susan 152
Nelson, D. C. 207, 226, 241
Neo-Nazis 199
Netherlands, The 12, 183, 187, 189
New Deal 49, 218
New England (US) 3, 204, 224, 241
New Left 47, 125
New Right 132, 133, 141; *see also*
  Employment, UK; Employment, US;

Family, US; Poverty, US; Women, US
New South 54
New York City: 133; and Education
17, 18, 26, 27, 28, 29, 33, 38, 44,
225, 227, 228
New York Civil Liberties Union 227
New York Herald Tribune 70
New York State 32, 33, 35, 39, 44, 45
New York Times 41, 68, 225, 227–8,
233–4
Newark, N.J. (US) 119, 232
Newham (UK) 178, 179
Newnham, A. 235
Nicol, A. 239
Nixon, President Richard M: 131,
140, 141, 142; and 'Southern
Strategy' 141; and 'law and order'
141
Noble, D. 242
Non-discrimination contract clause
(UK) 113
Nordholt, Eric (Chief Police Officer,
Amsterdam) 189
North African workers in France 16,
183, 186, 192
North-Western Regional Health
Authority (UK) 149
Northern United States: in anti-bellum
period 206, 207; and Civil Rights
Movement 55, 56, 66; and Great
Migration 49, 121, 220; and
institutional racism 29, 42, 121,
140; and maintenance of plantations
system, 213; and Northern blacks
and Civil Rights Movement 56;
Northern industrialists and First
Reconstruction 137; and urban
uprisings 76

Oakley, A, 157, 235
Observer (UK) 13, 225, 240
Ocean Hill-Brownsville
(demonstration district, Brooklyn)
(US) 27, 30, 32, 33, 34, 38, 39, 40,
43, 45
O'Connell, Daniel 207
O'Connor, Justice Sandra Day 143
O'Daniel, Pappy 60
O'Dell, Jack 72
Office of War Information 52
Oil Workers International (CIO) 61
Oldham, Lancashire (UK) 169
Oliver, Rev. C. Herbert (President,

Ocean Hill-Brownsville District, US)
32, 45, 227, 228
O'Neill, John 39, 43, 227
Open Enrolment 29
Oppenheim, C. 237
Orange Lodges 169
Orbach, Maurice, MP 98
Organisation for Economic Co-
operation and Development (OECD)
194, 195, 240
Osborne, Cyril, MP 160
O'Sullivan, John 129
Owen, Chandler 61
Oxford (UK) 4, 166

Pakistanis in UK 153
Pan-Africanism 53, 69
Panel on Decentralization (US) 227
Parry, N. 234
Pasqua, Charles (Minister of Interior,
France): 191; and Pasqua Laws of
1986 191
Pass Law Society 162
Patterson v. McLean Credit Union 145
Patterson, Sheila 79
Pax Americana 54, 220–1
Pax Britannica 54
Peace Information Center (US) 69
Pearson, M. 234
Permanent Wartime Economy 57, 142,
220
Perrucci, R. 231
Philadelphia Tribune (US) 52
Phillips, M. 231
Pieterse, J. N. 239
Pilisuk, M. 231
Pittsburgh (US): and Great Migration
50; and institutional racism 50
Place, T. 226
Plantations 3–4, 19, 48–9, 63, 115,
137, 166, 185, 204-05
Plessy v. Ferguson 65, 138
Polakow, V. 226
Police in Europe: 12, 16, 184, 192;
European Union 12, 16; and
Schengen Agreement 12; and
violence against migrants and settler
communities 16; and France 16,
184; and membership in the *Front
National*, France 16; and
stereotyping immigrants and settlers
as criminals in France 184; Germany
and stereotyping immigrants and

settlers as criminals 184; The
Netherlands and police racism 184;
and stereotyping immigrants and
settlers as criminals 184
Police in UK: 21–2, 116–21, 124–5,
131, 152–3, 175-6; and black
uprisings 22, 117, 119, 131; and
black youth 117-18, 120-1; and
Brixton 22, 117, 119–21, 131; and
community policing 21; and
immigration 117–18; and inner cities
116–17, 119; involvement in
'sectioning' black people in mental
hospitals 153; lack of confidence in
175–6; lack of police protection
against racist violence 152–3, 175–6;
and Lord Scarman's
recommendations 21; and police
violence 22, 119–20; and as part of
racist criminal justice system 118-19;
response to uprisings 124–5; and
Southall 119; and 'Sus' 117–18; and
Toxteth, Liverpool 120; and white
youth 131
Police in US: 14, 16, 20–2, 75-6, 114,
116–17, 119–20, 124–5, 132–3,
139, 144, 196–7, 206, 216; and
acquittal of police charged with
violence against blacks 22, 119–20;
acquittal of police charged with
killing blacks 132; and Baltimore
132; and black uprisings 22,
119–20, 132; and community
policing 125; and deaths in custody
14, 132; and Detroit 119–20; and
employment of black officers 125;
and increase in police powers 132–3;
and Kerner Commission 76, 114,
117, 124–5; and Los Angeles 22,
119–20, 132–3; and maintenance of
slavery 196; and maintenance of *de
jure* segregation 197; and Miami
132; and New York City 132; and
as part of racist criminal justice
system 118, 206; and police racism
75; and police violence 14, 21–2,
119–20; and restrictions on police
powers 139, 144
Police Support Units (PSUs) (UK) 125
Policy Review (UK) 129
Policy Studies Institute 153, 154, 174,
178, 226, 239
Political and Economic Planning (PEP)

Report 81 (UK) 96-9, 231
Pomerantz, C. 229
Poniatowski, Michel (Minister of
Interior, France) 190
Poor People's March 77
Pope-Hennessy, J. 224, 236
Portugal 12
Post-liberal consensus 22-3, 226
Potts, L. 239
Poverty in UK: 152, 155, 168, 170,
237, 239; and health implications
152, 155; and higher rates for blacks
152; and historic levels 170; and
relationship to labour markets 168,
170, 239
Poverty in US: 14, 20, 22, 37, 48, 77,
129, 141, 143, 232, 242; and
Culture of Poverty explanation 48,
129, 232, 242; and denial of effect
of poverty on uprisings 22, 29; and
effects on racial/ethnic children 77;
and feminisation 20; inherent in
structure of US society 77; levels of
143; and 1992 Los Angeles uprising
22; and Moynihan Report 141; and
New Right explanations 141
Powell, Enoch, MP 81, 83–4, 104; and
racialisation 20, 143; responses by
Labour Government and 82–4;
responses by sections of white public
81, 83
Powell, Adam Clayton Rep. 250
Prasher, U. 235
Prior, A. 239
Prisons in Europe: 16, 189–91; and
increasing levels of imprisonment of
young people from immigrant and
settler communities 16, 189–90;
France 16, 189–91; and membership
of prison officers in the *Front
National*, France 16; and
imprisonment of refugees and
asylum-seekers 191; and increasing
levels of imprisonment of young
people from immigrant and settler
communities 189–90; Germany and
increasing levels of imprisonment of
young people from immigrant and
settler communities 189–90
Prisons in UK: 13, 118, 135, 154-5,
182, 189; and disproportionate
imprisonment of Afro-Caribbean
men and women 13, 118, 189; and

increasing levels of imprisonment 182; and 'sectioning' of black prisoners to mental hospitals 154-5; and Steven Thompson 154-5; and young people 135

Prisons in US: 13–14, 20, 118–19, 208, 222; differential sentencing for possession of crack and powder cocaine 14; disproportionate imprisonment of African-American men and women 13, 20, 118–19, 220, 222; imprisonment of free blacks in ante-bellum North 208; and George Jackson and Soledad Brothers 119; and one of the two highest levels of imprisonment in the world 222

Protest: 58, 63, 71, 199–200; against *de jure* segregation 63, 71; against NAACP support for anti-Communist purges 58; marches against neo-Nazis in Germany 199–200

Public Order Act (UK) 88

Puerto Rican(s): 31, 37–8, 45, 64, 122; children 31, 37-8, 122; parents 37,45

Pulse 161, 235

Quiles Law of 1992 (France) 191

Qureishy, Bashy 189

Qureshi, T. 240

Race and Class (UK) 21, 201, 224–6, 228, 231–4, 236–42

Race and class: attempts to prevent linkage 47, 50; Communist Party of the United States (CPUSA) attempts to link the two 50; interconnections 17, 19, 23–4, 47

Race card 10, 12–13, 21, 25, 117, 176–81, 196, 201–3, 225

Race Relations: Act 1965 (UK) 79, 81, 85–95, 112; Act 1968 (UK) 79, 81–3, 95–113; Board (UK) 83, 91, 94, 95, 96, 98, 105, 109, 111, 231

Race Riots (UK) 173, 237

Race Riots (US) 46

Racial discrimination: 7, 14, 23–4, 60, 79, 87–9, 97, 113, 144–5, 149–50, 175, 184, 219, 231

Racial discrimination in UK: 23–4, 79, 87–9, 97, 113, 150, 175, 184, 231;

anti-discrimination legislation 79, 87–9, 97; and employment in National Health Service 23–4, 149–50; and immigration legislation 184; non-discrimination contract clause 113, 175

Racial discrimination in US: 7, 14, 60, 144–5, 219; anti-discrimination legislation 219; and differential sentencing decisions over crack and powder cocaine 14; and employment 7, 14; and foreign policy implications 219; and investment 7, 14; and location of toxic waste dumps 14; Supreme Court decisions 144-5; use in Cold War 60

Rai, M. 224

Rampton Mental Hospital (UK) 155

Randolph, A. Philip 61, 74

Rathzel, N. 192, 240

Reagan, Ronald (President, US) 10–11, 14, 22, 142–3, 145–6, 195, 221–2, 225, 233, 238, 240

Reconnection for Learning (US) 227

'Red Belt' around Paris (France) 196

Redbridge (UK) 178

'Red Squads' 63

Reed, A. 242

Refugee Forum and Migrants Rights Action Network, The 16, 186, 201, 225, 239, 240

Regional Health Authorities (UK) 149

Rehnquist, W 14

Reid, M. 192, 240

Republikaner Partei (Germany) 183, 196, 197

Resler, H. 237

Rhodes, E. Washington 52

Richard, Ivor, MP 92

Richardson, Abby 212

Richmond v. Croson 143

Rickets 155

Riggs v. Duke Power Company 141, 144

Ringer, B. B. 233, 241

Roberts, B. 231, 239

Roberts, Robert 172

Roberts, W. 226

Robeson, Paul: 58–60, 68–9, 77, 218, 229–30; and anti-Communist purges 59–60, 68–9, 77; and fight for black rights 58; and need for fundamental economic restructuring 218; and

support for African independence 69
Robeson, Paul, Jr. 59, 229–30
Robinson, Jackie 70
Rockefeller, Governor Nelson 70
Roe v. Wade 140
Roediger, David 206, 207, 224, 242
Rogers, D. 26, 28, 29, 226, 227, 228
Rogers, Joel A. 52
Rogers, M. 237
Rolston, B. 2, 224, 236
Roma People 184
Roosevelt Administration 9
Rose, Paul, MP 92
Rosen, Sumner 63, 229
Rosenberg, E. 212
Rosenberg, J. 212
Rosenthal, R. 227
Rowan, Carl T. 70
Rowley, Margaret 70, 230
Runnymede Bulletin 201
Runnymede Trust 201

Sacco, N. 212
Safe Third Country rule 15
Sage Race Relations Abstracts (UK, US) 201, 224, 225, 226, 232, 241
Sassen, S. 239
Save the Children Fund in Scotland 201
Saxton, A. 242
Scafe, S. 234, 235
Schauble, Wolfgang (Christian Democratic Union, Germany) 197
Schengen: Agreement/Accord 12, 15, 192, 240; Information System 12
Schlesinger, Arthur, Jr 71, 74
Schleswig-Holstein (Germany) 197
Schmalz-Jacobsen, Cornelia (German Commissioner for Foreigners) 188
Schmidt, Emerson P. 62, 229
School for the Educationally Subnormal (UK) 123
Schuyler, George 52
Schwerner, George, 111
Scientific Management 214
Scientific racism 19, 129, 215–16, 226, 232
Scott, Nicholas, MP 105, 106, 108
Scottish Ethnic Minorities Research Unit (UK) 179, 241
Scribner's Monthly (US) 212
Searchlight (UK) 201, 240
Searle, C. 177, 228, 237, 238

Second Reconstruction 14, 22, 136, 140, 142, 143, 230
Second World War: and Africa 68; and black radicalism 52, 56; and industrialisation of South and Southwest 49; and Keynesian Accommodation 47; and origins of Civil Rights Movement 56; and post-Second World War period and anti-Communist purges 47
Selznick, G. 41
Senate Internal Affairs Committee, US 63
Seniority System 56
'Separate but Equal' 18, 55, 65, 102, 107, 213
Shanker, A. 35, 39, 40, 41, 43, 44
Shaw, G. 233
Sheffield: City Council (UK) 178, 238, 241; Racial Harassment Project 178, 238, 241
Sherman, H. J. 233
Shine, C. 242
Shockley, William 129, 232
Sickle Cell Anaemia 147, 159
Simpson, A. 192, 240
Sinclair, Sir George, MP 105, 106
Sivanandan, A. 128, 132, 225, 231–4, 236–7, 239–42
Skinheads 199
Slaughterhouse Cases of 1873 (US) 137
Slave uprisings 48, 209
Slavery 1, 3–6, 48, 138, 165–7, 185, 204–9, 224, 236, 241
Slough 86
Smaje, C. 226
Smedley, A. 225
Smethwick 81, 86
Smith, A. D. 225
Smith, D. J. 239
Smith, G. 237
Smith, J. G. 239
Smith, Susan J. 3, 224, 225
Smith, William French (Attorney General, US) 134
Smout, T. C. 225, 236
Social Democratic Party (Germany) 16, 186, 188, 195–6
Social dislocation 10, 15, 185
Social mobility 28
Social programmes 82, 134
Social Wage 10, 15, 115, 130, 142,

166, 181, 186, 188, 201, 222
Socialist Party (France) 187
Society of Labour Lawyers 86, 98
Soledad Brothers 119
Solid South 56
Sorenson, Reginald, MP 85
Soskice, Sir Frank, MP (Home
  Secretary) 86, 87, 90, 91, 92, 93, 95
South Africa 20, 68, 69, 183, 184,
  222
South Shields (UK) 173, 237
Southern Christian Leadership
  Conference (SCLC) 66, 70, 72, 74,
  77
Southern radicalism 63, 225, 241
'Southern Strategy' 141
Spain 12
Special Patrol Group (UK police) 116,
  125
Spencer, D. 45, 228
Spencer, M. 240
St Paul's, Bristol (UK) 132
St Pauli Fans Gegen Rechts (St Pauli
  Fans Against the Right) (Germany)
  200
Stanfield, J.H. 7, 224–6, 239, 241
State Department (US) 68, 69
State racism 7, 8, 12, 14, 25, 46, 50,
  117, 132, 144, 184, 216, 219, 220
Statewatch (UK) 192, 201, 239
Stein, Annie, 122, 232
Stephens, Thaddeus 136, 139
Stereotypes in Europe: link between
  and state racism 186
Stereotypes in UK: Anti-African 3,
  236; Anti-Irish 2–3; of Afro-
  Caribbean family as pathological
  159, 161; of Afro-Caribbean women
  as irresponsible 159; of Asian
  women as compliant 159; of Asian
  illegal immigrants 177; historical
  upper-class stereotype of white
  working class 168; negative
  stereotypes and educational
  outcomes 123; and post-Second
  World War immigration 20; and
  racist immigration legislation 161
Stereotypes in US: of African-
  American family as pathological 48,
  134, 141, 232-3; anti-Semitic 41; of
  'special treatment' and maintenance
  of racism 139
Sternberg, S. 41

Stevas, Norman St John, MP 92
Stewart, Ollie 52
Stone, I.F. 43, 227
Strayer, G.D. 228
Street Committee Report 81, 97–8,
  101-03, 108, 113, 231
Street crime: UK 117; Europe 189
Street, H. 231
Structural racism in UK 20-1, 23, 174
Structural racism in US: 10, 20, 22,
  55–6, 60, 67, 131, 133, 217, 220;
  and Civil Rights Movement 55–6,
  60, 67
Student Non-Violent Co-Ordinating
  Committee (SNCC) 66, 70, 71, 72,
  74, 230
'Sub-Employment Rate' (US) 121
Suburbanisation 9–10, 18, 219; *see
  also* Family, US; Federal
  Government; Whites US
Sumner, Charles 139
Sun (UK) 12, 228, 237
Sunday Times (UK) 99, 230–2
Supreme Court 14, 22, 45, 55, 58,
  137, 140, 142–6, 213
Surinamese (The Netherlands) 183
'Sus' 117–18, 159, 234
'Swamp' 81 117; 'Swamping speech'
  176
Swinton, D. H. 233

Tabb, William 130, 233
Takaki, R. 212, 242
Talmadge, Eugene 60
Television 55, 64, 65, 84, 120, 178,
  230
Tenant farmers 63, 149
Texas 61, 62, 229
Thatcher, Margaret (Prime Minister,
  UK) 6, 10–11, 117, 125, 128–9,
  158, 161, 176-8, 181–2, 189–90,
  225, 228, 232–3, 237–8, 240; and
  Thatcherism 176, 178, 181
Theoharis, A. 229
Third World Voice (Denmark) 189
Thompson, Steven 155
Thorndike, Edward 215
Thorneycroft, Peter, MP 90, 91, 92,
  103
Times, The (UK) 99, 100, 132–3, 180,
  230–1, 233
Title I, Elementary and Secondary
  Education Act (UK) 38

Toffler, A. 226
Tompson, K. 238, 241
Toporowski, J. 240
Torkington, Ntombenhle Protasia
  Khotie 153, 157, 235
Tower Hamlets (UK) 178
Townsend, P. 234, 235, 237,
Toxteth, Liverpool 120, 126, 232
Trades Unions in Europe: 186, 195–6;
  and exclusion of immigrant workers
  186
Trades Unions in UK 100, 133, 161,
  174, 181, 187
Trades Unions in US 38, 47, 68, 115,
  122, 142, 186, 211, 214, 220, 222
Trades Unions and exclusion of black
  workers 186–7, 211, 214–15
Trades Union Congress (TUC) (UK)
  85, 99, 100, 102
Treadwell, D. 233
TREVI (Organisation of Ministers of
  Interior in European Union) 189,
  192, 240
Triangular trade 3, 166, 204
Tross, Dr J.S. Nathaniel 53
Truman, President Harry S.: and Civil
  Rights 57; and anti-Communist
  purges 63, 65
Tucker, M. B. 226
Turks (Germany) 184, 188, 196
Tuscumbia 13, 213
Tuttle, W, 242
Twelfth Earl of Meath 171
Two Bridges (demonstration district,
  New York) 33, 34, 35, 225

Underclass 10, 134–5, 141, 172, 176,
  222, 225, 233, 242
United Bronx Parents Association 37
United Federation of Teachers (US) 26,
  33, 35, 36, 38, 39, 40, 41, 43, 44,
  45
United Nations 12, 15, 20, 69–70, 237
United States v. Cruikshank 138
United Steelworkers v. Weber 144
Universal Negro Improvement
  Association (UNIA) 50
Uprisings: UK 21, 114, 116, 121, 129,
  132–3; US 21, 45, 55–6, 72, 76,
  141, 232

Vanzetti, B. 212
Veterans' Administration 9, 219

Vietnam War 70, 77, 114, 230
Virdee, S. 226
Vittoz, S. 242
Von Niedig, Norbert (Head,
  Germany's Central Office for the
  Recognition of Refugees) 194
Voting Rights Act 1965 (US) 75

Wagner Act 60
Wallace, George 56
Wallraff, G. 239
Walsh, D. 238 , 241
Waltham Forest, London Borough of
  (UK) 178, 241
Walvin, J. 5, 224
Wardle, Charles, MP 180
Wards Cove Packing Co. v. Antonio
  144
Warren, Chief Justice Earl 140, 145
Washington State Board Against
  Discrimination 110
Watkins, Steve 149, 150, 234
Watts (Los Angeles) and urban
  uprisings 120
Webber, F. 239, 240
Weir, M. 242
Welfare: 10, 12, 20, 60, 70, 76–7,
  121, 133–4, 141, 143, 147, 162–4,
  166, 175, 180–2, 186, 190, 195,
  217–18, 220, 224, 226; capitalism
  209, 217, 220; mothers 134; state
  77, 147, 162, 164, 166
West Indies/Indians 3, 69, 123, 153,
  155, 159, 166, 178, 181, 209, 232
West Midlands foundries (UK) 174
Westegaard, J. 237
White Evangelical Christians 222
Whitehead, M. 234, 235
Whitelaw, William, MP (Home
  Secretary), 125, 129, 135, 232
Whites in UK: and the Conservative
  Party 11, 13; and the Labour Party
  11; opposition to black migrants 11;
  overcoming racism 232; and racial
  hierarchy 11, 51; and racial violence
  153, 173, 178; resistance to racist
  ideology 165
Whites in US: benefits of whiteness
  1–2, 8–11, 18, 26, 28–9, 46, 48–9,
  141, 205, 207–8, 211–12, 214, 219;
  black antagonism to 26, 41, 72; and
  Civil Rights Movement 55–6, 66,
  72, 78; construction of whiteness 7,

12, 206-7, 224; Democratic Party and 221; opposition to affirmative action 14, 141, 144, 221; opposition to school desegregation and decentralisation 26, 28-30, 32-3, 40; poor 13, 48, 134, 137, 211–12, 216, 219; and racial privilege 10, 17–18, 26, 28–9, 46, 48–9, 141, 205, 207–8, 211–12, 214, 216, 219; Republican Party and 221; resistance to racial identity 7, 13, 17, 19, 165, 204, 208–9, 223; Southern 46, 48, 63, 138, 205, 214, 216, 219; suburbanisation 9–10, 18, 219

Wilcox, P. 32
Wilkins, Roy 70, 74
Williams, E. 224, 236
Williams, J. 226
Williams, L. A. 225
Williams, Shirley, MP 92
Williams, W. A. 229
Wills, G. 232
Wilson, Charles (IS 201 Administrator) 44
Wilson, Charles E. (General Electric) 57
Wilson, Harold (Prime Minister): and charges of black anti-Semitism 40 ; and anti-discrimination legislation 85
Winstanley, Dr Michael, MP 106
'With all Deliberate Speed' 66
Women in UK: and employment law 174; increase in number in medical schools 154; and consequences in of cuts in social and welfare provision; Afro-Caribbean and access to ante-natal provision 156-8; Afro-Caribbean and appropriate diet 157; Afro-Caribbean and contraception 158; Afro-Caribbean and disproportionate levels of imprisonment 13, 189; Afro-Caribbean and health 152, 157; Afro Caribbean and employment in National Health Service 150–1, 163; Afro-Caribbean and militancy 163, 231; Afro-Caribbean and racially segmented labour market 150, 157; Afro-Caribbean and stereotypes of fecklessness 159; Afro-Caribbean and unemployment 121; Asian and access to ante-natal provision 156–8;

Asian and childbirth 156; Asian and consequences of cuts in social welfare provision 121, 164; Asian and disproportionate emphasis of health education material on birth control 158; Asian and employment in National Health Service 150–1, 163; Asian and immigration rules 176; Asian and stereotypes of compliance 159; Asian and virginity tests 161, 235; Asian and X-rays as part of immigration procedures 176 middle-class and successful access to ante-natal provision 157; Muslim and access to ante-natal provision 157; white, working-class and poor women and contraceptives 158; working-class women and appropriate diet 157; working-class women and ante-natal provision 156–7
Women in US: black and Civil Rights Movement 67; black and discrimination 14; black and disproportionate levels of imprisonment 13; black and exclusion from the Keynesian Accommodation 115; black and the First Reconstruction 136; black and New Right attacks on gains 142; black and Reagan/Bush Supreme Court attacks on gains 143–4; black and scapegoating 222; black and stereotypes of aggressive black women 13, 213; white and the construction of racially privileged identity 212; white and New Right attacks on Second Wave 141–2; white and Reagan/Bush Supreme Court attacks on gains 143–4; white and Second Wave of Feminism 67, 140; white and struggle for equal pay and rights 64; white and stereotypes of black male attacks on 13, 135, 213
Woodhouse, C.M., MP 89
Woodruff, W. 236
Working class in Europe: acceptance of white workers of racial hierarchy 181, 183–8, 191, 195; exclusion of immigrant working class from working-class institutions 195; failure of trades unions 186–7, 195;

political powerlessness 198; rejection of racist ideology 198; support for the Far Right 190, 196–7

Working class, black in UK: 23, 121, 128, 131, 148, 150–2, 156, 163–4, 173–4; and Asian immigrant workers 175, 180; and Asian women 121; and consequences of cuts in services 125, 148, 163–4, 195; and economic restructuring 131; and entry into racially stratified labour market 148, 150–2, 156, 163–4, 174; and National Health Service 148, 150–1, 156, 164; and militancy 161, 164; and rise of Afro-Caribbean petit-bourgeois stratum 131

Working class, black in US: 8, 50–1, 53, 61, 63–4, 121, 131, 134, 206, 211, 216; Chinese immigrant workers 212; and health 157, 163

Working class, white in UK: and acceptance of racist ideology during period of English colonial dominance 168, 170–2, 174; and acceptance of scapegoating of Afro-Caribbeans and Asians as responsible for shortcomings in public services 160, 162–3, 180–1; and acceptance of system in which they were disrespected 163, 171; and Afro-Caribbean women 121, 151, 156, 163–4; and consequences of economic restructuring 166, 180–2, 202–3; and consequences of cuts in services 125, 148, 163, 195; and decline in material concessions from the State 202; and exclusion of immigrant workers from working-class institutions 100, 174, 180; and failure of trades unions 180, 186–7, 195; and post-war Keynesian Accommodation 174, 181; and the Labour Party 187; and political powerlessness 172–3, 181; and racial stratification of labour markets 100, 151, 174; and rejection of racist ideology 168–70, 186–7, 198; and support for Thatcher 182

Working class, white in US: declining income 142; and Democratic Party 221; and economic restructuring 78, 130, 134, 142; and failure of trade unions 221; and Herrenvolk Democracy 46, 206–7, 209, 224; and institutional racism 19–20; and political powerlessness 8, 19, 25, 47, 78, 115, 142, 209–12, 214, 216, 220, 222–3; and post-war Keynesian Accommodation 115, 130, 142, 220; and racial privilege 8, 19–20, 46, 210, 214; and rejection of racist ideology 208, 216, 222–3; and repression of those who challenged dominant ideology 212, 220–1; and white identity 7–8, 61, 64, 209–11, 214, 222–4

Working Group Against Racism in Children's Resources (UK) 201

Yavner, L. 228
Yellow Star Movement (UK) 88
Yorkshire Post 100, 231
Young people in UK: 116–18, 120–1, 128–9, 132, 135, 140, 162, 171, 189, 231, 234; and Afro-Caribbean Youth 116–17, 120–1, 128–9, 132, 135, 231, 234; and Asian youth 128; and imperialist education 171; and white racist youths 162; and white working-class youth 131–2
Young people: in US 140; and Europe and immigrant children born in Germany 188; and stereotyping black youths in The Netherlands 189
Young, Whitney 71

Zegeye, A. 24
Zinn, H. 229, 230